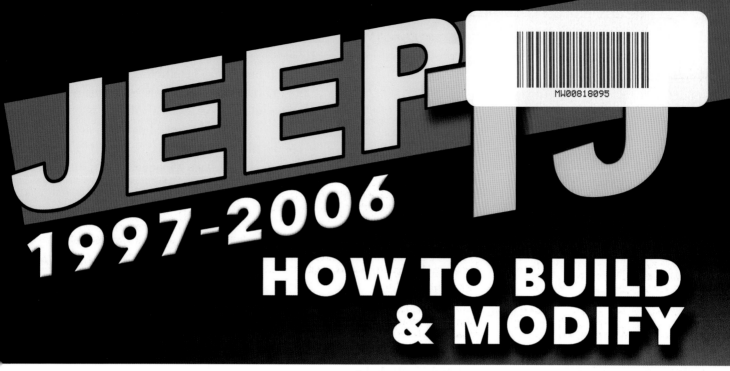

JEEP TJ

1997-2006

HOW TO BUILD & MODIFY

Michael Hanssen

CarTech®

CarTech®

CarTech®, Inc.
838 Lake Street South
Forest Lake, MN 55025
Phone: 651-277-1200 or 800-551-4754
Fax: 651-277-1203
www.cartechbooks.com

Edit by Bob Wilson
Layout by Monica Seiberlich

ISBN 978-1-61325-428-8
Item No. SA427

Library of Congress Cataloging-in-Publication Data

Names: Hanssen, Michael, author.
Title: Jeep TJ 1997-2006 : how to build and modify / Michael Hanssen.
Description: Forest Lake MN : CarTech Books, [2018]
Identifiers: LCCN 2017061674 | ISBN 9781613254288
Subjects: LCSH: Wrangler sport utility vehicle–Maintenance and
    repair–Handbooks, manuals, etc. | Jeep   automo-
    bile–Maintenance and repair–Handbooks, manuals, etc. | Automo-
    biles–Maintenance and repair–   Handbooks, manuals, etc. |
    LCGFT: Handbooks and manuals.
Classification: LCC TL215.W73 H36 2018 | DDC 629.28/722–dc23
LC record available at https://lccn.loc.gov/2017061674

Written, edited, and designed in the U.S.A.
Printed in China
10 9 8 7 6 5 4 3 2 1

DISTRIBUTION BY:

Europe
PGUK
63 Hatton Garden
London EC1N 8LE, England
Phone: 020 7061 1980 • Fax: 020 7242 3725
www.pguk.co.uk

Australia
Renniks Publications Ltd.
3/37-39 Green Street
Banksmeadow, NSW 2109, Australia
Phone: 2 9695 7055 • Fax: 2 9695 7355
www.renniks.com

Canada
Login Canada
300 Saulteaux Crescent
Winnipeg, MB, R3J 3T2 Canada
Phone: 800 665 1148 • Fax: 800 665 0103
www.lb.ca

CONTENTS

DEDICATION

To my wife, Jennifer, and to my son, Austin, who both probably understand the phrase "It's a Jeep thing" better than anyone.

ACKNOWLEDGMENTS

After many years of running a Jeep lifestyle website called jeepfan.com, I found myself an author of a Jeep CJ book. Fresh off the completion of the CJ book, I was busy writing this one. This lifelong obsession with the Jeep has kept me active in the Jeep community for more than 40 years. There have been so many people along the way who have appreciated my love of this vehicle and so many who have helped me grow my knowledge and abilities. First and foremost is my family, my wife Jennifer and son Austin, who have listened to countless hours of talk about Jeeps, accompanied me on trail rides, answered help "come hold this" requests with builds, and so much more. My wife once asked me why I like Jeeps so much. I'm not sure I was ever asked that so simply, but after thinking about it, I really can't say. Perhaps, like many of us, we like them just because of the way they make us feel. The look, the experience, the common ground that most of us Jeepers share. I'm not sure it matters.

My father, who truly is responsible for all of this since he introduced a Jeep into my life at three years old, spent countless hours on his Jeep, which later became my first Jeep and our first build. My father scared the wits out of me on the trail with this 1970 CJ-5 when I was a kid; this thrill of off-roading eventually spread to me, allowing me to scare passengers in my own Jeep. The look on someone's face when you tell them they might want to put on their seat belt for this section of trail is priceless.

Special thanks to my favorite parts suppliers, installers, and manufacturers, who helped me with the good stuff: Quadratec, OK 4WD, Extreme Terrain, ARB, Novak Conversions, TeraFlex, Off Road Only, and Genesis Offroad. An extra shout-out to the great people who work at these places and went out of their way for me; Jim, Vinson, Eric, Trevor, Peggy, Frank, and Sean.

Thanks to the followers of jeepfan.com, a site I have run since 1997. It has allowed me to share my knowledge of the Jeep and connect with people all over the world.

Lastly, I must not forget my close circle of Jeep friends: Ralph, Mike, Glenn, Matt, Bryan, Brian, Rich, and Mark, who always provide an opinion, advice, and a helping hand.

INTRODUCTION

The Jeep line has been in production since 1941 and has given us many models, each with its own special qualities, but the TJ series could be considered one of the pioneers of a new era of Wrangler. The 1997–2006 Wrangler redesign led to huge refinements in on- and off-road handling, options that further improved interior comfort and the continuation of what made this style of Jeep the legacy it still is today.

What's So Special about the 1997–2006 Jeep TJ Series?

The arrival of the TJ in the community was fascinating to watch because this new, redesigned Jeep became dominant in such a short amount of time. The YJ and CJ series almost moved into the back seat overnight. The aftermarket experienced a rebirth because this new model required new equipment not yet offered. It also prompted the birth of a new aftermarket with companies specializing in TJ-specific equipment.

Interestingly, because of the JK (the successor to TJ), the TJ has moved into the space that the CJ and YJ found themselves in after the introduction of the TJ. Building and modifying the TJ is becoming easier and more affordable as the used prices for the TJ have fallen. The TJ is destined to become a classic Jeep, just like the models before it.

I've been building and modifying Jeeps since 1984 and have been

The suspension redesign on the TJ quickly proved itself off-road. The TJ grew to dominate the off-road in a very short time. With only a minor lift and larger tires, the already-capable TJ could tackle serious trails.

Attending an event that focuses on the Jeep shows how huge a following this vehicle has. The annual All Breeds Jeep Show in York, Pennsylvania, put on by PA Jeeps draws hundreds of Jeeps every year.

continuously working on my 1978 CJ-5, 2004 TJ Unlimited, and 2016 JK Rubicon Unlimited. These Jeeps have seen many modifications and trail time through the years. They have seen many versions of lift kits, engine rebuilds and modifications, a frame replacement, lockers, tires, wheels, etc. The list goes on and on and is still going. The 2004 TJ Unlimited is a big part of this book and so much of what was done to it aligns with the concepts discussed here.

Before we begin, I want to stress that safety is the number-one concern when working on your Jeep. Don't take chances, plan ahead in the work, get help when needed, and be aware of your surroundings. Certain modifications to a Jeep can alter the way it drives. Lift kits and larger tires will affect road handling and stopping ability. Low quality or incorrect components can cause failures, damage, and potential injury. Be safe out there.

Butler, Pennsylvania, is considered the birthplace of the Jeep. It is here that the Bantam car company created the initial design that became the Jeep. The Bantam Jeep Heritage Festival held annually in Butler draws thousands of Jeeps. The Butler Jeep Invasion is one part of the festival where Jeeps line the streets of Butler. It's a must-attend event for a Jeep lover.

This is the project Jeep that is the subject of much of this book: a 2004 TJ Wrangler Unlimited. This Jeep has proven to be so much fun to work on and drive. It's common for Jeepers to refer to the TJ Unlimited as an "LJ," which is an unofficial designation never used by Jeep.

THE WRANGLER TJ, A DEPARTURE FROM THE PAST

In January 1996, Jeep unveiled the new Wrangler at the Detroit Auto Show. This model would replace the Wrangler YJ; its full redesign was a drastic departure from what the line featured for more than 50 years. In 1990, Jeep began development of the successor to the YJ and after six years of development, design, and testing, the new Jeep Wrangler, generally referred to as a TJ, was ready for the public.

Brilliant Suspension Redesign

Along with a body redesign (that was an evolution to the prior models), the most notable change was the introduction of a coil spring suspension, replacing the traditional leaf springs. The coil spring system was based upon the system found in the front of the Jeep Cherokee XJ and in the front and rear of the Grand Cherokee ZJ. The Wrangler's Quadra Coil suspension system uses upper and lower control arms connected to the frame and the solid Dana front and rear axles. The single-rate coil springs

The new Wrangler looked similar to the previous versions, but the underneath left most Jeep owners staring in disbelief. In the beginning, many old-school Jeep owners criticized many of the new features found on the TJ. In the end, Jeep did not disappoint, and the new Jeep exceeded the previous models in many ways. (Jeep is a registered trademark of FCA US LLC)

provide minimal friction, free articulation, and smoother operation; they improved the ride in both on- and off-road conditions. In addition, a front and rear track bar retain the axle location while front and rear sway bars control body roll during cornering. The difference in suspension performance from any Wrangler or CJ before was like the difference between night and day.

The Jeep community, in love with the return to round headlights, was unsure of the new design and many were promising to hold out and not buy a Jeep without leaf springs. Jokes and general resistance to change ended quite quickly after new Jeep owners started putting their new suspensions to the test both on- and off-road. The free-moving design of the coil spring setup allows

The Wrangler Quadra Link suspension uses a single coil spring and shock per wheel along with an upper and lower control arm. Weather and time can take its toll with the appearance of the Jeep suspension, but the function remains reliable. Fresh springs and shocks will breathe new life into the Jeep's ride.

the suspension to absorb changing road surfaces and navigate obstacles smoothly, efficiently, and exceptionally well. In many and most ways, the coil-spring design is superior to leaf springs.

With the new suspension, both existing companies and many new companies scrambled to create modifications to allow lifts and increased performance. It was evident that the new Jeep could be modified easily to increase off-road performance in a variety of ways, ranging from inexpensive spacers to complex long-arm systems. All of this will be explored in chapter 6. Even with a simple lift and larger tires, the new suspension, which was cautiously received by the Jeep community, shone as a winner for Jeep and off-road drivers.

Models and Trim Levels

The new Wrangler brought new models and trim levels to the line, some maintaining the sporty nature of the Jeep while others added a

The Wrangler TJ returned to the iconic round headlights found in similar Jeep models prior to the YJ. For an unusual new look, the TJ moved the turn signal lights from below the headlights to the fenders for better visibility and space.

level of class and sophistication, to a very special model designed for the off-road enthusiast.

Models

The Wrangler was available in two main models within its nine-year run: the Wrangler (TJ) and Wrangler Unlimited (TJU). In addition to the new suspension, the TJ featured improved climate control and additional safety equipment such as airbags and anti-lock brakes. The Wrangler TJ shared many specifications of the prior Wrangler YJ, including wheelbase, solid axles, door handles, tailgate, and engines.

A complete 3-inch lift kit from TeraFlex for the TJ that includes lift springs, tuned shocks, sway bar disconnects, adjustable FlexArms, and an adjustable front track bar is staged for installation. TeraFlex is considered as the maker of the first lift kit for the TJ. The redesign of the suspension spawned many new TJ-centric companies.

The redesigned body lowered the grille height and increased windshield angle to improve aerodynamics and fuel efficiency.

Common items across the series were the standard or optional 4.0L I-6, an upgraded design of the tried and true AMC I-6 that was introduced in Jeep vehicles in 1986. The 4.0L saw a few changes within the nine-year run of the TJ that resulted in a few extra horsepower and increased torque. The TJ was the last

The 4.0L 6-cylinder engine was available in the TJ through its entire run, either as an option or as standard equipment. The engine was well matched to the TJ, providing excellent low-end torque that was very useful off-road and sufficient horsepower to keep the Jeep moving in traffic. The refinements in the 4.0L fuel-injection system increased the reliability and efficiency of this engine.

The Wrangler TJ shared the same 94-inch wheelbase as the CJ-7 and Wrangler YJ. This size proved to be almost perfect for the Jeep off-road. It's short enough to stay nimble on a tight trail but allows just enough room to seat passengers comfortably along with some gear. The new styling of the TJ retained enough of the iconic Jeep look to make the vehicle instantly recognizable.

The Wrangler Unlimited debuted in 2004 and received kudos from the Jeep community. Similar to the old CJ-8 (also known as the Scrambler), the new Jeep was 15 inches longer; it added 10 inches behind the door opening and 5 inches in the rear. This stretched Jeep featured increased interior room: valuable space for gear and people. (Jeep is a registered trademark of FCA US LLC)

Jeep vehicle to use the 4.0L and when the model ended in 2006, the last of the AMC-era engines ended with it. The continued appearance of the Dana 44 rear axle with disc brakes as an option or standard equipment makes you wonder why it wasn't offered all the way through.

In 2002, Jeep began offering the dual-top group; it allowed a new Jeep owner to purchase both tops right from the factory. This popular and cost-effective option continued through the JK series.

Wrangler: The Wrangler TJ model was available for the full run of the TJ series. The replacement for the Wrangler YJ featured two doors and the same wheelbase and relative size as the YJ. This size proved itself since the CJ-7 was introduced in 1976 and continued to prove itself through this model.

Wrangler Unlimited: In 2004, Jeep unveiled the Wrangler Unlimited, sometimes unofficially referred to as an LJ, which offered an additional 10 inches of wheelbase and an extra 5 inches of rear cargo space. It was a welcome addition to the line that added much needed room to a small vehicle. With the added length came improved handling both on- and off-road. The Unlim- ited shared many similarities to the Jeep Scrambler without the excess rear overhang. The limited-run numbers and three-year availability keeps the used prices high for this model TJ. If history repeats itself, the Wrangler Unlimited will continue to be in demand, keeping prices up well into the future.

Wrangler and Wrangler Unlimited Compatibility and Interchangeability: The Wrangler and Wrangler

The Wrangler Unlimited's extra 10 inches of wheelbase (compared the Wrangler) improved street driving considerably. It also adds the advantage of being longer than the standard 94-inch length, which on the trail can be the difference between stuck or not stuck.

Brief Wrangler Specs

Wheelbase: 93.4 inches
Length: 155 inches
Engines: 4.0L I-6 (1997–2006), 2.5L I-4 (1997–2002), 2.4L I-4 (2002–2006)
Transmissions: 5- and 6-speed manual, 4-speed automatic
Transfer Case: NP231 (standard), NV241 (Rubicon)
Axles: Dana 30 front (standard), Dana 44 front (Rubicon), Dana 35 rear (standard), Dana 44 rear (Rubicon)
Hard and Soft Top

Brief Wrangler Unlimited Specs

Wheelbase: 103.4 inches

Length: 171 inches

Engines: 4.0L I-6 (2004–2006)

Transmissions: 5- and 6-speed manual, 4-speed automatic

Transfer Case: NP231 (standard), NV241 (Rubicon)

Axles: Dana 30 front (standard), Dana 44 front (Rubicon), Dana 44 rear (standard and Rubicon)

Hard and Soft Top

Unlimited share almost all of the same parts with the exception of items directly impacted by the increased length. These items include: body tub, frame, tops, roll bar, rear driveshaft, and fuel/brake lines. Almost all other items are fully interchangeable. Nearly all aftermarket parts such as lift kits, bumpers, and so on, will work across models; double-check with the manufacturer or reseller especially when looking at long-arm lift kits, body protection, tops, and rear driveline.

Trim Lines

The TJ featured many trim levels in its nine-year run; at least 15 different trims were available. Some were standard; others were special limited model-year editions.

Standard Editions

SE: The bottom trim level that came standard with the I-4 engine and limited creature comforts. The 4.0L I-6 and automatic transmission were optional additions.

X: This model, introduced in 2002, sits between the SE and the Sport. The 4.0L I-6 and manual transmission were standard; automatic, four-wheel disc brakes, and Trac-Lok differential were optional.

Sport: This is the most common version of the TJ; it included the 4.0L I-6 as standard. Popular options included air-conditioning, speed control, 30-inch tires, and upgraded sound system. A Dana 44 with the Trac-Lok differential and disc brakes was an option through the run.

Sahara: The Sahara included many features found in the Sport but added appearance and interior enhancements such as special decals, wider flares, and premium sound. A Dana 44 with the Trac-Lok differential and disc brakes was an option through the run.

Rubicon: Jeep introduced the Rubicon in 2003 and started a model that became extremely popular with the off-road crowd. The Rubicon, named after the famous trail in the Sierra Nevada mountain range, was equipped with features designed for off-road use. Larger off-road tires, body and underbody protection, Dana 44 axles equipped with air lockers, and a 4:1 low-range transfer case set this Jeep apart from all of the other special trim models. The Wrangler Unlimited was available as a Rubicon in the 2005 and 2006 models. It is estimated that only 10

The Wrangler Sport is the most popular model in the TJ line and was available throughout the model's run. It features many of the most popular options such as the reliable 4.0L 6-cylinder engine and attractive exterior. An array of options including a hard top and an air conditioner made this model extremely popular. (Jeep is a registered trademark of FCA US LLC)

For the Jeep owners who were looking for a little more class and refinement, the Sahara featured many appearance and interior upgrades. From an off-road perspective, the Sahara was equipped with wider fender flares that could cover larger tires. (Jeep is a registered trademark of FCA US LLC)

The Rubicon is difficult to ignore for its out-of-the-box off-road capability. Jeep hit the nail on the head, especially considering its need to satisfy so many requirements in a vehicle. The front and rear lockers, 4:1 transfer case, and Dana 44 axles are the stars of this model. (Jeep is a registered trademark of FCA US LLC)

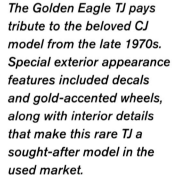

The Golden Eagle TJ pays tribute to the beloved CJ model from the late 1970s. Special exterior appearance features included decals and gold-accented wheels, along with interior details that make this rare TJ a sought-after model in the used market.

The Willys model of the TJ featured military styling and decals. The green color and basic utility look made this Jeep a favorite of some Jeep owners. At Jeep shows, the Willys models are often arranged together to show them off as a group. These Willys TJs are on display at the PA Jeeps All Breeds Annual Jeep Show in York, Pennsylvania.

percent of Wranglers in the available years (2003–2006) are Rubicon models; this low percentage has dramatically increased the used market value of the Rubicon. I will discuss the advantage and/or disadvantage of buying a Rubicon in the following chapters.

Notable Special Editions

Of the numerous special edition models, a few stand out, such as the Golden Eagle and Willys editions. The Golden Eagle, available in 2006, paid homage to the Golden Eagle trim line found in the CJ series that ran in the late 1970s. The Golden Eagle featured special colors, exclusive interior trim and seats, and unique decaling. The 30-inch tire group and special gold-trimmed alloy wheels completed the package.

The Willys edition, available in the 2004 and 2005 model years, was a throwback to Jeep's military days of the MB and M38. This model featured army green paint with special military-look decals. Camouflage seats and special interior accents made this Jeep a favorite for some people. Those who attend Jeep shows and events can find groups of Willys owners sticking together.

Other Special Editions

Some editions were very limited and were only available for a single year or part year. Many offered special decaling, paint, and interior trim on a standard TJ base. With the exception of the Rubicon, most special editions were nothing more than visual features. Models include: 60th Anniversary Edition, 65th Anniversary Edition, Apex Edition, Columbia Edition, Freedom Edition, Rocky Mountain Edition, Sahara Edition Unlimited Rubicon, and Tomb Raider Edition.

Why Build and Modify a TJ?

Shortly after the TJ was released, it became immediately apparent that Jeep did something correct. In fact, Jeep hit the nail on the head; the TJ was superior off-road. It seemed that aftermarket parts for the CJ and YJ gave way to the TJ overnight. Companies were quick to release all kinds of items for the new model. New TJ owners flooded Jeep events and trails, wanting to put the new Jeep to the test.

In its stock form, the TJ is rather capable, but its limits can be reached rather quickly, even on moderate trails. This is because of its limited ground clearance and suspension travel. This sounds funny to say because the TJ had more ground clearance and suspension travel than almost any other vehicle available at the time. Jeep always tends to be conservative with its offerings because it needs to make the Wrangler appeal to everyone, since it's generally known that most Wranglers are never used off-road. In addition to the general appeal, safety standards need to be met as does driving comfort and so on. Many consider the "off the lot" version of the Wrangler just a template ready for customization.

Luckily, the TJ's off-road performance can be drastically improved without much effort or expense. The simplest and least expensive method can consist of a 2-inch spacer kit and 31- to 32-inch mud-type tires mounted to stock wheels, which will result in about an extra 3 inches of ground clearance at the center skid plate. This simple lift method combined with the larger, better-designed tires for off-road will increase performance so dramatically that many owners go this route and never look back.

While the simple lift method is cheap and effective, it doesn't provide the performance or clearance that most Jeep owners (who actually use their Jeeps off-road) desire. Interestingly, a Jeep owner can perform most modifications to the TJ in his or her own garage. The simplistic nature of the Jeep lends itself well to the do-it-yourself crowd. In this book, I explore so many topics that most folks can do at home with perhaps only a slight "step above" set of garage tools.

At the time of this writing, it has been 10 years since the last TJ rolled off the line. It made way for the Wrangler JK, a more refined and improved successor to the TJ that was the first removable-top Jeep available in a four-door version. The JK retained the similar but improved Quadra Link coil suspension that worked so well in the TJ. In addition to the JK, the entire Jeep community is waiting anxiously for the release of the successor to the JK, the Wrangler JL. The Wrangler JL is an evolutionary change to the line rather than the revolution that was experienced from TJ to JK.

Lower Cost of Entry

Now that the TJ has moved into classic Jeep status, finding one at a reasonable price for a build and modify project is a reality. With such good performance right out of the box and an inexpensive price tag, finding extra funds for modifications might be more reasonable than buying a JK or JL. The aftermarket support for the TJ is not what it was in the TJ's prime, but many reputable companies still make and develop products for the TJ.

Finding Your Project

If you don't already own a Jeep and are looking for a TJ to modify and take off-road, there are some things to look for. This is a simple list and doesn't dig extensively into each topic. In the following chapters, these topics are dealt with more thoroughly.

Rust

Compared to older Jeep models, rust is not nearly as problematic on TJ Jeeps but can still be a problem in certain areas of the United States. A TJ that spent its life in areas that

A TJ fording some nearly frozen water on a winter trail run at Anthracite Outdoor Adventure Area (AOAA) in Pennsylvania. The TJ, even in a modest near-stock form, is very capable on a variety of terrains.

The Wrangler JK arrived in 2007 and established dominance quickly, as did the TJ in 1997. The JK Wrangler Unlimited offered a never-before-available four doors that brought new Jeep owners to the community who may never have considered a two-door Jeep.

Depending on your skill level, buying a basket-case Jeep can be a nightmare. These Jeeps may come at a low price tag but finding all the parts may significantly increase the cost before any real work is started. On the other hand, a parts Jeep may have the necessary components for an already started project.

Rust is part of life, especially for those Jeep owners who live in areas that experience winter weather. Body rust can occur nearly anywhere on a TJ, but it is most often seen where the steel is welded together. Fixing light rust will keep it from spreading and creating a larger problem.

A rusted-through frame on a Jeep can be big trouble, while normal surface rust is relatively harmless. Many TJ frames rust from the inside out and it's often too late by the time you see it. Notable rust areas are the rear section of the frame and at the frame mount of the rear control arms. Keeping the frame clean, both inside and out, will help with preservation.

have harsh winters and road salt may exhibit major or minor rust issues, especially if the Jeep was neglected. Minor body rust or frame surface rust is common and may not be a cause for concern. Minor body rust is common at the bottom of the side rockers, fenders, and rear corners. This is often thanks to road cinders and stones thrown up from the tires.

Major rust can be a cause to stay clear of a particular Jeep. The TJ is well known for major frame rust issues behind the rear wheels. Very often, the frame will rust from inside out, hiding the severity until it pokes through. Sticking your fingers in the frame holes when looking at a Jeep will help to determine if the frame is sound. Repairing a rusted frame is a big job, and many who do so often replace the Jeep's entire frame or a large section of it.

Major body rust is not common except with the most neglected and weathered Jeeps. If you find a Jeep with major body rust, it will likely also have major frame rust. Staying clear of these Jeeps might be the best advice unless the price is right and your restoration skills are up for the challenge.

Engine

It's likely that a TJ will have a 4.0L I-6; it is a more desirable engine compared to the standard 4-cylinder engines found in some X and SE models. The 4.0L engine is extremely reliable and will live a long life when maintained properly. Even in stock form the engine is very capable and power output is well balanced for even hard off-road use. For those looking to do an engine swap, finding a TJ equipped with a 4-cylinder will save extra money.

When looking at a used Jeep, look for leaks on or under the engine. Minor leaks are normal due to age and can often be easily remedied. Easy starting and smooth, quiet running are typical signs of a well-maintained engine.

With the Jeep running, check the dash for proper temperature, oil pressure, and charging readings. In addition, a check engine light that is on can indicate trouble. The computerized engine of modern vehicles is a double edge sword. These engines are equipped with many sensors that can malfunction with age, which then results in expensive diagnostics and repair. Reading the code with a code reader or through the speedometer using a particular key combination often results in a vague answer raising more questions.

The illuminated check engine light isn't something to be ignored. Auto parts resellers can often determine the problem for free using the OBD port and a code scanner. Sometimes the problem can be as simple as a loose gas cap or bad sensor.

Transmission

Choosing a manual or automatic will be a matter of preference. The TJ series used eight different transmissions through the years with the best coming in the last few years with the NV3550 manual, NSG370 manual, and 42RLE automatic. In general, all of the TJ transmissions were reliable and capable, and none should be

Pulling the dipstick and examining the color and smell of the fluid can indicate the condition of the automatic transmission. Deep brown or black fluid with a burned smell can indicate that the transmission hasn't been serviced for some time or has been overheated.

The Dana 44 was available as standard equipment in a few models of the TJ, most commonly seen in the Rubicon and Unlimited. The Dana 44 is easily identifiable by its egg-shaped cover, compared to the oval shape of the Dana 35 and the rounded shape of the Dana 30. This differential uses the semi-floating style of axle shafts and an 8.5-inch ring gear.

particularly avoided. The later models are labeled "best" because of their increased heavy-duty capabilities.

A drive test is the best way to determine the shape of a transmission. If it operates smoothly through all gears and shows no signs of leaks below, it may be in good shape. On automatic-equipped Jeeps, smelling the transmission dipstick can indicate condition. The presence of a burned smell and fluid that is dark brown/black can indicate the transmission was overheated, potentially leading to an expensive repair.

Rear Differential

The Dana 44 with disc brakes was an option on most trim levels through the entire run of the TJ. When looking at buying a TJ, being able to spot a Dana 44 rear is helpful and will add to the value. The Dana 44 is much stronger than the Dana 35. Moreover, the design difference doesn't use the C-clip axle retention as found in the Dana 35; that's a definite advantage.

Previous Modifications

Purchasing a Jeep that has been already modified can save money, especially if the modifications were done properly. A downside to existing modifications is that the Jeep

may have been used hard off-road, something easily spotted by examining the condition of the skid plates. Deep scrapes underneath usually indicate rock crawling, which may not be a problem, but it is a good indicator of previous use.

Extensive suspension modifications such as long-arm kits by a previous owner can be a cause for concern. Even when installed properly, these can dramatically impact street driving. Often, long-arm systems relocate the control arms that are sometimes bolt on or weld on. Weld quality with suspension systems is extremely important from both a performance and safety perspective. A test drive through varying road conditions will indicate the stability and performance of the system.

Wiring hack jobs can be a nightmare to diagnose and can present a fire hazard when not installed correctly. Look for random wiring under the hood and under the dash. If possible, determine the purpose of the wiring from the previous owner.

Take a Friend

When setting out to look for a Jeep, take a Jeep friend along to serve as a voice of reason and a second set of eyes. Discuss what each will look for before arriving at the poten-

This Wrangler TJ Rubicon has a good balance of on- and off-road capability. The factory Rubicon Dana 44 rears are equipped with factory lockers and 4.56 gears. Combine these with a 3-inch lift and 33-inch tires and you will maximize off-road capability while keeping streetability.

tial new purchase. Make the friend promise to not let you purchase the Jeep if too many red flags come up. The team approach to a purchase (or not) will typically result in the best decisions.

Rubicon Versus Non-Rubicon

A common question is "Should I buy a Rubicon?" The answer is not always clear, but usually it involves two things: How much will you spend on the initial purchase? How will you use the Jeep? A Rubicon will fetch a much higher price than a standard model. The most important things that set the two models apart are:

- Air locker–equipped front and rear Dana 44 axles.
- 4:1 NV241 Transfer Case
- Rear disc brakes
- Authentic Rubicon Hood Decal
- Special Moab wheels with larger tires

All other Rubicon features are less important, such as the marginal factory body protection, extra skid plates, and 1-inch-wider flares. The 16-inch Moab wheels and factory rear disc brakes are a nice feature. The factory rocker guards are relatively light-gauge steel to keep weight down, but they offer minimal improvement to side protection. Many Rubicon owners replace them with aftermarket heavier rocker guards.

Dana 44 Axles

The Dana 44 front in a Rubicon is more a Dana 30 with a Dana 44 center section. The axle shares outer components with the Dana 30, including axle shafts and knuckles. Axle tubes in a Rubicon Dana 44 are considerably smaller in thickness

It only takes a flick of a switch to activate the Rubicon air lockers, locking the differential to provide maximum traction. The factory switch only allowed three locker options: off, rear, or both. This served the Jeep well in most situations. Some Jeep owners modify the system to allow independent front and rear operation.

and diameter than a true Dana 44 front. In reality, a Dana 30 will withstand a considerable amount of trail abuse with 35-inch tires or smaller. Aftermarket axle shafts and trusses can significantly upgrade both the Dana 44 and 30.

Lockers

The factory air lockers in the Rubicon are not to be confused with ARB Air Lockers. The principle is similar but the construction and reliability are different. In general, an ARB Air Locker is considerably stronger and will stand up to larger tires and extended use.

The Rubicon featured factory body protection for the side rockers panels. On the trail, objects can often come in contact with this vulnerable area and cause damage. The lighter-gauge steel diamond plate provided basic protection to the area. Often Jeep owners replace the factory guards with heavier-gauge steel guards that include sliders for added protection. (Jeep is a registered trademark of FCA US LLC)

Along with the lockers, the NV241 transfer case is one of the more important items that separate a Rubicon from other TJ models. The 4:1 low range and no-slip yoke rear output flange makes this transfer case fully trail ready in stock form. In addition to the transfer case, the Rubicon air locker compressors are seen to the left tucked away from harm.

4:1 Transfer Case

The 4:1 low-range ratio in the NV241 Rubicon transfer case is especially useful off-road, especially in a Jeep equipped with a manual transmission. The lower ratio allows more control when navigating difficult trail obstacles. The NP231 transfer case found in all other TJ models runs a 2.72:1 ratio. In chapter 4, these two transfer cases and their options are discussed in more detail.

So Is It Worth It?

In the beginning, buying a Rubicon made sense because the equipment was covered under the factory warranty. The fact that the newest TJ is more than 10 years old means that a warranty is no longer a consideration. Choosing between the two models is never clear. However, purchasing a non-Rubicon model will often save enough money to equip a Jeep similarly with higher-quality components that then results in a better-built Jeep.

For the Jeep owner who only exposes his or her Jeep to mild off-road use and keeps tire sizes within the 33-inch range, a Rubicon will serve the owner well with minimal modifications (such as a lift). Those who are out to modify their Jeeps further and want to push off-road limits will likely benefit from a standard model. In the end, it will come down to the goal of the Jeep and the budget.

This heavily built TJ features many modifications and upgrades while still maintaining its ability to drive on the street. Aftermarket axle upgrades, a lift kit, and larger tires are just some of the items visible on this Jeep.

The Blueprint for Building and Modifying

In this book, I will explore building and modifying a TJ for maximum performance on- and off-road. This dual-purpose need forces us to consider all modifications that may severely impact street driving. Building a Jeep with a purpose will help you stay focused on what's important for performance and stay within your budget. It's easy to succumb to parts and size lust; in recent years, Jeep owners have been building their Jeeps larger and larger. In the past, 33-inch tires were considered big; now, with the popularity of the JK and JL, it seems that 37-inch tires are "entry level."

The Challenge

The reason we take our Jeeps off-road is to put the vehicle and driver in situations that force both to perform at their best to overcome the challenge. This challenge is, in effect, the same regardless of the level of the Jeep's build. An extensively built Jeep will require increased difficulty to get the same challenge. This cyclical effect is what causes Jeep owners

Pros and Cons to Purchasing a Rubicon

Pros
- The 38-percent difference in transfer case ratio is useful off-road without impacting street performance; this is especially useful in Jeeps equipped with a manual transmission.
- Most TJ Wranglers are factory equipped with a Dana 35 rear axle. This axle has known reliability issues mostly surrounding its C-clip design.
- Factory Rubicon models are just special for their originality.
- The NV241 transfer case doesn't use a slip-yoke (See chapter 4).
- Factory 4.10 differential ratios are well suited for up to 33-inch tires.
- Factory rear disc brakes.

Cons
- Increased purchase price.
- Off-road abuse by previous owner is more likely.
- Aftermarket selectable lockers are stronger.
- A 4:1 transfer case is less significant with an automatic.
- Regearing for 33-inch or larger tires is often needed.

Of all the modifications possible for a TJ, new tires and wheels seem to stand out more than anything else. Choosing the proper size tire and wheel for your Jeep is an early decision to be made. These BFGoodrich Mud Terrain tires in the 285/75R16 size mounted to 16 x 8 Quadratec Rubicon Extreme wheels are a good fit on a lifted TJ.

You shouldn't necessarily be scared off by high mileage. A well-maintained TJ can exceed expectations of some other vehicles. The 4.0L is known for long life and reliability; the 4.0L in this Jeep with more than 193,000 miles still runs smooth and strong. Higher-mileage Jeeps can save money because their lower purchase cost allows for more to be spent on upgrades.

All these things and more are taken into consideration in the following chapters. At the end of each chapter you will find a "Putting It All Together" seciton, where I lay out the best options for our Jeep.

Unveiling the Project

The star of this book is a 2004 Jeep Wrangler Unlimited that was purchased used in bone stock condition. This white TJ is equipped with a 4.0L I-6, automatic, Dana 44 rear, and disc brakes. At 193,000-plus miles, the Jeep still runs well, likely due to its previous owner's proper maintenance habits. The Jeep shows its age and use; it has paint chips, light body and frame rust, and an overall filthy underside that we will clean up during the project.

Through these chapters, the Jeep will be transformed into the ideal Jeep defined above. Lift kit, larger tires, lockers, new wheels, bumpers, and much more will be added with details along the way.

to keep building their Jeeps for the chase of the challenge.

Of course, this cyclical effect causes Jeep owners to spend more money on modifications, which require heavier parts to tolerate the increased loads put on the drivetrain from harder trails. This often results in the increased likelihood of broken parts and damaged body parts. These modifications also result in poor street driving and the need to trailer the Jeep to the trail, adding even more cost.

Keeping It Real

As stated earlier, the goal is to find maximum off-road and on-road performance. This forces a determination of the reasonable street driving compromise without giving in to the desire for overbuilding. All off-road build components will impact street driving in some way. Much-larger tires cause poor gas mileage unless gears are changed. Larger tires increase stopping dis-

tance and are much louder on the street. Many off-road tires handle poorly in rain and snow. Lift kits will alter street ride and handling, in addition to raising the center of gravity.

The Jeep featured in this book is a 2004 TJ Wrangler Unlimited in completely bone stock and ready for a transformation. A stock Jeep is an excellent starting point in a used Jeep intended as a project. Finding one is often the bigger challenge. This Jeep will find itself with a new look and will be ready for a new life upon completion.

FACTORY ENGINES AND ENGINE SWAPS

It's commonplace for owners of classic Jeeps such as AMC-era CJs (1972–1986) and earlier to swap engines because of the low-performance engine options in those years. In addition, swapping a tired old engine in a Jeep that's 30 or more years old is quite simple thanks to simple computer controls or even a lack of computer controls altogether. These engines often have simple emissions controls and may be exempt from emissions inspections.

Engine swapping is much less common with the TJ. It's only recently that changing engines has become more popular because of the TJ's age. In many parts of the United States, vehicles are required to pass emissions testing that can present a challenge to the Jeep owner who hasn't thought the swap through. In this chapter, I will explore swapping engines in greater detail and provide some guidelines to help with planning.

Factory Engines

Only three engines were offered with the TJ series: two different 4-cylinder models and one 6-cylinder. All were good engines. Unlike the series before the TJ, all of the engines offered used modern multi-port fuel injection (MPFI) that improved reliability and performance. The end of the Wrangler TJ series also marked the last use of the AMC engine, the 4.0L, which was replaced with the Chrysler 3.8L and 3.6L Pentastar V-6 of the JK series.

The Power Control Module

Perhaps before jumping into engines, discussing the Power Control Module (PCM) might be prudent. As modern vehicles evolved, the introduction and development of computerized systems increased their presence to the point that almost all of a vehicle's systems are controlled or monitored by the PCM. If you have had the pleasure of owning a CJ, you may understand the simple nature of its computer-less system; it's easy to troubleshoot and diagnose problems. While the complexity of the newer systems can seem daunting, these systems allow components, espe-

In the past, swapping a small-block Chevy into an older Jeep such as an AMC-era CJ was common, easy, and relatively inexpensive. The modern TJ presents some complexity with a swap because emissions requirements are stiffer now. A swap with an engine of the same year or newer will often satisfy emissions requirements. (Photo Courtesy Ben Mann)

cially the engine, to produce more power while maintaining efficiency and clean operation. The PCM in the TJ years is mounted on the passenger's side of the firewall in the engine compartment. It operates, monitors,

The Chrysler Pentastar V-6 is the latest engine found in the JK Wrangler. The 3.6L has a smaller displacement than the 4.0L but thanks to modern technology, such as variable valve timing and dual overhead cams, this small engine puts out an impressive 285 hp, a big jump over the 190 hp of the 4.0L.

The power control module (PCM) controls and monitors almost all of the engine operations, making the engine more efficient and producing optimum power output. These modules are easily replaced in the event of a failure even though they are extremely reliable. The factory attempts to find a balance of performance versus efficiency. This allows the aftermarket to make add-ons to the PCM to improve performance.

and adjusts most of the engine functions, including spark timing, air-fuel ratio, idle speed, and much more.

2.5L MPFI 4

The 2.5L is an AMC-built engine introduced in 1984 that was designed specifically for use in Jeep and Eagle vehicles. It shared some components and specs from the I-6; however, it is not a "cut down" version of the I-6. The version of the 2.5L used in the 1997–2002 TJ was an MPFI design and was labeled as the Power-Tech I-4. The engine produces 121 hp at 5,250 rpm and 139 ft-lbs of torque at 3,250 rpm. Even with its small horsepower and torque ratings, with the correct gearing and low range this engine will keep a Jeep moving on the trail without issue.

2.4L DHOC 4

The 16-valve 2.4L replaced the 2.5 in 2002 and continued until 2005. Running dual overhead cams and four valves per cylinder allowed the engine to produce 147 hp at

Both of the 4-cylinder engines perform as well as they can, which is very limiting in a TJ. The small-displacement engine struggles on the highway when larger tires are added to the Jeep and the gears aren't addressed to correct the effective ratio. The underpowered engines really perform their best off-road when using the Jeep's low range.

5,200 rpm and 165 ft-lbs of torque at 4,000 rpm. This engine (in a number of variations) was used in many Chrysler vehicles until it was discontinued completely in 2005, when Chrysler's World Engine replaced it. Like the 2.5L, this small engine is capable of keeping a Jeep moving with the proper gears.

2.5L and 2.4L Performance Upgrades

Many argue that there isn't much more to be pulled from the 2.5L or 2.4L without spending more than a 4.0L swap would cost. Many Jeep owners have reported that most upgrades available do not make the difference that justifies the expense. Often it is reported, in an unscientific way by Jeep owners, that the improvement in performance seems to diminish as the Jeep's engine controls work to control fuel input/exhaust output effectively. They conclude that as the engine adjusts it eliminates any gains. The investment is not worth the gain.

Several companies make performance mufflers for the Jeep that are often part of a cat-back system. This one from Banks is on a 4-cylinder TJ; its free-flowing design adds a little horsepower and some added engine tone. The cost of these systems is often not worth the minimal gain. However, if the system is in need of a replacement, it might be a worthwhile replacement. Most cat-back systems are stainless steel for long life.

Performance computer chips offer improvements in varying conditions by adjusting spark timing and air/fuel ratio. Installation is simple and can be done in less than 30 minutes. Chips from Jet and Superchips are available in varying forms and stages for TJs of all years. These modules typically install at the PCM and are placed inline with one of the PCM's plugs.

The stock 4.0L is almost the perfect engine for the TJ, its modern fuel injection and engine technology only adds to the reliability of this engine. Putting out approximately 190 hp and 235 ft-lbs torque, it is well matched to the size and weight of the TJ. It's not uncommon for a well-cared-for 4.0L to last more than 250,000 miles.

Clean, Less Restricted Air: A new or, even better, reusable-style air filter alone can improve engine performance. These filters allow increased airflow and improve throttle response as well as fuel mileage. K&N filters are possibly the most popular reusable, high-flow filters available.

Exhaust: PaceSetter makes a direct replacement header for the 2.5L and 2.4L that provides increased exhaust flow that results in performance improvement. In addition to the header, a few companies such as Banks make cat-back systems that improve exhaust from the catalytic converter to exhaust exit.

Computer Modules and Programmers: Adding a modified computer module to the Jeep can improve performance by altering the Jeep's programming. These modules install easily but often require installation of a performance exhaust and lower-engine-temperature thermostat to achieve maximum performance. Jet Performance Products makes modules for the Jeep 2.5L that

are available in multiple performance stages.

Gearing: Most agree that regearing a TJ with a 4-cylinder will provide the most noticeable improvement to performance compared to other modifications. Adding larger tires will drastically degrade engine performance because of the larger tires' effect on overall ratio. Most 4-cylinder–equipped TJs came with 4.10:1 ratios; often, regearing to 4.88 or lower will bring life back to the small engine. Gearing and its impact will be explored further in chapter 5.

Stroker, Turbo Charger, Supercharger, and More: In recent years, availability of performance parts for both the 2.5L and 2.4L has been diminishing due to less interest in aftermarket modification of these engines. As stated earlier, there is a money line to cross for a swap to a larger engine that is more cost effective and that will produce better results. Some of the fanciest and most expensive supercharger kits and turbo kits for the 4-cylinder engines produce 170–190 hp in the stock 4.0L range.

For those willing to spend the money for the challenge of squeezing more out of their small engines, stroker engines are available that can

push the engine size of a 2.5L up to 2.7L. The 2.4L engines have a bit of a larger aftermarket following due to their use in a variety of Chrysler vehicles. Once again, being conscious of cost versus benefit will save you money that may be used better elsewhere.

4.0L MPFI I-6

The 4.0L remained rather consistent through its final nine-year run. It experienced some slight design changes and a small bump in horsepower and torque. The 1997 4.0L produced 181 hp at 4,600 rpm and 222 ft-lbs of torque. The 2001 and later produced 190 hp and 235 ft-lbs of torque.

The 4.0L was so well matched to the Jeep both on- and off-road, providing excellent torque at low engine speeds; it was a definite advantage in slow off-road driving conditions. While the 4.0 isn't a high-horsepower engine, it is capable of providing a pleasant driving experience on the street. Combine the low-end torque with excellent reliability and you can debate the merits of an engine swap away from the 4.0.

Slight variations in the run generally brought improvements as the years ticked by. The tubular exhaust

Cold air induction systems come in many forms from several different companies. All use a similar concept of a free-flowing reusable air cleaner that is protected from engine heat by an enclosure. This enclosure brings in fresh, cooler air from the grille area or cowl. These systems usually result in a gain of a few horsepower and a little extra fuel economy.

manifold, which was prone to cracking, was replaced with an improved cast version in 2000. The distributor also disappeared in 2000 and was replaced with a one-piece three-coil rail system. The Jeep's PCM controlled the spark timing after the distributor was removed, which meant that manual adjustments were no longer possible or needed. These improvements just added to the 4.0L's reliability.

4.0L Performance Upgrades

The trouble with modern computer-controlled engines is that the computer attempts to maintain predetermined performance characteristics even after modifications. Rewriting the programming is not technically possible but programmers and performance modules attempt to piggyback on the Jeep's computer and alter programming along the way. Even then, gains are minimal and the cost often exceeds the reward. It is a truth that is common to many performance upgrades, so a good piece of advice is be cautious of engine performance modifications; it's often money better spent elsewhere. That being said, I list many of the common add-ons that can make some improvement, whether it is in fuel mileage, throttle response, or power.

Clean, Less Restricted Air: A new or, even better, reusable-style air filter can improve engine performance alone. These filters allow increased airflow and improve throttle response as well as fuel mileage. K&N filters are possibly the most popular reusable, high-flow filters available. A cold air intake system (CAI) can improve engine performance further by replacing the entire air cleaner assembly with a less-restrictive system that isolates the air cleaner to allow it to receive cooler outside air rather than hot underhood air. Airaid, Volant, and K&N are some of the more popular makers of CAI systems. Most of these systems are installed with simple tools in a short amount of time.

Replacing the CAI System

1 *The stock air intake system on a TJ isn't particularly bad but improvements in the style of the filter and keeping the air pulled into the intake as cool as possible will add some horsepower and fuel efficiency. Most cold air intake (CAI) systems replace the filter box with an open element housed in an isolated box to separate the air intake from underhood heat.*

2 *Loosen the clamp attaching the intake tube to the box and pull the tube from the box. Remove the airbox lid and air cleaner. Remove the three internal bolts to allow removal of the factory airbox. Then remove the bolt on the passenger-side radiator bracket.*

3 Pull out the PCV tube and air temperature sensor (if equipped) from the intake tube and remove the factory intake tube. With all the components

removed, installation of the new components can proceed.

4 Unbolt the radiator support and install the heat shield, passing the radiator support through the rear wall of the shield. Tighten the bolts.

5 Install the intake tube to the heat shield and throttle body. Install the PCV tubing and the aFe air cleaner.

6 Make sure that all of the bolts are tightened and install the trim seal on the heat shield. The installation is now complete. Test-run the engine and check for vacuum leaks or loose connections.

Exhaust and Headers: The TJ 4.0L exhaust options are plentiful from cat-back systems to entire replacement systems that include performance pipes and low-restriction emissions-legal catalytic converters. Some of these systems give the Jeep a nicer exhaust sound and tone, as well as improve performance through less restriction.

The factory exhaust manifold on the TJ can be either a tubular-steel or a cast-iron design, depending on the model year. Some model years have manifolds that are prone to cracking; typically, these manifolds can be replaced with a direct fit high-flow header that will mate up with the stock Y-pipe tubes or aftermarket tubes. For maximum exhaust performance, replacing the entire system from the header to the catalytic converter to the muffler and the exit is recommended.

A TJ exhaust system can be broken down into three sections, from front to back: the manifold, catalytic converter section, and cat-back section. The exhaust system configuration changed a few times in the TJ era. The 1997–1999 (earlier) versions used a manifold that converged from two sets of three tubes merging into one then those two sets into one with a single large catalytic converter. From 2000 to 2006, the manifolds used a dual three-tubes-into-one design using two pre-cat converters that

The TJ 4.0L used a few different manifolds through its run; some years used a tubular steel design similar to a header and others used a cast-iron design. Earlier versions used a straight 3-into-1 to 2-into-1 collector design; later versions used a 3-into-1 with dual output design. The latter used small catalytic converters right after the manifold followed by a 2-into-1 collector.

merged the two into one, followed by a larger converter. The later design used four oxygen sensors to measure oxygen levels before the pre-cats and after.

Performance exhaust systems are not cheap but often can last for the lifetime of the Jeep because most are stainless steel. If your Jeep has high mileage and is in need of replace-

ments to the exhaust, consider a high-performance system. Magna-Flow, Borla, Flowmaster, and aFe make replacement and performance exhaust components for the TJ.

aFe Performance Exhaust Installation

If you need to replace a rear main seal or oil pan gasket, now is the time to plan for that. Removing the oil pan usually means dropping the exhaust, so you might as well do both.

This TJ has more than 193,000 miles and the check engine light is illuminated, indicating a problem with the catalyst system. Onboard diagnostic (OBD) codes can be viewed on a TJ by turning the ignition key on three times in 5 seconds. The cycle is on, off, on, off, on. The speedometer will display any code generated by the Jeep. In this case it was P0432 indicating that the catalyst system was below efficiency. The issue is likely an oxygen sensor, but

The TJ exhaust always crossed under the engine in some location (depending on the year) to allow the pipe to run down and eventually exit on the passenger's side of the Jeep. The crossover was most often below the oil pan. Dropping the oil pan requires the removal of the exhaust system because of this crossover.

O2 sensors are a necessary evil in modern engines. These sensors measure the oxygen level in the exhaust gases, which allows the computer to adjust the fuel mixture to achieve optimum burn efficiency. Later-model TJs used four sensors that read O2 before and after the catalytic converters. When replacing sensors, check with a reseller to make sure the proper sensor is used because Jeep used a variety of sensors.

the old cats are way past their useful life. The muffler is not leaking yet, but the outer shell is falling off from rust. Replacing the whole system is money well spent. A performance system from aFe was chosen; it included new catalytic converters, mandrel-bent pipes, and a free-flowing muffler all constructed of 409 stainless steel. The factory manifold is in good condition and will be retained. All four O2 sensors will be replaced as well with the system.

Before starting the project, disconnect the battery and properly support the Jeep to allow easier access from underneath. The center skid plate will need to be removed to allow access to the catalytic converter and other sections. Support the rear of the transmission/transfer case with a stand or jack. Remove the transmission mount nuts and then the six skid plate bolts. If the Jeep has an automatic transmission, you may need to deal with the transmission

pan skid plate. Lower the plate and move it out of the way. It's easiest to start removal of the old system from the rear and move forward.

1 *Remove the center skid plate by supporting the rear of the transmission/transfer case, remove the mount nuts, and remove the six frame bolts. The muffler and catalytic converter are easily accessed with the center skid plate removed. This difficult-to-reach area can trap mud and trail debris that increase rust potential and wear, so use this opportunity to clean here.*

2 *A reciprocating saw makes removal of the old system quicker because unbolting old clamps may be almost impossible thanks to rust. Cut the pipes between the muffler and tailpipe, muffler and catalytic converter, and the catalytic converter and crossover pipe.*

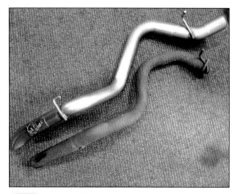

3 *The aFe tailpipe is compared to the stock pipe. The stainless-steel construction will allow this pipe to serve the Jeep for a lifetime and the smooth mandrel bends along with the larger diameter pipe allow the exhaust to flow more freely. The hangers attach at the exact stock locations, which eases installation.*

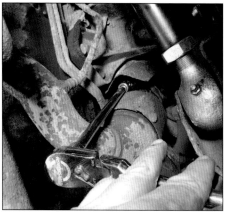

The later-model TJ dual mini catalytic converters are located right after the manifold. They are equipped with a downstream O2 sensor immediately after the mini cat. The crossover pipe goes under the engine oil pan, taking the exhaust to the passenger's side.

With the rear sections removed, the crossover and lead pipes are next to come out. These are difficult to reach and will require patience. Unplug the lower O2 sensors before removing the bolts. With the lead pipes unbolted, remove the lead pipe and crossover.

Because of this Jeep's excess mileage, all of the O2 sensors (four in this case) will be replaced, so their removal from the old lead pipes isn't necessary unless the sensors are to be retained. At this point, the upper O2 sensors are unplugged and removed, followed by installation of the new sensors. Access to the sensors with the lead pipes removed is much easier.

4 *The aFe performance muffler, compared to a stock muffler that is rusting away. The smaller size and freer-flowing internal design adds horsepower to the Jeep along with a pleasing exhaust tone. The stainless-steel construction will likely allow this muffler to serve the Jeep for its lifetime.*

Attach the sensors back to the wiring harness. Then install the mandrel-bent section of the lead back to the main catalytic converter. Install the supplied band clamp loosely.

5 *Installing the new O2 sensors is easy with the lead pipes out of the way. Each sensor should come with some installation lubricant that aids installation and prevents the sensor from seizing over time. Tighten to manufacturer's specifications; be careful of the wiring hanging from the sensor.*

6 *Install the new O2 sensors in the lead pipes' section and tighten to the manufacturer's specifications. Raise the section in place and loosely bolt the section to the manifold with the four bolts. Observe the front driveshaft clearance and adjust to prevent rubbing.*

7 *Position the aFe converter in place to line up with the factory bushing hanger. The aFe directions indicate to cut the lead pipe 3.25 inches from the end when using the aFe converter. Tighten the supplied band clamp loosely.*

8 *Complete the installation by installing the muffler to the converter at the flange and attaching the tailpipe to the muffler using the supplied band clamp. The factory hanger locations should match up.*

After everything is installed loosely, begin tightening from front to back until everything is properly tight and fitted in the hangers. Be certain to attach all of the new oxygen sensors to the factory wiring. Start the Jeep and listen underneath for leaks. After 50 to 100 miles of driving, check all bolts. In this case, the check engine light went off without interaction because the system was functioning properly. Clearing codes will vary depending on the year of the Jeep and the particular code. Some codes will clear with the battery disconnected while others require an OBDII device.

Throttle Bodies and Spacers: The 4.0 throttle body simply serves as an air regulator, unlike a traditional carburetor that regulates air and fuel. The throttle position sensor on the throttle body provides feedback to the computer to indicate the position of the throttle so that other engine systems, such as the fuel injection, are matching the engine needs of the driver. Performance throttle bodies that use a larger opening are available; they allow an increased volume of air to pass through the throttle opening, allowing more fuel to be burned, thereby increasing power. Painless makes bolt-on throttle bodies that feature a 70- and 72-mm bore as opposed to the factory 60- to 62-mm bore.

Several companies make throttle body spacers that are designed to alter the flow of the air moving into the engine, allowing increased efficiency. Airaid, Hesco, and aFe make throttle spacers that can be installed in less than one hour.

Superchargers: For those dying for more horsepower, and have money to burn, a supercharger will add a 40- to 50-percent horsepower increase and a 30- to 40-percent increase in torque. At the time of this writing, a supercharger kit for a 4.0L costs in the range of $3,000 to $5,000. That's a lot of money to go from 190 to 270 hp. It's likely still less expensive than a V-8 swap with much less fabrication and hassle, but the numbers aren't as impressive as a V-8 on its own. In addition, a supercharger can be hard on an older, high-mileage engine.

Sprintex continues to make a bolt-on supercharger system for the TJ while many other companies have discontinued their systems due to the age of the TJ. The Sprintex system mounts directly to the top of the intake and relocates the throttle body, unlike many older or home-made systems that pressurize the entire intake system with a separate mounted supercharger feeding air through a tube to the throttle body.

Jeep owners have used Eaton M90 superchargers from late 1990s to early 2000s GM vehicles to create custom installations. Boosted Technologies took this practice a step fur-ther by making a true bolt-on system that uses an M90 twin-rotor design supercharger mounted to a custom adapter on the intake manifold and relocating the throttle body. The supercharger pulley is located near the power steering pump and runs off the engine's serpentine belt.

Programmers and Performance Computer Modules: Like the 4-cylinder engines, Jeep owners can add a performance computer module or programmer to their Jeeps. These components work similarly in that they alter the original programming to allow the engine to increase power and efficiency. Modifying fuel ratio, spark timing, and other points often accomplishes this. Some modules are fully adjustable and some require high octane fuel as well as changing engine thermostat to allow the engine to run cooler. Most modules attach to the PCM directly and can be installed in less than an hour.

Stroker: A stroker is an engine that uses a crankshaft from a different engine or a custom crankshaft to increase the stroke of the engine, resulting in increased horsepower and, more significantly, torque. For many Jeep owners, this is an attractive way of gaining some increased performance without the expense and complexity of an engine swap. A stroked engine fits in the same space and requires no adapters, fabrication, or electrical modifications, and it shouldn't create any emissions nightmares.

A 4.0L can be commonly (safely) stroked from 4.6L to 4.7L; some have pushed the engine to a 5.0L. A common trick is installing a crankshaft and connecting rods from a 4.2L (258 ci) into a 4.0L and increasing the bore up to .060 inch. This method almost "squares" the engine, meaning that the bore and stroke are almost identical. Some builders will use the 4.0L connecting rods and special pistons to further increase low-end torque, but this method is often more costly and uses non-stock pistons. The horsepower and torque differences between using the long or short rods is likely trivial. An off-road Jeep will benefit from the added cubic inches in either way.

It is common to include an array of performance parts in a stroker engine. Keith Black pistons are a popular high-performance piston, as are performance camshafts from Elgin or Crane. Several camshaft duration/lift options are available to suit the need of the application. Edelbrock makes an emissions-legal performance aluminum head for the 4.0 that increases and improves flow in both the intake and exhaust ports. It should be noted that the Edelbrock Performer head will work with the 1997–2006 TJ 4.0L, but a 1997–1998 exhaust manifold or headers must be used. In addition to the internals, higher-output fuel injectors are often included.

A stroked 4.0L combined with a free-flowing exhaust, larger throttle body, higher-output injectors, and cold air intake may be the ultimate I-6 combination without the hassle or expense that comes from an engine swap. It is common to see gains of 40 to 50 hp and 60 to 80 ft-lbs of torque. Building a stroker at home is no small task, and it is probably best left to those with engine-building experience. Golen Engines, Titan, and Hesco make full and partial 4.0L stroker kits for the TJ.

Cooling: Keeping the engine cool, especially on the trail where the Jeep is likely maintaining a slow speed for extended times, can put stress on the system. In general, a

Direct-fit aluminum radiators can do a better job of displacing engine heat than the factory radiator. These radiators usually use more cores and full-aluminum tanks. Many aluminum conversion radiators are used for swaps that are direct fit to the Jeep to match the engine.

4.0L, even with the stock cooling system, is very capable of maintaining proper engine temperature even on the hottest days on the trail. Over time, if this system is neglected its capacity is diminished and overheating problems, which are bad in general but worse on the trail, may appear. Performance upgrades, primarily internal engine mods, will increase the amount of heat that the engine generates, which increases the load on the cooling system. In short, this is not a common condition in a Jeep with a 4.0L. Regular flushing, inspection, and (especially) keeping the radiator fins clean will make this system perform at its optimum level.

Hood vents are extremely useful for reducing underhood temperatures. Some Jeep owners install vent kits or purchase aftermarket hoods with integrated vents. A Jeep that experiences slow off-road conditions in hot environments will benefit from a vented hood.

Gearing: If you don't go to a full-on engine build, such as a stroker, changing gears can have a dramatic impact on the Jeep's per-

The 4.0L can be stroked to increase displacement up to 4.8, often using a crankshaft from a 4.2L along with bored cylinders. Several companies, including Hesco, ATK, and Clegg, make stroker kits as well as fully assembled engines that are ready to install. (Photo Courtesy Titan Engines)

formance by getting the engine back to its designed power range. Adding larger, heavier tires will effectively alter gear ratios, causing a reduction in engine RPM at the same speed. Performance and fuel mileage will suffer if the engine falls too far below its designed power range.

The 4.0L is a well-known low-RPM-torque engine that will operate in the 2,000-rpm range at 65 mph. Finding the proper gearing to keep the engine at peak RPM will enhance both performance and fuel mileage and that will make the driving experience better. Gearing and ratio choices are discussed in chapter 5.

Swapping Engines

Swapping engines in Jeeps is common and has been performed countless times, stretching all the way back to the earliest CJs. For many Jeep people, it seems impossible to satisfy the hunger for more power. As time moved on, engines became increasingly sophisticated and complex, mostly to improve vehicle emissions and improve fuel mileage. There was a time in the mid- to late 1980s when swapping engines became almost impossible, especially when the Jeep needed to pass an emissions test.

Luckily, the aftermarket caught up to the times and began offering components to make swapping a modern engine into a TJ easier than ever. We are in good times now. Modern engines make more power than ever, maintain fuel economy, and stay within required emissions standards.

As with any swap choice, many choices do not make sense because of complexity or poor aftermarket support. What may seem like a good idea at the time will turn into a money pit and time waster. A few companies, such as Novak Conversions and Advance Adapters, specialize in Jeep engine conversions; they make components ranging from adapters to radiators that make a conversion almost easy. Keep in mind that any swap will have its challenges. The key to success in a swap, even before the first bolt is removed, is preparation and planning. Because there are so many options and combinations, it's nearly impossible to give full step-by-step instructions for a swap; I will provide some ideas and common practices.

Jeep to Jeep Conversion: 2.5L and 2.4L to 4.0L

Swapping from a Jeep 4-cylinder to a 4.0L is a rather straightforward process and is much easier if a donor

Jeep is available. Enough differences are present to make finding parts afterward extremely difficult and expensive. Exact-swap processes are a bit different when using engines from other Jeeps; because the model years vary slightly; it's another reason to get everything possible from the donor Jeep. Many folks who have done this swap recommend staying within a year or two for maximum compatibility. Engine mounts, exhaust, power steering lines, and much more will be impacted from the swap. Certain 4-cylinder transmissions will not mate to the 4.0L, namely the AX-5.

Non-Jeep Conversions

Swapping in a non-factory engine brings an array of potential issues. Fitting and mounting the engine, determining the transmission, and finding adapters, mounts, and radiators are just the tip of the iceberg. Many hidden gotchas can appear that will eat up a lot of time and money. Almost all of the factory gauges operate from input of the PCM; in most swaps, replacing the entire gauge cluster with aftermarket gauges is necessary. Fuel lines and sizes, transmission shifter location, and power-steering connections are additional items that will need addressing. The steering shaft, front axle, frame rails, and firewall are all elements that can interfere with a swap. It's a given that a non-Jeep swap will require a custom exhaust system. There isn't a lot of room under a TJ; snaking larger-diameter exhaust tubes, especially a dual exhaust, can get very tricky.

GM V-6 and V-8

These two engines can add some incredible power to the TJ, and

The TJ's 4-cylinder engine is in process of being removed for replacement with a Magnum 5.9L from a Jeep Grand Cherokee. The more body parts that are removed the easier it is to get to everything. Take time to label everything. (Photo Courtesy Ben Mann)

swapping a modern GM engine is easier than ever. Of course, swapping a pre-computer, non-fuel-injected engine may be the first thought of some Jeep owners, especially those who have performed swaps in earlier-era Jeeps. In many areas that require emissions inspections, swapping a non-computer, non-fuel-injected engine for a TJ engine may cause the inspection to fail. Some people believe that using an earlier-style engine will be less expensive and result in more power, but swapping modern, emissions-friendly engines can often cost less and result in more power and efficiency. Emissions laws often permit engine swaps only when the donor engine is the same year or newer than the recipient, depending on the state where it will be registered.

The Generation III and later V-8 from GM is so compatible in the Jeep that a swap can be easy, clean, and efficient. Novak Conversions has been a leader in engine swaps in Jeeps for many years and it has adapted to the changing times to provide solutions for newer Jeeps. The Gen III and later engines still use the same bellhousing pattern as in the past; attaching an older manual or automatic is rather simple.

Novak indicates that obtaining the engine and transmission from the donor vehicle, along with all of its electronics, is a key step for success. The PCM can be custom programmed to match the particular transmission, especially a manual transmission. Of all swaps, the GM V-8 is believed to be the most simple. Obvious items that would be impacted (other than those that are part of the engine/transmission combination) are radiator, driveshafts, fuel lines, gauges, and much more.

The Generation III and later GM V-8 engines are some of the easiest swap engines available. When mated with a GM transmission, which easily adapted to the NP231 or NV241, the power and reliability of this combination will make any Jeep owner happy. Custom computer programming is readily obtained for a (nearly) plug-and-play conversion. (Photo Courtesy Novak Conversions)

The Mopar Magnum 5.9L that was used in Dodge vehicles, including the Jeep Grand Cherokee, offers an almost Jeep-to-Jeep swap. This engine is based upon the older Mopar LA engine that offers excellent power and torque in a modern-style engine. This engine was mated to a NV3550 transmission using a NP 231 transfer case. (Photo Courtesy Ben Mann)

Mopar, Including Hemi

The Hemi swap is more of a novelty rather than being practical. The cost of the engine plus the long list of swap details makes this engine an impractical candidate for a TJ. Companies such as AEV specialize in Hemi conversions and produce a conversion kit that makes the swap much cleaner and easier. For those with money to burn, Mopar offers crate Hemi engines that are complete and ready for a custom installation. This kind of engine swap requires a compatible transmission and stronger axles capable of dealing with the power output.

Using a Mopar V-8 such as a Magnum 5.2L or 5.9L from a Jeep Grand Cherokee or Dodge vehicle is a common swap that can keep the Jeep "feel." Advance Adapters makes mounts, radiators, and transmission/transfer case adapters for this swap. Like most other swaps, obtaining as much from the donor vehicle as possible will ease the installation. Companies such as Auto Computer Exchange can customize the engine's ECM to match the Jeep.

Diesel

There is a certain group of individuals who have a deep-rooted love for a diesel engine in a Jeep. It is a polarized argument; you're either on one side or the other. It's similar to the old Ford versus Chevy and chocolate versus vanilla arguments. Never a clear winner; it just comes down to preference.

Diesel engines offer unique characteristics when compared to gasoline engines, especially in the low-end torque and high-fuel-efficiency categories. By design, the diesel engine offers much more low-RPM torque than a similarly sized gasoline engine. The demands of a trail Jeep are well matched to a diesel, sometimes so much so that some people question why it was never available from the factory.

The expense of the diesel engine and the items required to do the swap often exceed the amount of money saved by the gain in fuel efficiency. For those who really do want to swap in a diesel, the Cummins 4BT engine is a favorite among the Jeep community. When taken care of, the 4BT engine is known for exceeding 500,000 miles and can be converted to run alternative fuels.

Typically, a transmission swap is required with a diesel conversion. Popular transmissions are 4L80e HD automatic transmission or NV4500 manual transmission. Many other components, including radiators, exhaust, and electronics, must be custom matched to the swap for success. Jeff Daniel's Jeep Customization and Bruiser Conversions is a well-known shop for diesel swaps.

Putting It All Together

The project Jeep is being built for performance on- and off-road. This particular application does not require a massive amount of horsepower and torque. In fact, too much of either can lead to broken components and poor fuel economy. This Jeep is being built for slow trail running and off-road conditions that will make better use of low gearing and low-RPM torque rather than high horsepower.

Because the 4.0L engine performs so well in a TJ right out of the box, spending extra money for improving performance should be considered after items that make a bigger difference off-road are installed first. A quality CAI system and a performance exhaust system will give the largest improvement in the TJ 4.0L; these items may be the first of the modifications a Jeep owner may do.

Swapping a 4.0L in place of a 4-cylinder engine is not terribly complicated and can be done at a reasonable cost for a significant improvement. Having access to the donor Jeep will reduce the expense and complexity of the swap.

Retaining an already-installed 4.0L is more cost effective. It also eliminates the almost endless potential for problems, including adapters, fitment, exhaust, emissions, and electronics compatibility.

V-8 and other non-factory swaps should be performed in accordance with your local emissions laws. A modern, fuel-injected engine with all of its necessary components will perform best in a TJ. The GM V-8 is one of the simplest and most-developed engines swapped for a TJ engine. Planning and preparation are the keys to a successful swap.

Diesel swaps are popular among certain groups of Jeep owners. The most popular diesel for swapping is the Cummins 4BT engine, which is sized well for the TJ. It puts out impressive torque, which is especially useful on the trail, as well as excellent fuel mileage on the street. Several ways of mounting and adapting are available for diesel engines that make this swap not too difficult.

The 4.0L is a well-matched engine for the TJ and serves the Jeep well in almost all driving situations. There was much fear in the Jeep community when Chrysler announced it was being discontinued and replaced with a new engine in the new JK model. Adding a few performance modifications, watching gearing, and performing proper maintenance will allow this engine to power a Jeep for years.

TRANSMISSIONS AND TRANSMISSION SWAPS

The engine has much to do with the "personality" of a Jeep, but the transmission may play a bigger role in the Jeep's overall capability. A Jeep and its intended use are quite different from most other vehicles that spend their lifetime on the street. A properly matched transmission will only make the Jeep's use in both on- and off-road conditions better. The transmission is the first part of the three components that are part of the crawl ratio calculation. Crawl ratio is defined and explored in chapter 5.

Factory Transmission Offerings

The Wrangler TJ was equipped with eight different transmissions through its production run. When Jeep changed a transmission model, it was often an improvement over the previous version. Of the five manual transmissions and three automatics, the 42RLE automatic and the NSG370 manual are standouts. These models were installed in Jeeps after 2003. However, the reality

The factory automatic is easily spotted by the shifter sitting in the center console or the presence of a transmission skid plate in front of the main center skid plate. The 4-speed automatic uses the same shifter as the 3-speed. The fourth gear, also known as overdrive, is engaged and disengaged by a switch on the dash.

is that all of the transmission models are a good fit for the TJ; in fact, the NV3550 is a commonly swapped transmission. Transmission choice among Jeep owners is a matter of personal preference and, like many things, the debate on manual versus automatic continues.

Manual Transmissions

A manual is the more common type of transmission found in a TJ, with the exception of the TJ Unlimited, which was more commonly fitted with an automatic. Jeep owners often prefer a manual transmission for added control off-road, increased fuel economy, and the fun. Manual transmissions are much simpler in

Determining the particular manual shift in a Jeep is difficult by looking only at the shifter. The exception is the NSG370, which has six speeds. The manual transmission is much more common in the TJ series except for the Unlimited, for which the automatic tends to be more popular.

design and create less heat, which, in general, increases life and makes them more reliable. All of the five manual transmissions featured an overdrive gear that kept engine RPM speeds lower, increasing fuel efficiency.

When building and modifying a Jeep, it is helpful to know the first gear and last gear ratio; this is used to calculate overall crawl ratio and highway cruise RPM. Both of these concepts are explored in chapter 4.

Aisin-Warner AX-5

This fully synchronized light-duty 5-speed transmission was used until 2002 in 2.5L-equipped TJ Jeeps. Its light-duty design makes this transmission a poor candidate for a larger, more powerful engine and/or hard off-road abuse. The 21-spline output shaft makes a Jeep equipped with this transmission have a NP231 transfer case equipped with a 21-spline input. Many transmissions and adapters use the 23-spline input.

First gear: 3.93:1
Fifth gear: 0.85:1

Aisin-Warner AX-15

This fully synchronized medium-duty 5-speed transmission was used from 1997 until 1999 in 4.0L-equipped TJs. The AX-15 had wide use in Jeep vehicles, including the YJ Wrangler and XJ Cherokee, and is capable of handling the 4.0L easily along with swapped mild V-8 power. The split cast-aluminum case transmission uses a 23-spline output shaft and an internal hydraulic clutch release bearing. The numbers on the lower part of the case identify the AX-15. This requires a chart listing the many part numbers. An easier way is to check the intermediate plate that is aluminum on the AX-15 and steel in the AX-5.

First gear: 3.93:1
Fifth gear: 0.79:1

NV1500

This fully synchronized light-duty transmission was only found in the 2003 and 2004 2.4L engine–equipped TJ. It is likely the least desired or sought after transmission of the TJ line. This transmission is up to the task of handling the 4-cylinder engine but not much more.

First gear: 3.85:1
Fifth gear: 0.80:1 or 0.83:1

NV3550

This fully synchronized medium-duty 5-speed transmission was used from 2000 until 2004 in 4.0L-equipped TJ Jeeps. This popular transmission is capable of handling the 4.0L power as well as mild swapped V-8 power. It is more than capable of withstanding off-road abuse and its low first gear is a good contributor to overall crawl ratio. There are a couple of things to note. First, the NV3550 is a rather noisy transmission that is even noisier in a Jeep with no carpet. Second, it doesn't use standard gear oil; it uses the more expensive and more difficult to find Synchromax oil.

First gear: 4.01:1
Fifth gear: 0.79:1

This NV3550 sits ready to go into the Jeep's frame, freshly mated to the Magnum 5.8L V-8 from a Grand Cherokee. This popular 5-speed transmission, found in Jeep vehicles as well as Dodge trucks, has a respectable low first gear and will handle mild V-8 power. (Photo Courtesy Ben Mann)

NSG370

This fully synchronized medium-duty 6-speed transmission was used in 2005 and 2006 TJ Jeeps with the 4.0L and 2.4L engines. The final two years of the TJ saw the best manual transmission in the run. For the first time, the same transmission was used with both engines, reducing production costs for Jeep and providing an excellent transmission for a V-8 swap for either engine. The NSG370 incorporated many modern improvements that reduced transmission noise and improved shift quality. The 6-speed offered a wider gear range, allowing for increased fuel efficiency and an impressive first-gear ratio. This

The NSG370 was the first 6-speed manual used in a Jeep vehicle. It is so well matched to a Jeep that it remained for the entire 10-year run of the Wrangler JK model and beyond. Its 4.46:1 first gear and overdrive gives a wide gear range that works well on- and off-road.

transmission went on to serve the JK Wrangler as the only manual for its entire 10-year run.

First gear: 4.46:1
Sixth gear: 0.84:1

Clutch

All Wrangler TJ Jeeps used a single disc–style clutch with a hydraulic master cylinder and slave cylinder release configuration. The clutch master cylinder is mounted on the firewall next to the brake booster. Depending on the transmission, the slave cylinder configuration varies. The benefits of a hydraulically operated clutch are easier clutch operation for the driver, longer and more reliable operation, and tolerance for both body and/or engine/transmission lifts.

Clutch Upgrades

Replacing the clutch with a stronger, high-performance unit such as those offered by Centerforce

All TJs have a provision for a clutch master cylinder even if they were not factory equipped with a manual transmission. When swapping from automatic to manual, adding a master cylinder is only a matter of opening up a few holes and installing. Swapping a whole pedal assembly from a manual-equipped Jeep is the most common practice in this kind of swap.

Centerforce Dual Friction and Centerforce I- and II-series clutches offer greater holding power and are a great upgrade for a problem clutch. The centrifugal weights increase holding power without increasing pedal pressure. A day of off-road driving will give the clutch leg of a Jeep owner a workout; less pedal pressure creates less fatigue. (Photo Courtesy Centerforce)

can improve clutch performance off-road. The dual friction clutch withstands slow off-road driving when clutch usage can be excessive. A Jeep owner often uses the Jeep's clutch more in one day off-road than possibly several weeks' worth of everyday street driving.

Some money-to-burn upgrades can include the following. Russell makes a braided stainless-steel hydraulic clutch line for the TJ. The stainless braid prevents deterioration and protects the line from rubbing and thrown objects. The construction of the line is firmer, resulting in a more positive pedal feel. B&M produces performance short-throw shifters for the NV3550 and the AX-15.

Automatic Transmissions

The three automatics offered in the TJ were all excellent transmissions and are extremely capable of serving the Jeep in all situations. As

Learning the two-foot driving technique with an automatic adds an incredible amount of control for the driver and the Jeep. If you can hold the brake while operating the gas when navigating rocks and other obstacles, you can help prevent damage from bouncing. It takes some practice and is even useful with a manual transmission.

stated earlier, the later model 42RLE is generally considered the best and most desired. Interestingly, the 30RH and 32RH, previously known as the TorqueFlite 904 and 999 respectively, were well-known transmissions used over a 23-year span of various Jeep vehicles.

As in the manual transmission section, the first- and final-gear ratio will be listed to serve as a guide for calculating crawl ratio and cruise RPM. An automatic creates an increase in torque at slow speeds from the transmission's torque converter. This allows a higher first-gear ratio without much sacrifice to crawl ratio. A 2.74:1 first gear in an automatic is not a direct comparison to a 4.46:1 in a manual transmission because of the torque multiplication from the converter.

30RH

The 30RH, previously known as the TorqueFlite 904, was used in

2.5L-equipped Jeeps from 1997 until 2002. The lighter-duty automatic is well suited behind the 2.5L but is not considered a good candidate for more powerful V-8 engines. Adapter options are scarce for the 30RH, making other transmission choices more attractive.

First gear: 2.74:1
Third gear: 1.00:1

32RH

The 32RH, previously known as the TorqueFlite 999, was used in 4.0L-equipped Jeeps from 1997 until 2002. This small-sized heavier-duty automatic can handle the power of the 4.0L and many V-8 swaps. Adapter and upgrade options are generally plentiful for the 32RH.

First gear: 2.74:1
Third gear: 1.00:1

42RLE

The 42RLE became the only automatic offered through 2003 and up to 2006 with both 2.4L- and 4.0L-equipped TJs. The first 4-speed automatic offered in this style of Jeep

The all-electronic 42RLE was the most advanced automatic in the Wrangler until the end of the TJ series. The overdrive allows for lower axle gears without increasing highway cruise RPM. Its low-hanging, thin-walled automatic transmission fluid pan needs protection from trail obstacles. A factory skid plate offers mild protection at best.

was of a heavier-duty design that was well equipped to handle the power of the 4.0L and V-8 swaps. The transmission is electronically controlled to manage shift points based on sensor input. In addition, the 42RLE is equipped with a converter lock-up mechanism to further increase fuel efficiency. Interestingly, the 42RLE uses a higher overdrive than all other TJ transmissions; it helps with highway-cruise RPM when running lower gears.

First gear: 2.84:1
Fourth gear: 0.69:1

Automatic Upgrades

Upgrades and modifications for the factory automatics are sparse, but a few companies make some upgrades. Skyjacker and Rubicon Express make a deep transmission pan for the 32RH that increases fluid capacity, resulting in cooler operation. The increased fluid prevents a neutral drop condition that is caused by fluid starvation when climbing steep hills; it makes the transmission seem to be in neutral. Because the 32RH is essentially the TF999, shift kits, heavy-duty torque converters, heavy clutches, and other internal upgrades are available from companies such as TCI, B&M, and TransGo.

The 42RLE transmission has limited upgrade options. Some Jeep owners add a larger cooler to help with heat because the 42RLE is known for running hot. TransGo makes a few internal upgrade options for this transmission, including shift kits and improved-flow valve bodies. The transmission is entirely electronically controlled, so traditional internal transmission modifications such as shift kits, are really not possible. If your Jeep is equipped with this transmission, take care of it and enjoy it.

The TJ is equipped with a large transmission cooler from the factory. Nevertheless, adding an extra cooler such as a Derale electric fan–equipped cooler, especially to a Jeep that is off-roaded in hot environments, will aid in keeping the transmission cool.

Transmission Care and Maintenance

In general, both the automatics and manuals will be trouble-free if they are properly maintained. Checking and/or changing fluids according to the Jeep recommended schedule is the first step. It would be beneficial to change the fluid more often on a Jeep that sees a lot of off-road use, especially when water crossings and driving in deep mud are involved. A little water can contaminate the lubricant and cause excess wear and other problems.

Heat is a big enemy to the automatic. Slow off-road driving raises the temperature of the transmission because of the slow speeds and low volume of air moving through the

When looking at purchasing a used Jeep, smelling the automatic transmission fluid on the transmission dipstick will indicate if the fluid was overheated because it will smell burnt. Fluid color on the stick should be a lighter to medium brown. Look for the presence of leaks around the pan or torque converter dust cover.

The aluminum transmission cooler sits between the grille and the radiator. Heat is the biggest enemy to an automatic transmission, because the cooler sits in front of the radiator. It often can become a trap for trail debris such as mud and dirt, lessening its cooling ability. Keeping it clean will extend the life of the transmission.

cooler. To make matters worse, the transmission cooler sits forward of the radiator and will collect mud and dirt that comes through the grille. A clogged cooler will only contribute to increasing the transmission temperature. Be sure to clean the cooler thoroughly after every off-road adventure. Check the fluid regularly and note the smell and color of the fluid. If it smells burnt or is black in color, heat may have been high, and you should consider a flush.

Transmission Swaps

Like engine swapping, changing a transmission is a common practice for Jeep TJ owners. A transmission swap is often part of an engine swap, but many Jeep owners will change the transmission to one that offers improved strength and better gear ratios. Transmission electronics in modern automatics can cause headaches during a swap. These transmissions typically require input from the engine and even the vehicle to

Adapting a transmission to any number of engines or transfer cases is often easily done with adapters from Novak Conversions or Advance Adapters. The NP231 and NV241 use the same mounting surface; it accepts adapters easily by its design. (Photo Courtesy Novak Conversions)

operate properly; they usually pair best with an engine that was original to the transmission. Swapping manual transmissions will often offer the path of least resistance because they do not interact directly with the Jeep's computer system.

When planning out a transmission swap, determining your overall

gear ratio impact on important numbers such as crawl ratio and cruise RPM can help in making a decision. See chapter 4 to learn more about these numbers. Also consider the drivability of a swap before taking it on, especially if you are retaining the factory engine. Older transmissions are strong and some offer extremely low first-gear ratios. However, often these transmissions are 3-speeds that look like a 4-speed. They have three regular driving gears plus the extra-low "granny" gear.

Almost every transmission swap will require modification of the center skid plate mount. Many transmission-to-transfer case adapters integrate a mounting location. Skid plate mounting holes in the frame are fixed, and adjusting the mount location is often done at the transmission mount rather than moving the skid plate. An additional option for the need to customize the transmission mount is to use a replacement or fabricated skid plate.

New driveshafts are likely going to be needed when a transmission swap is performed because of length changes. If the NP231 is going to be retained, it is best to install a slip yoke eliminator (SYE) kit at the same

When swapping a transmission, the Jeep owner must often deal with the center skid plate alignment. With most swaps the transmission mount will not align with the factory mount, which requires modification. Many transmission-to-transfer case adapters include a mounting location. (Photo Courtesy Ben Mann)

time as a swap. This will replace the factory slip yoke from the rear of the transfer case. This conversion requires a new driveshaft; doing this at the same time saves having the rear driveshaft altered twice.

Luckily, the speedometer cable for a TJ is housed in the transfer case instead of the transmission. A swap that retains the NP231 or NV241 will not require any modification or conversion to retain speedometer function.

Manual Swaps

Swapping a manual transmission will likely offer more options and easier installation. Both Novak Conversions and Advance Adapters make adapting non-factory manual transmissions simpler. Consider contacting them before starting a swap; their expert advice can save you time and money.

Converting a TJ transmission to a manual transmission from an automatic isn't an overly complicated process and adding the clutch components (such as master cylinder and pedals) is almost a bolt-in procedure. The mounting location for the slave cylinder is present even on an automatic-equipped Jeep. Finding a clutch pedal setup with all the components from another TJ will make adding a clutch to a factory automatic Jeep an easy job.

Most non-Jeep manual transmission swaps will require customization to the Jeep floor to accommodate the new shifter and its location. Depending on the transmission, this can interfere with the factory center console and, in some cases, cause it to be completely removed or altered drastically.

NV3550: This Jeep transmission is among the stronger of the factory 5-speeds, and swapping one can almost be a bolt-in procedure. The transmission will attach readily to the 4.0L but may require some alteration of the output because some TJ transfer cases used different inputs. This 5-speed retains good drivability and is capable of handling V-8 power. Adapting to the NP231 (23-spline) or NV241 transfer case can be done natively.

First gear: 4.01:1
Fifth gear: 0.79:1

NV4500: This heavy-duty transmission is well suited for both V-8 swaps and retaining the 4.0L. This transmission was offered in Dodge and GM trucks, which makes it compatible with engines from both automakers. There are differences between the two; the Dodge version is often used with a swap that does not involve a GM engine. Swapping this transmission will offer an excellent low-ratio first gear while adding an overdrive. According to Novak, this transmission swap may be best left to those swapping a higher-powered V-8 engine because this transmission offers the strength needed for the engine but it also comes at a typically high price along with adaption complexities. Adapting to the NP231 (23-spline) or NV241 transfer case can be accomplished with adapters.

First gear: 5.61:1 and 6.34:1 (early GM)

Fifth gear: 0.73:1

NSG370: This 6-speed factory transmission is another Jeep transmission that can swap into an earlier-model TJ with minimal modification. This transmission is quite strong and will adapt to GM V-8 and V-6 engines readily. The low first gear and overdrive makes this transmission well suited for a Jeep used both on- and off-road. Adapting to the NP231 (23-spline) or NV241 transfer case can be done natively.

First gear: 4.46:1
Sixth gear: 0.84:1

Installing a set of pedals when swapping an automatic to a manual in a TJ is easily done. The TJ factory pedal assembly is modular and can be fitted with either style of pedals.

The NV4500 is a strong transmission that can be a good swap candidate for factory and non-factory Jeep engines. Adapters for both ends are readily available. Its low first gear and overdrive allow excellent crawl ratios and cruise RPM. The biggest drawback of this transmission is in its cost, which remains relatively high, compared to other options.

Other Manual Transmissions to Consider

There are many choices; they will depend on the type of driving situations and how the Jeep will be used. Because we are building a TJ for maximum performance on- and off-road, many of these options will not make the most sense for this situation but are still worth considering. The following are 4-speed manual transmissions but are driven most of the time like a 3-speed. The extra-low "granny" gear is extremely useful on the trail but nearly useless for everyday street driving. This creates a situation where the gear span is wide and the lack of overdrive will impact highway cruise RPM. Calculating this is key when planning a swap.

In many cases, using an older transmission with the 4.0L will require the bellhousing to have a provision for a crank position sensor, which is an integrated part necessary for proper engine operation. Using non-Jeep engines may or may not require this provision. Some conversion bellhousings will have this provision integrated; checking with the manufacturer is best when selecting the component.

T-18: The T-18 was a factory Jeep transmission in the AMC-era CJ; it used an extra-low first gear. The heavy-duty transmission comes in many forms but the Ford and Jeep versions seem to lend themselves much better to adapting. Adapting it to the 4.0L is simple with the proper bellhousing, crank position sensor, and a custom pilot bushing. Adapting to the NP231 (23-spline) or NV241 transfer case can be accomplished with adapters.

First gear: 6.32:1
Fourth gear: 1.00:1

The SM420 is a compact transmission with an insanely low-ratio granny gear. This transmission will mount readily to many engine types and adapt to either the NP231 or NV241. Swaps of older 3-speed manuals are often left to Jeeps that spend more time off-road. (Photo Courtesy Novak Conversions)

While some similar-year non-Jeep automatics use the same mount pattern as the factory Jeep transmissions, adapting a non-factory automatic to an NP231 or NV241 usually requires an adapter and possibly a new tailshaft for the automatic. Like many transmission adapters, the frame mount is integrated into the adapter. (Photo Courtesy Novak Conversions)

SM420: The SM420 is an aging transmission used from 1947 to 1967 in many GM trucks. This popular transmission is readily available and parts are abundant. This heavy-duty 4-speed features a super-low first gear. This transmission will mate easily to a GM engine and to a 4.0L with an adapter, a new mainshaft, and crank position sensor. Adapting to the NP231 (23-spline) or NV241 transfer case can be accomplished with adapters.

First gear: 7.05:1
Fourth gear: 1.00:1

SM465: The SM465 is a newer heavy-duty 4-speed transmission than the SM420. These were used in GM trucks from 1968 until 1991 and exist in a few varieties. Like the SM420, the SM465 will mate to GM engines readily. Adapting one to a 4.0L will require an adapted bell-housing, release arm, release bearing, clutch disc, and crankshaft position sensor. Adapting to the NP231 (23-spline) or NV241 transfer case can be accomplished with adapters. The SM465 is rather tall and can often hang lower than the transfer case. This can cause skid plate issues unless you plan carefully.

First Gear: 6.55:1
Fourth Gear: 1.00:1

Automatic Swaps

Swapping in an automatic can be a much more complex process, depending on the engine being used. In reality, swapping a non-factory automatic into a Jeep that already has an automatic may not make much sense because, in the case of the TJ, factory automatic transmissions will serve just fine. If the factory transmission needs repair, it will often be an easier and more cost-effective option to repair it than to do a swap. Almost all automatic swaps into a TJ are because of engine changes.

Swapping an automatic for a non-factory transmission will create the need to deal with many variables that result from a swap. Especially with an automatic, the Jeep owner will have to deal with shifters, shifter cables, and linkage. It's often likely that the factory shifter will not work with a non-factory automatic. Fortunately, many aftermarket companies including B&M and Lokar make custom universal shifters. The factory center console will probably also

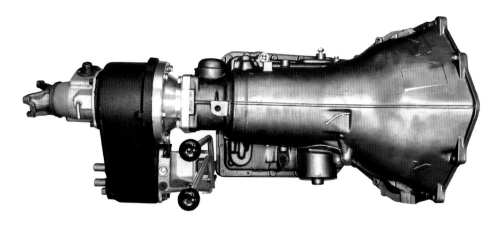

The GM TH350 and the 4L60 are strong automatics that can handle even well-built V-8 swaps. The two have a similar size, will bolt directly to most GM engines, and are easily adapted to the TJ transfer cases. The 4L60 4-speed automatic features a useful overdrive gear for reducing street-driving RPM even when running lower-ratio axles. (Photo Courtesy Novak Conversions)

interfere with custom shifter installations. Removal or customization of the console is often needed to install an aftermarket shifter properly.

In addition, cooler lines will likely have to be altered or replaced because of cooler line location and/or configuration. Silly little details such as dealing with the transmission dipstick and center crossmember can make completing the project an extra hassle.

TH350: This is a compact aluminum-case GM 3-speed automatic transmission with a tremendous amount of aftermarket support. It mates easily to GM engines and can be adapted to the 4.0L with adapters. Adapting to the NP231 (23-spline) or NV241 transfer case can be accomplished with adapters.

First gear: 2.52:1
Third gear: 1.00:1

TH400: Jeep vehicles in the AMC era used this heavier-duty aluminum-case GM 3-speed automatic. Like the TH350, this trans-

The little details are often most time-consuming and expensive in a swap. Making provisions for items such as a clutch slave cylinder can be a challenge on one-off swaps. When using a popular transmission, you can often find bolt-in products for the many details. (Photo Courtesy Novak Conversions)

mission has a lot of aftermarket support, ranging from shift kits to torque converters. This transmission mates easily to GM engines and can be adapted to the 4.0L with adapters. Adapting to the NP231 (23-spline) or NV241 transfer case can be accomplished with adapters.

First gear: 2.48:1
Third gear: 1.00:1

TH700R-4 / 4L60 / 4L60-E: The 4-speed automatic from General Motors is similar in size to the TH350. Many versions of this transmission are found through the years as it continued to evolve with the changing automotive times. In 1993, the TH700 was renamed the 4L60 and the 4L60-E became a fully electronic-shifting model. The addition of an overdrive gear as well as a converter lockup makes this an excellent modern transmission for swapped engines. These transmissions will mate directly to GM engines, but using a 4L60-E will add a level of complexity because of the need for the transmission to interact with the engine's PCM. The 4L60-E is best used with its original factory engine as part of a full engine/transmission swap. These transmissions (with the exception of the 4L60-E) will mate to a 4.0L with adapters. Adapting to the NP231 (23-spline) or NV241 transfer case can be accomplished with adapters.

First gear: 3.06:1
Fourth gear: 0.70:1

The Devil Is in the Details

Transmission swaps often require many little details that won't pop up until you are knee-deep into the project. Items including shifter location, clutch master cylinder/slave cylinder, reverse lights wiring, and so much more will have to be tackled. Driveshafts will probably need to be lengthened and/or shortened to deal with the differences in transmission length. Many companies, including Tom Woods and Reel Driveline, make custom driveshafts well suited for off-road use. In addition, contacting Novak Conversions or Advance Adapters with details before begin-

Transmission choice will continue to be a source of campfire debates within the Jeep community. Any choice will result in a capable off-road Jeep when it's properly paired with a balance of engine, transfer case, and axle gearing.

ning the swap will help it to be successful.

Putting It All Together

Because the goal here is to build a Jeep TJ for maximum performance on- and off-road, some things need to be considered. We have determined that the 4.0L engine will give best results for the needs of the Jeep. A transmission that is well suited to the 4.0L is the next decision to make.

Of course, the decision whether to use a manual or an automatic will come down to personal preference. Manual transmissions offer somewhat more control in downhill situations while automatics reduce broken parts and help in uphill situations. Traversing a rock field with a properly geared manual and a skilled

driver can look graceful. Similarly, a skilled driver who can drive an automatic with one foot on the gas and one on the brake can traverse the same field with the same grace. As with many things, the debate goes on.

The factory transmissions will all be a good choice for the Jeep we are building, but the NSG370 manual and the 42RLE stand out as the top of the factory transmissions.

If an engine swap is in your Jeep's future, consider matching the transmission to the engine for the best result. The TJ deserves a modern engine and transmission.

For our type of Jeep, money saved from a transmission swap (that is, not paying for the transmission, adapters, and other parts) can be used on components that more dramatically improve performance.

TRANSFER CASE AND DRIVESHAFTS

The transfer case sits attached to the rear of the transmission and serves a rather simple purpose. It lowers the overall gear ratio, making off-road driving easier by allowing more control. In addition to low range, it splits the engine power between the front and rear axle. By decreasing vehicle speed while increasing engine speed, the engine can turn the wheels with less effort. The transfer case is the second part in the three components that make up the crawl ratio. Crawl ratio is defined in chapter 5.

The driveshafts connect the power moving through the transmission and transfer case. They appear to be just tubes with some universal joints (U-joints). However, these components need to be well matched to the Jeep for best performance and long life.

Speedometer

It should be noted that the speedometer sensor gear is located in the transfer case. All TJs use an electronic speedometer connection with a gear installed in the tailhousing. If you change axle ratios and/or tire sizes, you must replace the gear with a properly matched gear that will correct the speedometer for an accurate speed reading. Engine and automatic transmission operation, as well as performance, are based on vehicle speed. An inaccurate speedometer reading can cause odd automatic transmission shift operation.

Modes, Naming, and Part-Time Four-Wheel Drive

Transfer cases can offer several operating modes that determine

Unlike earlier-model Jeeps that used a cable connecting the transfer case to the speedometer, the TJ uses an electronic unit connected to the PCM via a wire. Reliability is greater because there is no cable to wear out and/or break. Replacing the speedometer gear for ratio changes is simple and many configurations are available.

Off-road use is what the TJ is designed for, and the transfer case is the key component that splits engine power to the front and rear axles. Making that connection complete is the driveshaft, which perhaps suffers the most abuse off-road. Constant direction changes and torque pressure from obstacles focuses an incredible amount of stress on the driveshaft.

where the power is sent. TJ factory transfer case operating modes are two-wheel drive, four-wheel-drive Hi, neutral, and four-wheel-drive Lo. Jeep used names for the transfer cases in its vehicles; some of those names continue to confuse new Jeep owners. The TJ series only ever used the Command Trac (NP231J) and ROCTRAC (NV241OR) transfer cases, both of which were part-time four-wheel drive.

Some Jeep vehicles offered full-time transfer cases; the TJ was only ever equipped with part-time models. The part-time versus full-time mode often confuses Jeep owners and has led to worn parts and poor fuel mileage for some. Part-time transfer case–equipped Jeeps are designed for use in poor

Speedometer Gear Selection

Many variations of speedometer gears are available to fit most tire and gear ratio combinations. Use the chart provided to find the proper gear for your application.

Locate the appropriate tire size and match it to the axle gear ratio to find the proper speedometer gear. It's always recommended to replace the O-ring on the mount when replacing a gear. Installation is simple and requires only a wrench.

Tire Size to Axle Gear Ratio

Tire Size	36	35	34	33	32	31	30	29
5.38 Ratio	42	43	N/A	N/A	N/A	N/A	N/A	N/A
5.13 Ratio	40	41	42	43	N/A	N/A	N/A	N/A
4.88 Ratio	38	39	40	41	43	N/A	N/A	N/A
4.56 Ratio	36	37	38	39	40	42	43	N/A
4.10 Ratio	32	33	34	35	36	37	38	39
3.73 Ratio	28	29	30	31	32	33	34	35
3.55 Ratio	27	28	29	30	31	32	33	34
3.07 Ratio	N/A	N/A	N/A	N/A	26	27	28	29

(Measurements in inches)

Swapping Gears

A replacement speedometer gear can be installed rather quickly. Removing the sensor from the transfer case tailshaft is a matter of removing the retaining bolt, unplugging the wire, and pulling out the sensor assembly.

Remove the plug from the sensor and then the bolt and retaining bracket. Gently pull the sensor from the transfer case. Some gentle prying may be needed.

The original gear (right) is compared to the replacement (left). The size of the gear will make the difference. Using the gear as a reference will aid in the proper selection. With a little force, the old gear can be pulled from the sensor housing. Install the new gear by pressing it into place using slight force. The new gear snaps into the sensor housing.

Install a new O-ring and place the assembly into the transfer case tail-housing and then install the retaining clip. The clip fits into notches in the sensor. Attach the sensor wire plug.

The TJ series used a transfer case selector lever located on the driver's side of the center console. The Z-gate–style shifter can be problematic with age, body lifts, and drivetrain modifications. A simple pull of the lever will allow shifting from two-wheel drive to four-wheel drive and other drive modes.

With the lever pulled all the way back, the Jeep will be in four-wheel drive low range. Shifting into or out of low range should be done at or near a full stop. A Jeep owner will occasionally need to move slowly in reverse to free up the driveline stress that may be holding the Jeep stuck in low range.

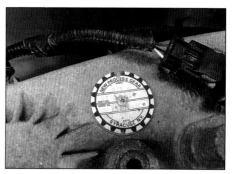

Identifying an NP231 is simple thanks to its round red tag attached to the rear of the transfer case next to the output shaft. The tag has the model number stamped directly on it. This transfer case is found in all TJs except the Rubicon; because of its 2.72:1 low range, it is well suited for the Jeep.

traction conditions such as snow and off-road. Two-wheel drive should be used only when driving on a street. Binding, wear, and poor mileage can occur when four-wheel-drive mode in a part-time transfer case is used on the street because the front and rear outputs are locked together.

Jeeps equipped with a full-time transfer case can operate in four-wheel drive even on a dry street. Full-time cases, such as the NP242 Selec-Trac found in the XJ and some others, have a differential within the transfer case that allows for slippage, relieving the binding and poor mileage.

Shifting

Since the TJ was never factory equipped with front locking hubs, simply pull the shifter to the four-wheel-drive Hi position to shift from two-wheel drive to four-wheel-drive Hi. Returning to two-wheel drive is the same procedure except that you push the lever back to the two-wheel drive position.

Shifting into four-wheel-drive Lo should only be done with the Jeep stopped and often is best done with either an automatic or manual transmission in neutral. You then pull the lever to the four-wheel-drive Lo position. It may be a small fight on many Jeeps to get the mode fully engaged. This is often due to an old linkage or the Jeep's need to move in either direction slightly to allow the gears to line up fully. Allow the Jeep to slowly move forward or reverse and try shifting again.

After some time in four-wheel-drive Lo, returning to two-wheel drive can be a challenge because the four-wheel-drive mode may have bound up the driveline. It is often easy to relieve the pressure by backing up several feet in a straight line.

Factory Transfer Cases

The Wrangler TJ was equipped with two different transfer cases during its run. The NP231 was a continuation from the Wrangler YJ and remains an excellent and reliable

transfer case for the Jeep. When the Rubicon was introduced in 2003, Jeep equipped the Rubicon models with the NV241OR transfer case, which was truly designed for off-road use. Jeep changed the forward output to the driver's side from the passenger's side starting with the YJ Wrangler, and it has remained there until today.

NP231J

It is frequently referred to as an NP231, Command Trac, or just a "231." Jeep began using this transfer case in 1988 in the YJ and XJ models and continued all the way until the end of the TJ series. The chain-driven part-time transfer case uses a split all-aluminum housing and is identified easily by the round red tag attached to the rear of the case.

The 231 uses a splined output that doubles as a slip yoke for the rear driveshaft; it adds considerable length to the case and some extra issues to the Jeep when a lift is added. The slip yoke allows the driveshaft to become shorter and longer during suspension movement. Earlier Jeep vehicles used a slip yoke within the driveshaft rather than the transfer case. Fortunately, several modification options are available to deal with the slip yoke. Input shafts were generally 23-spline except for some Jeeps equipped with 4-cylinder engines that used a 21-spline input.

The integrated rear output slip yoke on the NP231 adds several inches of length to the transfer case while at the same time shortening the driveshaft. This design works well for street-driven Jeeps but when used off-road the driveshaft is prone to being pulled from the yoke when the suspension is extended, especially on lifted Jeeps.

The transfer case chain drive in both the NP231 and NV241 keeps the transfer case operation quiet and allows for easy shifting but the chain is subject to stretching and wear from extended four-wheel-drive use. Replacement chains are readily available from a few manufacturers. Heavier-duty chains that withstand more abuse are available from JB Conversions.

The chain-driven design makes for quiet running and light weight. Hard, long-time off-road use can take its toll on the chain, but most recreational off-road use will not impact the chain. The respectable low-range ratio is a good match for the TJ, and for most off-road use the ratio will perform well.

Low-Range Ratio: 2.72:1
High-Range Ratio: 1:1

NP231J Modifications and Upgrades

The 231 is capable of serving the Jeep as it is, but a few upgrades will make this case even better. In recent years, some upgrades have disappeared from the market and have become items sought after at swap meets and online. Some of the reasons for the diminishing upgrade options are less demand and age. Swaps are discussed later in this chapter, but often a 231 is swapped out with a 241 for less than the price of the upgrades. Before going too far with a 231, consider the 241 swap option.

Slip Yoke Eliminator: The slip yoke tailshaft on the 231 becomes problematic after the Jeep is lifted because the angle increases; the effective length of the shaft also increases because of the lift. This results in

increased driveline vibration and the possibility of the driveshaft being pulled off the shaft at full suspension droop. This condition is less severe in a TJ Unlimited because the rear driveshaft is about 10 inches longer. Nevertheless, it should still be dealt with for the best performance.

Aftermarket companies resolved this issue by refitting the transfer case with a fixed yoke tailshaft using a standard universal-joint yoke. Almost always referred to as a slip yoke eliminator (SYE), these kits can be installed at home in a few hours. Several versions of SYEs exist; some use an extra-short output shaft to help increase driveshaft length, which reduces angles and reduces and/or eliminates driveline vibration. Installation of an SYE will require the use of a new rear driveshaft. Jeep owners often equip their Jeeps with an SYE and a CV-style driveshaft. The fixed yoke on the transfer case moves the slip joint to the driveshaft, preventing the possibility of the shaft pulling out of the back of the case during full extension. Equipping the Jeep with an off-road-designed driveshaft (with an extended slip joint) will give the best performance.

TeraFlex, JB Conversions, and a few others make quality SYE kits

The slip yoke eliminator (SYE) is a common modification to the NP231 to eliminate the integrated slip yoke, allow for a longer driveshaft, and reduce vibration. TeraFlex makes a quality kit that includes a new output shaft, tailhousing, and yoke. Installation can be performed in a few hours with the transfer case still in the Jeep.

A comparison of the NP231 output shaft: the SYE shaft (top) and the factory slip yoke shaft (bottom). Seeing them side by side shows the length difference between the two designs. The shorter SYE lengthens the driveshaft, which reduces potential vibration by lowering the driveshaft angle.

that replace the output shaft and tailhousing to increase driveshaft length by at least 6 inches. The typical installation is to leave the transfer case in the Jeep and split it along the two halves. Many lift kits recommend or even require installation of an SYE; some complete kits include them. Some kits modify the existing shaft to accept the fixed yoke while most replace the entire shaft, which is often the best choice for reliability.

Lower Gears: Prior to the introduction of the Rubicon and its

Installing a Slip Yoke Eliminator

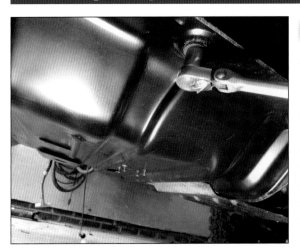

1 If a lift isn't available, raising the rear of the Jeep can allow easier access underneath. After the Jeep (and the transmission) is properly supported, remove the center skid plate to allow access to the transfer case. Remove the rear driveshaft and disconnect the front driveshaft at the transfer case yoke. Drain the fluid from the transfer case.

2 Gently remove the speedometer assembly and the front output yoke, followed by the output shaft seal and the snap ring located behind it. Remove the tailhousing and the eight case bolts at the case half.

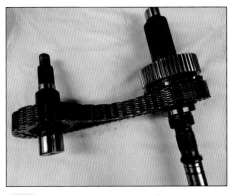

3 With all of the exterior components removed, carefully split the case apart and remove the rear cover. The front and rear output shafts and the drivechain are fully exposed. Simply pull the shafts rearward to remove the components.

4 Place the shaft on a clean surface. Remove the snap ring and take the hub out of the shaft. Install the new shaft into the original chain sprocket. Install the snap ring to retain the hub on the new shaft; verify that the snap ring is fully seated.

5 With the hub installed on the new shaft, assemble the gears and chain to match the way they were removed. Gently align the shaft spines and install the chain and shaft assembly into the transfer case's forward half.

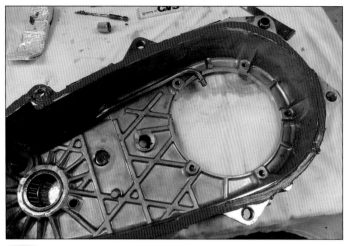

6 *Clean the case's mating surfaces. Apply a thin bead of a silicone-based sealer such as Permatex Ultra Blue RTV around the case half. Make sure the oil pump tube is properly located within the case's rear half.*

7 *Carefully place the case half to the front half and make sure that everything lines up and seats properly. Install the case bolts and tighten in a varying pattern of 20 to 25 ft-lbs. Install the oil pump over the rear output shaft; make sure the oil tube inside the case is inserted into the pump.*

8 *With the case together, and after making sure the housing mount is clean, apply blue RTV to the output housing. Install the output housing to the case and install the bolts; tighten to 26 to 34 ft-lbs.*

9 *Install the new rear driveshaft yoke followed by the front. It is recommended to place some RTV on the flat surface of the nut and apply thread locker to the threads; torque to 90 to 130 ft-lbs. Reinstall the front driveshaft, speedometer unit, and rear driveshaft.*

NV241OR transfer case, several companies produced low-gear sets for the 231 that lowered ratios from 2.72:1 to 4:1. This increase added some impressive change to the crawl ratio without any impact to street driving. These kits were costly because they replaced the entire front half of the case with a strengthened aluminum case fitted with the conversion. The kit uses stronger internal gears that substantially improve the 231 overall. TeraFlex's Low231 kit was the earliest kit

for a 4:1 ratio conversion.

TeraFlex no longer produces the 4:1 conversion because the NV241OR is such an easy swap instead. The 241OR cases can often be found for less money than the TeraFlex kit, and the 241OR case is superior to the 231 in many other ways. Finding a new old stock (NOS) kit is still possible and finding complete cases in the used market is relatively common, offering a good value.

Planetary Units: The stock 231 uses a planetary gear unit consist-

ing of three gears. Upgrading to a six-gear unit increases the strength of the unit. JB Conversions makes a complete six-gear planetary unit ready for the 231.

Wide Chains: A stock 231 uses a 1-inch-wide chain that can be a weak link, especially with hard four-wheel-drive use. The chain is prone to stretching and wear from the stress of larger tires and front lockers. JB Conversions makes a wide chain kit that replaces the chain along with the sprockets to increase strength

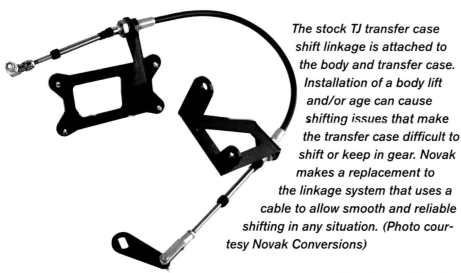

The stock TJ transfer case shift linkage is attached to the body and transfer case. Installation of a body lift and/or age can cause shifting issues that make the transfer case difficult to shift or keep in gear. Novak makes a replacement to the linkage system that uses a cable to allow smooth and reliable shifting in any situation. (Photo courtesy Novak Conversions)

and reduce wear. Some NP231 cases found in other-make vehicles can contain these wider chains from the factory. Swapping them into the Jeep 231 is possible; if done, proper fit and matching is important to prevent issues.

Shifters: The Z-gate linkage design of the 231 can be problematic with age and if the linkage operation is altered from modifications such as a body lift, engine lift, transmission swap, etc. These problems manifest as binding when shifting as well as popping out of gear. Novak Conversions makes a few 231 shifter options that rectify these issues. Perhaps the most common is the replacement cable–operated shifter linkage that separates the need for proper alignment of the shifter to the transfer case. After installation, shifts are precise and effortless; the factory shifter handle is retained to maintain a stock look.

NV241OR

When Jeep introduced the Rubicon in 2003, it became evident that Jeep was answering the call of Jeep owners who regularly off-road their Jeeps. The NV241OR transfer case was such a great addition to the Jeep that it only further solidified Jeep's

position as an off-road-capable vehicle. This heavy-duty transfer case equipped with both front and rear fixed yokes was nice on its own but adding the 4:1 low-range gear ratio made it just right. Interestingly, a NP231 fitted with all of the upgrades still doesn't match the reliability and strength of the 241. The direct-swap ability of the 241 to 231 quickly increased the value of a 241 in the used market while at the same time decreasing the popularity of deep 231 modifications.

Low-Range Ratio: 4.00:1
High-Range Ratio: 1.00:1

When Jeep introduced the NV241OR in the Rubicon in 2003, the Jeep community was impressed that Jeep would factory-equip a Jeep with such a great transfer case. The 4:1 low range combined with front and rear fixed yokes made this transfer case almost perfect for the Jeep.

NV241OR Modifications and Upgrades

The 241 is so well equipped that upgrades and modifications are almost nonexistent. Really, the only upgrade needed for the 241 is not actually within the transfer case but rather the problematic Z-gate–style shifter linkage found in the TJ. As with the 231, Novak Conversions makes a cable-style shifter linkage system that replaces the factory linkage completely while retaining the stock shifter handle. Shifting is precise and effortless after installation.

Transfer Case Swaps

Transfer case swaps in a TJ aren't very common thanks to the quality of the factory cases. A swap is often the result of an engine swap or if the Jeep is used for heavy off-road use that exceeds the demands of the 231 or 241.

NV241OR

Jeep owners who have 231-equipped TJs and desire the lower gears from a transfer case often look to swapping in a 241 from a Rubicon. This swap is a direct fit that can be accomplished without much, if any, modification. The swap almost always requires new front and rear driveshafts because of the yoke and length differences. During the swap, replacing the shifter linkage with an aftermarket one such as the Novak cable system makes for easier shifting but the factory shifter will work.

Finding a used 241 isn't particularly difficult and a few companies make rebuilt, ready to install 241OR transfer cases that will fit directly in place of a 231.

Dana 300

The Dana 300 first appeared in the 1980 AMC-era CJ. This compact, fully gear-driven case is still highly regarded as a superior transfer case in a Jeep because it has exceptional strength. Upgrades to a 4:1 gear set are rather simple, and the transfer case uses the same 23-spline input and mounting pattern as the 231 and 241. The biggest issue is the fact that the CJ used a passenger-side front output and the TJ uses a driver-side front output.

Down East Offroad makes a Dana 300 flip kit that relocates the shift mechanism to the bottom cover area (which is now the top because of the flip) while using a twin-stick design. Novak Conversions offers a Dana 300 clocking ring that allows for the flip, but shifter operation and other issues such as venting still need to be addressed.

The popularity of this swap has diminished thanks to the ease of swapping in an NV241. At the last report, the Down East Offroad flip kit is still available.

Atlas

The Atlas transfer case from Advance Adapters is legendary and is well known to withstand the most extreme off-road use. This aftermarket transfer case was designed specifically *for* heavy off-road use. It is constructed of a solid one-piece case made from T6 heat-treated aluminum and is completely gear driven. This case also uses a twin-stick design

shifter mechanism that allows for a whole variety of gear selection options, even unusual selections such as front-wheel-drive low range. The Atlas is available in a few versions and several different gear ratios, ranging from 2:1 to 5:1. This case is expensive but will live up to its reputation.

Other Transfer Case Swaps

It's quite rare to see swaps using other transfer cases in a TJ because the factory cases are so good and the standard non-factory options might offer a Jeep owner everything he or she might need. In unique swap cases for which non-Jeep transmissions are used, it may be necessary to use a transfer case better matched to the engine/transmission combination. Those kinds of swaps would likely be complex and best left to the experts.

Underdrives

There was a practice some years ago, possibly somewhere in the 1990s, when the quest for the ever-lower crawl ratio was running rampant. Off-road events often featured slow drags where Jeep owners would put their 100:1 crawl-ratio vehicles up against each other to see whose was slowest. Like many fads, it's gone and good riddance. Underdrives are units that most often sit between the transmission and transfer case, essentially lowering the drive ratio entering the transfer case that then multiplied the reduction even further. Achieving an 11:1 to

The Atlas by Advance Adapters is the ultimate transfer case for an off-road vehicle. It is available in many gear ratios and configurations. This case can withstand even the hardest use and powerplants.

16:1 reduction was not uncommon. Gears this low are often unusable for most off-road driving conditions. Super-low ratios are only good for extra-slow rock navigation; even then, they are probably too slow.

A common practice was to install a planetary gear reduction unit made by Klune-V. In a standard TJ, the Klune-V increased the driveline by 6.5 inches, requiring the installation of an SYE with a 231. Like many once-popular products, the Klune-V is no longer manufactured and has become available only as NOS or in the used market.

Other underdrive options, such as dual transfer cases, are not typically feasible in the TJ because of its short wheelbase. Proper axle gears and a single 4:1 transfer case fits the needs of 99 percent of Jeep owners.

Driveshafts and Upgrades

The driveshaft is the final component connecting the transfer case to the front and rear differential. The driveshaft doubles as a way of transferring the rotational torque of the engine to the differential while allowing the movement of the suspension to not interfere with the rotation. The U-joints on the driveshaft allow the operation to move in various angles and the slip joint allows the shaft to extend and compress during suspension movement. The driveshaft is often a weak link in the Jeep's driveline; it certainly does take a substantial amount of abuse off-road.

U-Joints: The job of the U-joint is to allow movement in an angle while transferring rotational force. That sounds simple, but the life of a U-joint in a vehicle is tough and in an off-road-used Jeep it's even tougher. U-joints experience a large amount

A stock TJ driveshaft is sufficient for the street and mild off-road use. Its thin-wall tubing can twist under the pressure created by lower gears and larger tires. Replacing the shaft with a thicker-walled, longer slip joint–style shaft will increase reliability and reduce breakage.

The TJ uses the 1310-style U-joint on the driveshaft ends. Greasable and sealed units are available; some consider the sealed units stronger because they are solid. Carrying a spare set or two in the Jeep's toolbox is easy insurance.

of constantly changing force. When driving off-road and navigating a rock field or attempting to traverse a goopy mud bog by quickly changing from forward to reverse and back again, the loading and unloading of force on the U-joint is massive compared to cruising down the highway.

The U-joint can be a weak point in the drivetrain, and, in many ways, it's a good place to have a weak point. Many Jeep owners carry spare U-joints or even a spare driveshaft in case of a failure. It is much easier to change a driveshaft on the trail than to change an axle shaft or differential.

The factory TJ uses seven U-joints within the driveline; five are within the driveshafts and two are located within the front axle. Driveshafts use the Dana Spicer 1310 style of joints with the exception of the factory CV-style joint.

Operating Angles: U-joint operating angles are often misunderstood, and failure to observe "the rules" leads to vibration and joint failure. For the majority of driveshafts used in a Jeep, you will find either a drive-shaft with a U-joint at each end or a constant velocity joint (CV joint) at one end and a U-joint at the other. Operating angles are different for both of them.

In a standard driveshaft with two U-joints, both yokes should be operating on a parallel plane extending from the yoke's shaft to each other. The larger the variations in the plane, the more out of phase the U-joints become, which causes a speed-up/slow-down condition that is felt as a vibration. Lift kits and transfer case lowering kits can increase the variation dramatically.

CV-style joints allow greater operating angles but work best when the yokes are pointing at each other. This means that the optimum setup will angle the axle side yoke to point at the transfer case yoke. In a stock TJ, the factory control arms are not adjustable and achieving the optimum angle isn't likely. Lift kits with adjustable upper and/or lower control arms allow for this adjustment to find the perfect vibration-free location.

U-Joint Upgrades: Some Jeep owners occasionally have a moment when

Lift kits increase the angle on a driveshaft, which will increase the likelihood of vibration, wear, and failure. A CV-style joint increases the working angle of a shaft and reduces vibration. (Photo Courtesy Ben Mann)

Vibration can be minimized with the addition of an SYE and a CV-style driveshaft. An optimal angle for a CV-equipped driveshaft is having the pinion pointed at the output yoke. This can only be done on a TJ equipped with adjustable suspension control arms.

the belief that bigger and stronger is always better. A U-joint may not be the best place to apply this unless the bigger picture is considered. A 1310 U-joint is common, quite strong, and inexpensive. Carrying them in a TJ is simple and compact. Let's say you upgrade your driveshaft and yokes to use a larger, stronger U-joint while still retaining the factory axles. It's possible that the weak link (often the U-joint) is no longer the U-joint but rather the factory ring and pinion or front axle U-joints. These components are not easy to fix on the trail and are much more costly. The U-joint could be considered disposable, like a fuse.

Slip Joints: While the U-joints allow for angle changes, the slip joint allows for length changes that occur during suspension movement. As discussed earlier, the factory NP231 uses a rear-integrated slip joint with a fixed-length driveshaft while the front slip joint is within the driveshaft. With the installation of an SYE, a new driveshaft with an integrated slip joint will be required. When replacing or upgrading a driveshaft, using one with a heavier joint with longer travel will allow the Jeep's sus-

When measuring for a new driveshaft, follow the provider's instructions to ensure the optimal length for the Jeep is acquired. Most require that the length be measured with the Jeep at ride height; measure from yoke to yoke.

pension to move freely without the joint binding or coming apart.

Shaft Upgrades: With the exception of replacing a U-joint, the entire shaft is often replaced as a whole. Many companies, including Reel Driveline and Tom Woods, make driveshafts designed for off-road that include longer slip joints and heavier tubes. The stock TJ driveshafts use thinner-wall tubes that can twist and fail much more easily from the torque and shock loads of off-road driving. This is exaggerated with larger tires and lower gears.

When replacing a driveshaft, it is recommended to take measurements as required by the specific manufacturer. This ensures that the shaft is proper length for the Jeep to accommodate the lift and/or other modifications.

Putting It All Together

Keep in mind that the Jeep we are building is for maximum on- and off-road performance. In addition, you want to find the best value for the money to get that performance. Either factory transfer case will serve the Jeep in this capacity.

The NP231J is an excellent transfer case for a TJ with a factory engine and up to 35-inch tires. Installation of an SYE and a rear CV-style drive-

shaft is an almost mandatory modification. The 2.72:1 low range is still respectable and usable.

An NV241OR may be the perfect transfer case for a TJ. It's strong and ready to go right out of the box. The 4:1 ratio makes for extra-low off-road crawling.

Swapping an NV241OR for an NP231 will be the best value over completely upgrading the NP231.

Thicker tube, extended slip-joint driveshafts will improve strength and reliability. Carry extra joints and the tools to change them on the trail.

Extended high-strength slip joints found in aftermarket driveshafts prevent binding and separation at full suspension movement. These shafts typically use larger, stronger slip joints that are superior to the factory driveshafts.

A new replacement driveshaft that is perfectly matched to the particular Jeep should provide vibration-free driving and reliable off-road performance. Maintaining the driveshaft by lubricating the joints, if possible, will extend the life.

AXLES AND TRACTION SYSTEMS

The term *axle* or *rear end* can refer loosely to the entire axle assembly instead of just a particular part. To be consistent, the word *axle* is used here to define the entire assembly rather than the axle shaft specifically. An axle assembly contains many components, most of which serve to alter the rotational direction of the driveshaft to forward and reverse rotation, which then propels the Jeep in one direction or another.

Within the axle assembly is a ring and pinion gear set. These gears serve the direct function of changing the rotational direction. The pinion gear is attached directly to the driveshaft and the ring gear is connected to the differential. The differential is responsible for transferring the rotation directly to the axle shafts while allowing changes in left or right wheel speed when cornering. During cornering, the outer wheel travels farther than the inner

wheel. If the axle shafts were connected directly, binding would occur, causing difficult steering, excess wear, and possible damage. The axle shafts, which support the weight of the Jeep, are directly connected to the differential and the wheels.

In addition to all of these jobs, the axle holds the brakes and has the burden of being the object closest to the ground; therefore, it receives most of the physical abuse by objects on the trail.

Axle Gear Ratio

The gear ratio is determined by the teeth on the pinion compared to the ring gear. Jeep used axle ratios in factory TJs over quite a span: 3.07:1, 3.21:1, 3.55:1, 3.73:1, 4.10:1, and 4.56:1. The 4.10:1 was a standard ratio in Rubicon models and the 3.73:1 was standard on the Wrangler Unlimited. Most of the other ratios were used dependent on the engine and transmission combination.

The gear ratio is simply the number of revolutions of the pinion to the ring gear. A 4.10:1 ratio means that the pinion will rotate 4.1 times for every single revolution of the ring gear.

The TJ retained the solid axles that were in every Jeep CJ and Wrangler model before it. The Dana 44 and Dana 30 models are excellent axles for the Jeep; they include many modifications and upgrade options. The Dana 30 (top) can be spotted because of its offset gear housing and the Dana 44 rear (bottom) is identified by the centered gear housing.

Crawl Ratio

The three components that make up the crawl ratio are the transmission's first-gear ratio, the transfer case low-range ratio, and finally the axle gear ratio. This number is a simple multiplication of the three numbers resulting in the final ratio known as the crawl ratio. The larger the number is, the lower the gear ratio. Occasionally, these numbers are confusing, depending on how they are used.

Numerically Greater = Lower Ratio
Numerically Lesser = Higher Ratio

An example is 35:1 versus 52:1. While 52:1 is numerically greater than 35:1 because 52 is a larger number than 35, 52:1 is a lower ratio. In this example, at 52:1 the engine rotates 52 times for every 1 revolution of the axle shaft; that translates to 17 more revolutions than 35:1. More revolutions translates to greater torque multiplication, resulting in less effort from the engine and slower, more controllable vehicle speed.

To put this into a real-world situation, I'll use two examples, one from an automatic-equipped Jeep, and one from a manual-equipped Jeep. You must think about crawl ratio differently depending on the type of transmission. An automatic will almost always have a higher crawl ratio than a manual. This is rarely a problem because the automatic transmission torque converter can multiply engine torque at slow speeds. The tire size is not factored into the crawl ratio so assume that all of the Jeeps in the example have 33-inch tires. Cruise RPM is a separate calculation that represents engine speed at a set highway speed; tire size is a factor in cruise RPM calculation.

Manual Transmission Crawl Ratio Example:
A TJ equipped with an NSG370 transmission, an NP231 transfer case, and 3.21:1 axle gears.

$$4.46 \times 2.72 \times 3.21 = 38.94:1 \text{ crawl ratio}$$

A Rubicon TJ equipped with an NSG370, an NV241OR transfer case, and 4.10:1 axle gears.

$$4.46 \times 4.0 \times 4.10 = 73.14:1 \text{ crawl ratio}$$

It's obvious that the Rubicon TJ's ratio is nearly twice as low as the other one. That's thanks to the 4:1 transfer case and the lower axle gears. The Rubicon, because of its crawl ratio, would navigate rocks and other trail obstacles with much less effort from the engine and the low gears would allow more control because of the slower speeds.

A change of axle gears in the non-Rubicon Jeep from 3.21:1 to 4.56:1 would alter the ratio significantly. So, 4.46 x 2.72 x 4.56 = 55.32:1 crawl ratio, which is a much more usable and controllable ratio. It's likely that this change in ratio would improve cruise RPM due to the increase in tire size over stock.

Navigating difficult obstacles can be a challenge in a Jeep with ratios that are too high or too low. Finding the right balance of off-road ratios versus street ratios is the key to a Jeep that works well in both situations. Greasy hill climbs can require some extra wheel speed that a too-low ratio may not be able to provide.

A lower gear ratio makes such a difference off-road and often a Jeep owner who experiences it for the first time after driving a higher-geared Jeep will suddenly understand what it means. The control that is gained is so significant that it makes driving easier and reduces the potential for damage from excess speed.

Highway-cruise RPM will vary among engine types and modifications. Finding the optimum RPM for your Jeep by selecting appropriate gearing will result in the best fuel mileage and performance. A 4.0L runs optimally in the 2,000- to 2,300-rpm range.

It's a fact that most Jeeps spend their lives on the street and most Jeeps that are used off-road serve double duty and actually spend most of their time on the street. This reality leads into the concept of finding the balance of performance that makes both driving situations acceptable.

Automatic Transmission Crawl Ratio Example:

A TJ equipped with a 42RLE automatic transmission, an NP231 transfer case, and 3.21:1 axle gears.

$$2.84 \times 2.72 \times 3.21 = 24.80{:}1 \text{ crawl ratio}$$

A Rubicon TJ equipped with a 42RLE automatic transmission, an NV241OR transfer case, and 4.10:1 axle gears.

$$2.84 \times 4.0 \times 4.10 = 46.58{:}1 \text{ crawl ratio}$$

Similar to the manual transmission example, the crawl ratio of the Rubicon is almost twice as low as the non-Rubicon Jeep. Again, because of the 4:1 transfer case and lower axle ratio.

A change of axle gears in the non-Rubicon Jeep from 3.21:1 to 4.56:1 would alter the ratio significantly. So, 2.84 x 2.72 x 4.56 = 35.22:1 crawl ratio, which is a much more usable and controllable ratio. It's likely that this change in ratio would improve cruise RPM due to the increase in tire size over stock.

Cruise RPM

Even though tires haven't been discussed, this is a good time to discuss cruise RPM. Because tires are a simple concept that is only considered here for their height, the details of the tires are irrelevant. Unlike crawl ratio, cruise RPM is the calculation of engine RPM and highway speeds. The Jeep we

Changing tires has an effect of altering the gear ratio because the tires cover more distance per revolution. This causes the cruise RPM to drop by effectively making the overall gear ratio higher. Lowering the axle gear ratios after installing larger tires can return cruise RPM back to an efficient level.

are building is meant for use in both on- and off-road driving, so cruise RPM is an important consideration.

All engines have a specific RPM at which they provide a balance of horsepower to torque that makes the engine run most efficiently and gives the best fuel mileage. An RPM too low for the engine will demand constant downshifting, and a too-high RPM can make for poor fuel mileage. Looking at the cruise RPM of the stock Jeep will often indicate what is most efficient. Keep in mind that engine speed is not always an indicator of fuel consumption. In these examples, a speed of 65 mph is assumed.

The 4.0L engine in a stock Jeep operates at around 2,000–2,300 rpm at 65 mph. Note, Jeep has had a habit of running the 4.0L in a lower RPM range to keep mileage

Crawl Ratio *CONTINUED*

down, but in normal highway driving at this RPM, the passing and hill power is almost nonexistent without downshifting.

The 2.4L and 2.5L engines operate at a little higher RPM than the 4.0L. The most common is 3,000 to 3,200 rpm at 65 mph.

For non-factory engines, it is important to know the optimum RPM speed for highway driving. This will play a part in finding the proper gear selection.

Tires Sizes and Cruise RPM: Increasing tire size will impact cruise RPM by slowing down the engine speed because the larger tire covers more distance per revolution. In effect, adding larger tires makes the gear ratios higher. The slower engine speed will cause the engine to fall below the efficient RPM, which robs fuel mileage and creates the need to downshift.

Example: A Jeep equipped with a 4.0L, 42RLE automatic (0.69:1 top gear), and 3.73:1 axle gears. With the stock 30-inch tires at 65 mph, the engine will run at 1,874 rpm. Increase the tire size to 33 inches with no other changes and the engine drops to 1,703 rpm, which is well below the bottom of the range.

By lowering the axle gear ratio to accommodate the larger tires, the appropriate cruise RPM can be restored. The same Jeep from above with 4.56:1 gears will run at 2,082 rpm. An increase from the original 1,874 rpm makes highway power better without the sacrifice to fuel mileage.

Several calculators are available online. The Grim Jeeper website has an extensive calculator that allows easy comparison along with preset ratios for many transmissions and transfer case types.

For manual calculation: MPH x gear ratio x 336 / tire diameter = cruise RPM.

So What Does This All Mean?

Calculating out the crawl ratio will help in making decisions to modify certain components of the Jeep. Crawl ratio and cruise RPM are extremely important factors that need to be considered for entirely different driving scenarios. It can be a compromise; some elements, such as the transfer case, impact only crawl ratio and not cruise RPM.

In general, transmissions and particularly transfer cases make the biggest impact to crawl ratio. Swapping a transmission with a lower first gear and/or a transfer case with a lower low-range ratio will drastically improve off-road performance with little change to highway driving. Altering axle ratios will have less of an off-road impact than on highway performance. It's all a compromise; find that low range and highway sweet spot at the same time.

Jeep owners often ask what an optimum crawl ratio is. In truth, there is no perfect answer. Attempting to achieve even higher numbers to lower the ratio further can actually have a negative effect. Gears that are too low become effectively unusable. There are times that wheel speed and/or vehicle speed is necessary. Excess low gears can make achieving the needed speed impossible. For our Jeep build, somewhere in the 50–70:1 range is good for a manual transmission and 35–55:1 range for an automatic. ∎

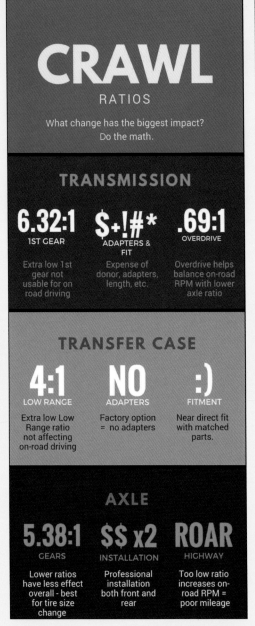

Calculating crawl ratio and cruise RPM before beginning modification to the Jeep's drivetrain will aid in determining the correct components. Taking into account the planned tire size, the engine's RPM band, and the transmission type are essential to calculating the optimum results. This graphic indicates the positives and negatives of certain modifications.

This mockup shows how the differential is oriented within the housing. The axle shafts (not shown) enter the carrier (top and bottom) to engage the side gears. Thanks to spider gears (center) that are attached to the carrier, they can move along the side gears, allowing the wheels to move at different speeds during cornering. This particular set is a Dana 44 Trac-Lok differential with 3.73:1 ratio gears.

Spider gears allow the wheels to move at different speeds when turning. This is often a mystery to Jeep owners. It often makes total sense only when a physical model or computer-generated video is available. Spider gears are a weakness in many axles, as well as the reason for spinning only one wheel.

Changing gear ratios impacts both cruise RPM and crawl ratio, so consider both calculations when changing ratios. Gear changes can be costly and most often must be done by a professional.

Traction Systems

A differential in most vehicles uses a carrier assembly to which the ring gear is attached. Within the assembly, smaller gears make up the gear set that allows the wheels to move at different speeds when cornering. These are typically referred to as spider gears. The spiders are made up of side gears that attach directly to the axle shafts while the differential pinions ride along a shaft within the carrier.

A differential of this design is referred to as an open differential, meaning that power is capable of going to each wheel or just one. Typically, the wheel with the least traction gets the most power. This simple setup works well in cars and vehicles driven in high-traction conditions (such as the street) but falls very short in poor conditions. If you see a vehicle in a low-traction situa-tion spinning one wheel, it's almost guaranteed that it has an open differential. Most TJs were equipped with an open differential in the front and the rear; this is obvious off-road when the Jeep is trying to traverse an obstacle and only one front and one rear wheel (the ones with the least traction) are spinning.

Several solutions are possible for increasing traction by sending the power to both wheels. These solutions vary in approach, price, and complexity.

When a Jeep flexes the suspension over an uneven surface, a tire that is extending from the Jeep will have to bear less weight. Even if the tire is almost off the ground, it will not impact a locker's operation. Both wheels will move at the same speed, which allows the tire on the ground to receive full power and get as much traction as possible. Even a limited slip differential will have difficulty in this situation.

Limited Slip

The limited slip differential, also known as a "posi" (short for positive), is the optional traction system that Jeep offered in the TJ as the Trac-Lok differential. The limited slip differential works by allowing a certain amount of torque to be applied to both wheels even in low-traction situations. The limited slip operates by using clutch packs on the differential's side gears that limit excess slip when there is a loss of traction. This is an effective system for slippery road conditions and light off-roading. However, in situations where a wheel may come off the ground, the limitations of the limited slip will be exceeded, causing loss of traction. The effectiveness of the limited slip over time diminishes as the clutch packs wear. Proper gear oil must be used in a limited slip–equipped axle. A properly operating limited slip may cause some odd driving behavior. The Jeep may lose traction and fishtail during hard

Many TJ models were available with a Trac-Lok differential in both the Dana 35 and Dana 44. These added traction that was better than a totally open differential. Over time, the clutch packs that made the limited slip operate wore and that diminished its effectiveness. A limited slip, like an automatic locker in rainy and snowy conditions, can engage, which causes the Jeep to fishtail.

acceleration when cornering or driving in very slippery conditions such as snow.

Lockers

A locking differential causes equal torque to be applied to both wheels (regardless of traction) by locking the side gears of the differential together, which effectively eliminates any differentiation. Lockers are extremely effective off-road and will provide maximum traction to one wheel even if the other wheel is in the air. Lockers come in a few varieties and operate in different ways, but they can essentially be boiled down to two different types: automatic or manual lockers. Expense, convenience, and durability are all considerations when deciding on a locker. Manual lockers offer the convenience of choosing when to engage the locker, but they often come at a higher price because they may include other necessary components for operating the system. Automatic lockers can be much less expensive but often introduce less desirable characteristics to normal street driving.

Manual Lockers: The driver actuates manual lockers in one of three ways: air, electronic, or cable. All three types operate by locking the side gears so that the axle shafts receive 100 percent of the engine power. That power is then transferred equally to both wheels. When disengaged, the differential operates just like a normal open differential. Manual lockers do not impact street driving as a limited slip or automatic locker will.

An air locker operates by using air pressure to engage the locker. It's an on-demand system that often includes an onboard compressor to provide the needed pressure for operation.

The TJ Rubicon is equipped with Jeep's version of an air locker. Small compressors located on top of the center skid plate send air to the front or rear locker with the flick of a switch on the TJ's dash. Rubicon lockers operate in a set sequence from the factory with a single switch for rear, both, or off. The factory setup does not allow operation of the front locker without the rear being engaged. Furthermore, neither locker will operate without being in four-wheel-drive Lo. It's not usually a problem for most situations, but some drivers may want to use a locker in two-wheel drive or four-wheel-drive Hi on occasion. Using the rear locker in four-wheel-drive Hi in the snow can be especially handy when extra traction is needed and shifting to low range is inconvenient. In reality, locker operation in two-wheel drive is only good for donuts. Several electronic hacks are available (through the Jeep community) that allow locker operation in any transfer case mode. You must understand the potential for unusual or unpredictable driving characteristics with a locker engaged at higher

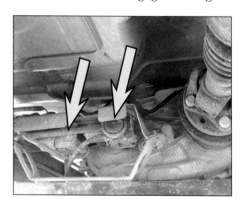

The small compressors (arrows) used for the factory Rubicon lockers are safely located on top of the center skid plate. These low-pressure compressors are insufficient to run tools or fill air tanks such as a regular onboard air compressor.

A Rubicon will have a switch on the dash not found in any other version of a TJ. The locker switch operates both the front and rear lockers. The front locker will only operate when the rear is engaged and neither locker will operate unless the Jeep is in low range.

speeds or street driving. The Rubicon air compressors do not have the capability to run other equipment or inflate tires.

Factory-offered locking differentials were a first for Jeep in 2003 with the release of the Rubicon. Likely based on the popularity of the ARB Air Locker, a factory-equipped locker system in a Jeep was impressive. The lockers are quite reliable and the fact that they were covered by the factory warranty was extremely attractive to new Jeep buyers. Even today, the Rubicon model lives on in the JK and JL with the factory-equipped electronic lockers.

The added traction is most noticeable when navigating rocks. The locker will keep both front wheels turning; this allows a tire to climb a rock rather than having to be pushed over it. You must note that an automatic locker in the front of a TJ can cause steering difficulty even on the street in two-wheel drive because of the lack of lockout hubs. However, many owners report that it is not a problem.

ARB Air Locker: Perhaps the most well-known aftermarket air locker is the ARB Air Locker. These lockers are known for their dependability and strength. Air enters the differential housing through a hose attached to an onboard air source. Typically, a Jeep owner installs an ARB compressor with electronically operated air

The ARB Air Locker kit includes the necessary components for installation. Air line, bearings, air collar, and air solenoid are the key components except for the differential. Installation requires specialized tools for installing a ring and pinion. For this reason, many choose to hire a professional to install the carrier.

solenoids that control the airflow. A professional will usually install an ARB Air Locker because it replaces the entire differential carrier assembly. When installing an Air Locker, consider axle gear ratios. Changing both at the same time can save money.

Installing ARB Air Lockers

Differential carrier installation is, in this case, the same as a stock replacement, which is covered thoroughly in your factory shop manual. Therefore, I will touch on the gear/locker assembly install only briefly and focus on the installation of the air compressor, air lines, and switches.

To save some shop labor costs, the axle assemblies were removed and prepped at home. Delivering the axles to a shop ready for installation will save a few hours of labor time. Be sure you do not remove the differential from the housing; most shops will want it installed for a beginning

reference. Supporting the Jeep properly is extremely important because with both axle assemblies removed, all of the weight will be placed on the

When installing a new locker, using a differential rebuild kit is recommended. Companies such as G2 make complete differential rebuild kits that include bearings, shims, seals, etc. Including these fresh components in the installation will make the axle like new.

support stands. Spend as little time as possible underneath.

Because of the desire to save some labor costs as well as prep for a lift kit install, axle assembly removal was the best option. Draining the oil is the first step of the long list of things to do to remove a Jeep's axle assembly. For more details on removing the axle, see chapter 6, where lift kits are covered in detail.

1 *Draining the gear oil for locker installation is the first step toward removal of the axle from the Jeep. If the oil looks like chocolate milk, water has likely entered the axle from either the breather tube or the wheel ends. Be sure to fix the seals before reinstalling the axle to prevent future water entry.*

2 *With the axles removed and cleaned, they, along with the ARB locker kits, gear sets, and rebuild kits, are loaded into the back of a four-door JK and delivered to OK Auto for installation.*

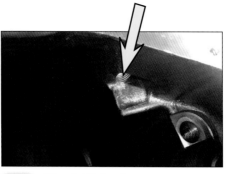

3 *After initial setup, measurements are taken, the differential is removed, and a hole is drilled and tapped in the top of the housing to accommodate the air line fitting that feeds the bearing collar that leads to the air locker's air passage.*

4 *Special marking paint is used on the ring gear during installation. The installer observes the wear pattern to properly set up the meshing of the pinion gear to the ring gear. The pattern left in the marking compound indicates what adjustments must be made to obtain an optimum installation. Proper installation leads to quiet gear operation and long life.*

5 *The ARB Air Locker, now installed in the Dana 44, uses a special air collar (seen under the bearing cap on the left) to allow the air to move into the rotating differential. You must make a small notch in the bearing cap to allow the copper tube from the collar to be routed to the air fitting in the axle housing.*

6 *The electric ARB air compressor kit can serve several purposes in addition to providing the Air Locker air pressure. You can install fittings to allow the compressor to supply an air tank capable of running air tools and filling tires. Onboard air systems are discussed in chapter 10.*

7 *Finding a suitable location for the compressor under the hood in a TJ isn't particularly difficult. Some owners use the small shelf located under the brake master cylinder or a higher, easier-to-reach location on the driver-side fenderwell. Make sure to account for room for the solenoids. The ARB compressor is adjustable and can fit into many locations.*

With the lockers installed into the axles, the labor-intensive step of reinstalling the axle housings into the Jeep must be completed. With that accomplished, the next part of the installation is finding a suitable location for the compressor, running air lines, and installing the wiring.

8 *Running air lines from the axles to the compressor should be done in a way to best protect the plastic line from debris and trail obstacles. Placing the line inside plastic wire molding is an added level of protection for the lines. In addition, install the lines to avoid high heat sources such as the exhaust.*

The ARB air compressor kit includes a complete harness for easy and proper installation of the locker switches. After the switches are fitted in a suitable location, wiring is a matter of following the diagram.

Finding a good switch location can depend on the year of the TJ; later models had a flat square area perfect for the three ARB switches. With the panel carefully removed, holes are cut for the switches. The wiring harness is routed through the Jeep and attached. A good circuit to power the locker's low-power side is the rear-window defroster circuit. A fuse tap was used to tap the circuit with a proper fuse for the locker system.

With all of the steps completed, test the locker operation. When

Locating the switches for manual lockers, such as ARB Air Lockers, will require some real estate somewhere in the dash area and within reach of the driver. The square area in the center area of the later-model TJ dash will accommodate the ARB switches nicely. ARB compressor kits come with a complete wiring harness, so you can properly wire a set of front and rear lockers.

using the ARB wiring harness and its switches, remember that the front locker will only operate when the rear is engaged. Neither locker will operate unless the compressor switch is in the "on" position. Periodic inspection of the locker components, especially the vulnerable air lines, will prevent a failure when the locker is needed.

Eaton E-Locker and Auburn ECTED Electric Locker: Both the Eaton and Auburn electric lockers operate similarly to the ARB, except that an electronic solenoid is used to engage the locker mechanism instead of the air-actuated mechanism found in the ARB. Electric lockers are simpler than air because only a wire needs to be run to the locker to allow operation. Installation does not require an air compressor or air lines, which saves in setup costs and reduces the potential for component failure. A damaged electrical connection from

a trail obstacle is also more easily repaired compared to a failed air line.

OX Cable Locker: The OX offers the ultimate in no-frills manual operation. A cable extends from the special OX differential cover to a shifter lever located within the driver's reach. The OX bare-bones approach offers greater reliability because very few points of failure are present. There is no need for an air or electrical system to operate the locker; this can save in both setup costs and complexity. The special heavy-duty OX cover holds the engage/release fork.

Automatic and Lunchbox Lockers: Automatic lockers will run in a normally locked mode but can unlock quickly to allow cornering without dragging a wheel. Most automatic lockers use the forward or reverse torque to hold the locker in the locked mode and will only unlock during cornering when power is not being applied. If the driver is applying too much power during cornering, the locker will lock, causing the inner wheel to drag; the sudden locking can often be violent and cause erratic vehicle movement. Most automatic

The Lock Right from Powertrax is an inexpensive automatic locker that installs in place of the spider gears. The locker relies on the strength of the differential's center pin to keep the axles locked together. Excess torque from the engine can shear this pin off, which will cause a complete failure. You must take care with spider replacement-style lockers.

lockers will cause a clicking, ratcheting, or clunking sound during cornering because the locker teeth slip over themselves. In addition to the clicking, lockers may engage suddenly; this can cause a banging noise and the vehicle may pull to the left or right when accelerating. Driving in the rain or snow with an automatic locker can be a hair-raising experience. The locker tends to stay locked in these situations, which can cause the Jeep to fishtail.

A Jeep owner must be willing and able to deal with the characteristics of an automatic locker. Some manufacturers offer automatic lockers that deal with everyday driving better; these styles usually cost more and may be more prone to failure because of their complex design.

Some automatic lockers replace the entire differential carrier while other less expensive systems replace the open differential spider gears. The latter is occasionally referred to as a lunchbox locker. These lock-

ers are typically not as strong as the full-carrier design but can be and are used for years. Failure usually occurs with broken center pins; fortunately, most locker manufacturers offer high-strength center pins to help with durability. In truth, driving style has the biggest influence on the reliability of these lunchbox lockers. Even a V-8 swap–powered TJ running 33-inch tires can run a lunchbox locker successfully for years with proper throttle control and respect for the components. Lunchbox lockers are a good introduction to an automatic locker. Jeep owners can often install a lunchbox locker with normal tools and without huge expense.

Detroit Locker: The Detroit Locker is the strongest and most popular of the automatic lockers. The Detroit Locker replaces the entire differential carrier assembly with a special carrier that contains components unlike traditional spider gears. When the Jeep is driven in a straight line, both wheels receive full torque. When cornering, the side clutches separate,

which allows a wheel to rotate with the corner. When power is applied, the clutches remain engaged and provide equal torque to both wheels, even if one wheel is off the ground. The strength and reliability of the locker is well established in many forms of motorsports. In most cases, a professional should install the Detroit Locker because the gears will need to be set up properly.

Powertrax: Powertrax makes a few versions of automatic lockers that fit into the lunchbox category. The most basic is the Lock Right; it's an automatic locker that uses a very basic design. This locker remains in the locked position and only unlocks when not under power or cornering. The Lock Right is known for abrupt locking and unlocking. When equipped in a manual-transmission TJ, it is common for the Jeep to pull to one side when shifting gears. The Powertrax No-Slip automatic locker is similar to the Lock Right but adds a synchronizing system that reduces the abrupt locking and unlocking.

The Detroit Locker is likely the ultimate automatic locker available. Its use in racing and other applications has helped boost its reputation. The Detroit replaces the entire differential and requires that the ring and pinion are set up to the locker. As with other automatic lockers, the Detroit makes noise when cornering and handling can be erratic. (Photo Courtesy Ralph Hassel)

Installing a Lock Right is possible in a home garage without specialized tools. The process of installation requires the removal of the axle shafts and the carrier center pin. Depending on the differential type and gear ratio, you may have to remove the entire carrier and ring gear to remove the center pin. The Lock Right installation manual gives specifics for the particular axle.

The Powertrax No-Slip is a popular front locker.

Spool: A spool is effectively a replacement for the differential. A spool either replaces a differential's spider gears or replaces the differential carrier. A solid connection is formed between the left and right axles and both remain locked in place, which causes the engine's torque to be applied evenly to each wheel. A spool is impractical in a Jeep that is used on- and off-road because cornering properties will cause one wheel to drag. The result is excess tire wear and driveline stress.

Factory Axles

The three models of factory axles offered in the TJ are practically the same as those offered in Jeeps going back to the CJ series. The axles were often strong enough for mild off-road use, even with larger tires. Breaking parts often comes down to driving technique rather than fragility of the parts. A heavy foot combined with a manual transmission can spell disaster for many components. Factory TJ axles always use the 5-bolt on 4.5-inch wheel hub.

Dana 30

The Dana 30 has been used in Jeeps since 1972 and is the most common front axle found in Jeeps from the CJ series up to the JK series. This axle was used in all TJ Jeeps with the exception of Rubicons. It is a lighter-weight axle that can serve well for a Jeep with tires up to 33 inches, although many Jeep owners have run 35-inch tires without incident. The Dana 30 axle shaft's U-joints can be a weak point, as can the outer stub shaft. However, the small ring and pinion is often strong

The Dana 30 found in so many Jeep vehicles is easily spotted thanks to its roundish-shaped cover. The Dana 30's popularity has created a vast market of upgrades and modifications that can greatly increase the axle's strength and reliability. A heavy-duty front cover can save the day when it smacks up against a rock.

Dana 30 Specifications

Stock gear ratio options: 3.07:1, 3.55:1, 3.73:1, 4.10:1, 4.56:1
Carrier break: 3.55:1/3.73:1
Open carrier: No Trac-Lok limited slip option
Ring gear diameter: 7.2 inches
Pinion shaft spline count: 26
Axle shaft spline count: 27, both inner and outer
Axle shaft U-joints: 5-760x/5-297x

A 4.56:1 ring and pinion from G2 is set for installation in a Dana 30, along with an ARB Locker. Many gear ratios are available from G2 and other manufacturers for the Dana 30, ranging from higher ratios to a low 5.38:1.

enough to withstand the abuse of off-roading, unlike the weaker components. The differential assembly is often the lowest point on a Jeep; the Dana 30 assembly is compact, which helps with ground clearance. Extra clearance is always better.

Dana 35

This carryover axle from the YJ series was almost universally hated because of its C-clip axle retention

design. A C-shaped clip is installed at the end of the axle shaft within the differential carrier to hold the axle within the housing. These clips are prone to failure, which can cause the axle to fall out the side of the housing. When this happens, the axle shaft can bend or damage other components, such as the brake lines and cables. Even though this axle has its issues, it can handle a lightly modified Jeep well. For serious off-road use, owners generally swap the Dana 35 for a Dana 44, an aftermarket axle, or a non-factory axle.

Its oval shaped cover and rubber plug easily identify the relatively undesirable Dana 35. Many TJs came equipped with this axle from the factory and they can successfully off-road with these for years with care without incident. It may not be worth spending too much money on Dana 35 upgrades because it's an easy sway for the commonly available Dana 44.

Dana 35 Specifications

Standard rear axle used on all TJs except the Rubicon and Unlimited

Stock gear ratio options: 3.07:1, 3.55:1, 3.73:1, 4.11:1, 4.56:1

Carrier break: 3.31:1/3.55:1

Optional Trac-Lok limited slip differential

Ring gear diameter: 7.5625 inches

Axle shaft spline count: 27

Rubber pressed-in fill plug

Dana 44

The Dana 44 has appeared in Jeep vehicles through the years almost since the earliest CJs of the 1940s and it was often the standard axle. Within the TJ series, it was either standard or an option, depending on the model. The Rubicon was the first Wrangler to include both front and rear Dana 44 axles with locking differentials. The Wrangler TJ Unlimited included a Dana 44 rear as standard. This axle has a vast amount of aftermarket support and many modifications and upgrades are available. This axle's strength and relatively compact size make it a good fit in a Jeep. Interestingly, the JK Rubicons have continued using the Dana 44 in both the front and rear.

The Rubicon's Dana 44 is fitted with the Tru-Lok differential. It uses a torque-sensing helical-gear limited slip that isn't prone to wear like a clutch pack–style limited slip. The limited slip offers better traction on the street in snow and rain, as well as light off-road driving. In addition to the limited slip, the Tru-Lok has air-engaged full locking capability for total traction. You should note that the Rubicon Dana 44 front axle uses smaller axle tubes and Dana 30 outers, which separates it from a traditional Dana 44 front.

Dana 44 Specifications

Optional rear axle used on 6-cylinder models; standard on Rubicon (front and rear) and Wrangler Unlimited (rear)

Stock gear ratio options: 3.55:1 (1997 only), 3.73:1, 4.10:1 (Rubicon)

Carrier Break: 3.73:1/3.92:1 (except Rubicon with thick gears)

Standard Trac-Lok limited slip differential on earlier-model TJs; optional on later-model TJs

Rubicon Dana 44: Tru-Lok limited slip with full lock

Ring gear diameter: 8.5 inches

Pinion shaft spline count: 26

Axle shaft spline count: 30

Front outer axle shaft spline count: 19

Threaded 3/8-inch fill plug

A 4.56:1 ring and pinion from G2 and an ARB Locker are set for installation in a Dana 44. Many gear ratios are available from G2 and other manufacturers for the Dana 44, ranging from higher ratios to a low 5.89:1.

The Dana 44 is easily recognized by its egg-shaped design; it can be confused with an aftermarket Dana 60, which is similar in shape but much larger. The Dana 44 front and rear were perfect for the TJ when the Rubicon was released in 2003. A heavy-duty cover will provide needed protection for the differential because they sit low and often come in contact with obstacles.

The Rubicon Dana 44 also uses what's known as a thick ring and pinion on the Tru-Lok differential; it will impact gear changes. Only thick-style gears will fit the Tru-Lok, which is limited to the 4.10:1, 4.56:1, and 4.88:1 ratios.

Factory Axle Modifications and Upgrades

Modifying the factory axles can help add strength and reliability to them. Many options are available for the Dana 30, Dana 35, and Dana 44. Common upgrades include lockers, higher-strength axle shafts, and U-joints.

Dana 30

Many Jeeps run the Dana 30 and it's more than up to the task of serving the Jeep off-road. The weakest point of this axle is the small axle tubes, outer axle stub shafts, and U-joints. Some upgrades can reduce the weak spots without the larger investment of swapping a Dana 44 or aftermarket axle.

Truss: Larger tires combined with hard off-road use can bend the axle tubes, which will cause worn or broken internal components. Several varieties of trusses are available from suppliers including Synergy and

Changing to RCV brand front axle CV joints is a popular upgrade to increase the strength and flexibility of the joint. In addition to the RCV joints, other manufacturers such as Ten Factory and Alloy USA manufacture higher-strength joints that will withstand the pounding better than stock.

JCR Offroad that can strengthen the Dana 30 to prevent a bent housing.

Axle Shaft Replacements: Ten Factory and Alloy USA make higher-strength axle shafts that use stronger materials to improve the performance of the Dana 30. Larger tires and lower gears increase the stress on axle shafts. RCV Performance manufacturers front axle replacement joints that replace the standard U-joint with a CV-style design that is twice as strong. The CV-style joints allow easier steering because the binding that can occur in a front axle U-joint is eliminated.

A way to shore up the smaller-sized tubes on factory Jeep axles is by using a truss. The added metal will increase rigidity and reduce the likelihood of a bent axle tube that can lead to worn and/or broken axle shafts and poor road handling.

Lockers: Almost every style of locker, from lunchbox lockers to air lockers, is available in a Dana 30. A lunchbox-style locker can work well in a Dana 30 for some inexpensive traction. A manual-style locker is a better option in a front axle to prevent difficult steering when in four-wheel drive.

Gears: A wide range of ratios is available, ranging from 3.07:1 to 5.38:1. The Dana 30 has a carrier break that requires a change when using 3.55:1 or higher ratios and 3.73:1 and lower ratios. It may be necessary to change a carrier when changing gears. Because most Jeep owners will choose a lower ratio, changing to the 3.73:1 and lower carrier is usually best, especially if a locker is added.

Dana 35

This axle has always carried a bad reputation, although it's probably not as bad as some folk might think. However, some things should be considered before dumping too much money into this unit. A factory Dana 44 is almost a bolt-in replacement for

The C-clip is the source of pain for many TJ owners who have experienced an axle leaving the side of their Jeep. A few companies used to make kits that eliminated the C-clip by using special axle tube ends or full-floating axles. In recent years, swapping the axle with a 44 or something else has become more cost effective.

this axle. It might not make sense to invest money into gears and lockers.

Truss: A few truss options exist to sure up the Dana 35 housing. Many Jeep owners will fabricate a truss for this axle.

Axle Shaft Replacements and C-Clip Eliminator: Ten Factory, Alloy, and G2 make high-strength axle shaft replacements. Warn used to make a full float kit that eliminated the C-clip. This upgrade, like many other TJ upgrades, has disappeared into the used market. As noted earlier, it may be a more cost-effective option to consider a swap for a Dana 44 instead of investing in the Dana 35.

Lockers: Almost every locker manufactured is available in a Dana 35 version, from lunchbox lockers to air lockers.

Gears: A wide range of ratios is available, ranging from 3.07:1 to 4.88:1. The Dana 35 has a carrier break that requires a carrier change when using 3.31:1 or higher ratios and 3.55:1 and lower ratios. It may be necessary to change a carrier when changing gears. Because most Jeep owners will go with a lower ratio, changing to the 3.55:1 and lower carrier is usually best, especially if a locker is added.

Dana 44 Front and Rear

The Dana 44 is so well built that often the only upgrades available are lockers and gears. The Dana 44 front found in the Rubicon is a bit of a hybrid; it shares some components with the Dana 30, including knuckles, U-joints, and outer axle stub shafts.

Truss: A few truss options exist to further shore up the Dana 44 housing. The 44 rear uses thicker tubes than the front, which uses the smaller Dana 30–size tubes. The front espe-

A front Rubicon Dana 44 from the factory is identified by the presence of the air line entering the top of the differential housing. Swapping a Dana 44 from a Rubicon is almost a bolt-in procedure that requires only the compressor, a switch, and a proper front driveshaft.

cially can use some extra support for heavier off-road use and larger tires.

Axle Shaft Replacements: Like the Dana 30 front, the Dana 44 front can benefit from an upgrade to higher-strength axle shafts and U-joints. Several companies, including Ten Factory and Alloy USA, make higher-strength axle components for the 44 front. In addition and similar to the Dana 30 front, RCV Performance manufactures front axle replacement joints that eliminate the standard U-joint for a CV-style design that is twice as strong. The CV-style joints allow easier steering because the binding that can occur in a front axle U-joint is eliminated. Several companies, including Ten Factory and Alloy USA, manufacture higher-strength axle shafts for the Dana 44 rear axle. It is an excellent replacement for a broken axle over a factory-style axle.

Lockers: Almost every locker manufactured is available in a Dana 44 version, from lunchbox lockers to air lockers.

Gears: Gear options and manufacturers for the 44 are almost endless, and ratios range from 3.07:1 to 5.89:1. When looking at gear options, remember that the thick gear ring and pinion set must be used. Be sure to consult your favorite reseller with your combination to ensure that you select the proper gears.

Axle Swaps

Swapping axles in a Jeep is a common practice and is often much easier than swapping engines or transmissions. Swapping components from one Jeep vehicle to another Jeep is the most common because of the lower cost and simplicity.

Aftermarket Dana 44 axles feature strength and clearance enhancements not found on the factory 44. The Dynatrac Dana 44 has a special differential housing that increases clearance and uses thicker axle tubes to prevent bending. These kinds of axles do not come cheap, but they will probably serve the Jeep for its lifetime.

A freshly modified Dana 44 in the rear of a TJ Unlimited. The new 4.56:1 gears, Air Locker, and heavy-duty cover dramatically increase the capability of the Jeep in many ways, including crawl ratio, cruise RPM, and durability.

Dana 44 Swap

Swapping a Dana 44 from another TJ is a bolt-in procedure. Minimal modifications are often required to get up and running. Frequently, driveshafts need to be changed and the brakes can be different. Most TJ Dana 44 axles used rear disc brakes. Using a Rubicon 44's axles will require the installation of the compressors and wiring.

Ford 8.8 Swap

This was a common swap to replace the Dana 35. This disc brake–equipped axle found in many Ford trucks and SUVs can be modified to fit a TJ. Installation of TJ suspension brackets is required; bracket kits are available from Ballistic Fabrication. Many varieties of lockers and gears are available for the 8.8.

Aftermarket Dana 44 & Dana 60

For even tougher axles, many companies, including TeraFlex, G2, and Dynatrac, produce custom-built heavy-duty axle assemblies ready to bolt into a TJ that are almost works of art. They are available with many locker options, gear ratios, lockout hubs, and more, and they feature thicker tubing, heavier mounting hardware, and ball joints. Be warned, these assemblies are not cheap, but it may be the last time you need to mess with your Jeep's axles.

Putting It All Together

Axles play a big part in a Jeep's capability. Gears and traction systems are extremely significant to the performance of the Jeep both on- and off-road. You should consider the many factors carefully that go into making these choices. This includes crawl ratio and cruise RPM. Find the low-range ratio that doesn't ruin highway RPM.

A Dana 44 rear axle combined with Dana 30 or Dana 44 front axle is an optimum combination for our Jeep configuration. Both can handle 33- and 35-inch tires with some upgrades that include stronger axle shafts and U-joints.

Swapping factory Dana 44 axles is the simplest swap for the most gain and least cost.

Manual lockers offer total traction with no impact on highway driving. Rubicon lockers or ARB Air Lockers will provide the best strength and reliability. Automatic lunchbox-style lockers are a great entry-level locker that can hold up, if the driver respects them.

Aftermarket axles are expensive but add a higher level of strength and reliability compared to any factory axle. Consideration of cost versus benefit should help in the decision. In most cases, factory axles will work just fine for our build configuration.

SUSPENSION AND STEERING SYSTEMS

The TJ Wrangler introduced the Quadra-Link suspension system to the Wrangler line. It was a massive improvement to the leaf-spring design found in the Wrangler and CJ before 1997. The simple design allowed smooth articulation and suspension movement that improved road driving and increased the Jeep's off-road capability. Like many other systems on the TJ, the Jeep's suspension is easily modified and upgraded to handle tougher off-road situations. Aftermarket support provides many choices and options for a Jeep owner.

Lift Kits

As with previous model Jeeps, lift kits are some of the most common modifications made to a Jeep. TJ lift kits are available in many forms and sizes but the most common are between 2 and 4.5 inches; variations in how the lift is achieved sets different lift kits apart. The purpose of the lift kit is to raise the Jeep, which increases ground clearance for components such as the center skid plate, bumpers, and fuel tank. In addition to ground clearance, the lift allows the owner to install larger tires that further increase ground clearance and add clearance for the differentials. Spring lifts not only raise the Jeep but also increase wheel travel.

The factory TJ coil suspension will get a Jeep through the trail better than many Jeepers believe, but its limits can be exceeded quickly when trying to tackle harder trails. A suspension lift increases chassis clearance and suspension flexibility and also allows larger tires for even more clearance. A good test of suspension flex is using a one-sided ramp to test a Jeep's ramp travel index (RTI). (Photo Courtesy Ben Mann)

This TJ Unlimited is equipped with a 4.5-inch suspension lift and 35-inch tires. A TJ lift usually maxes out at 4.5 inches with the factory control arm length and 35-inch tires. To run larger tires or increased lift, more drastic modifications must be made, but these mods will reduce street driving characteristics.

Compromises When Lifting a Jeep

Whenever a modification is made to a vehicle, characteristics related to that modified system change. In the case of lift kits, increasing vehicle height raises the center of gravity, which increases the possibility of a rollover. Driving characteristics of a lifted Jeep will be altered in several ways. Specific to the lift kit will be the increased body roll from the increased height. Some kits provide provisions to minimize roll by using heavier sway bars and variable-rate shocks.

A lift can cause brake lines to pull tightly during suspension movement. Many aftermarket companies offer quality extra-length brake lines or brackets that lower the front lines to compensate for the additional lift. Refer to chapter 8 for more details on brake upgrades and modifications.

Driveshafts and driveshaft angles may be affected depending on the amount of lift. More lift will cause the driveshafts to effectively extend

Factory brake lines can pull tight after a lift kit is installed and cause damage or rip the line. Longer aftermarket lines are available from TeraFlex and Goodridge that will not be overextended. Some lift kits include extension brackets that lower the hard line at the frame by approximately 1 inch to correct the situation.

and increase the angle in which they operate. Excess angle on a driveshaft can cause damage and the potential for joint failure. Another possible issue in a TJ equipped with an NP231 transfer case is with the slip yoke; it can allow the driveshaft to fall out because of the lift. Refer to chapter 4 for more details on driveshaft modifications and upgrades.

The steering system and driveline are also often impacted by the lift. Naturally, higher lifts will have more impact on all of these systems.

Suspension Lift Kit Types

TJ lift kits can be broken down into two main types: spacer and spring. Each has benefits and compromises, including installation difficulty and cost. On- and off-road performance will vary with each type but, in the end, both offer benefits. Choosing a lift for your Jeep is often based on your budget and the kind of off-road driving you do. For those on a tight budget or the light off-roaders, a spacer lift may suffice. However, those who can spend a bit more can improve the Jeep's performance to take on much more challenging trails.

Spacer Lift: Spacer lifts are quite simple and very effective at raising

The slip yoke eliminator (SYE) is an extremely popular and necessary upgrade to the NP231 when a Jeep is lifted. The already short rear driveshaft will suffer from the increased angles resulting from the lift. An SYE adds valuable length to the driveshaft and can decrease vibration caused by the angles. (Photo Courtesy Ben Mann)

A common starter lift kit consisting of simple spacers from 1 to 2.5 inches can add lift to a Jeep without replacing the springs or shocks. These inexpensive kits add valuable ground clearance and allow installation of larger tires without altering the ride of the Jeep. Many kits include shock spacers to account for the added height.

the Jeep. They are typically inexpensive and range in size from .5 to 2.5 inches. You simply install a spacer on the top of the coil spring, which raises the chassis for the lift. These kits retain the stock ride, and most spacer kits measuring 2 inches or less can use the stock-height shocks or extensions for the shocks.

From a wheel travel perspective, off-road performance isn't improved but the added chassis height and potential for increased tire size will provide valuable, extra ground

Lift springs are several inches taller than the factory springs. They frequently offer altered and variable spring rates to firm up the Jeep's ride while allowing increased suspension movement off-road. Increased wheel travel allows the tires to maintain contact with the ground, which preserves traction. Increased suspension height requires new, longer shocks that match the lift to prevent over-extension or bottoming out.

clearance. Axle articulation will be limited with a spacer lift. The stock springs and shocks cause a loss in downward travel because the shocks are overextended due to the lift.

Some spacer kits include shock extensions that will adjust the mounting location of the shock to put it at normal level to allow full travel. As an option, you can add new, longer shocks to deal with the extra height.

A typical 2-inch spacer lift will allow 31- to 32-inch tires to fit the Jeep comfortably without rubbing. A spacer lift is a great entry point for a Jeep owner looking to increase the Jeep's height and add larger tires without extra expense. Spacer lifts differ from spring lifts because the advertised size of the spacer will actually add that amount of lift. Many spring lifts result in variations of actual lift because of vehicle weight and spring

differences. TeraFlex, Rough Country, and Rubicon Express are a few of the companies that offer quality spacer lift kits for the TJ.

Spring Lift: A spring lift replaces the factory springs with taller springs that increase the Jeep's height and increase wheel travel, which allows more axle articulation. These increases allow for larger tires and provide more ground clearance. Increased suspension articulation allows the Jeep to traverse obstacles while reducing the likelihood of a wheel leaving the ground and losing traction. A spring lift provides the best performance off-road.

Components, Upgrades, and Modifications

Many components make up the suspension of the TJ Wrangler. Many of these can be enhanced or improved with some upgrades and/or modifications. Almost all of these components will enhance performance of the Jeep both on- and off-road.

Control Arms

The TJ uses four control arms per axle that control axle location with respect to forward and backward location. The arms, which are attached to the frame and axle, allow for movement in an arc along the control arms' axis. While the lower arm bears most of the forces, the upper arms keep the axle stable and aligned optimally during suspension compression and extension.

Factory control arms are stamped steel and have a bushing at each end. The front upper arms are the exception; they use a bushing that is held in the axle mounting points. Factory arms can take the punishment of off-road use exceptionally well,

unless the Jeep is used in activities such as rock racing and events in which higher speed is more frequent. The excessive forces in these activities can bend arms.

The factory arms control the front caster angle; this is used to keep the tires tracking straight down the road and maintain center. The Jeep uses about 4 degrees negative caster in the front that can be adjusted using cam bolts found at the axle side of the lower control arms. Installing a lift can drastically affect the caster angle, causing the Jeep to wander on the road. An alignment after a lift is essential to maintain the angle and keep the Jeep driving properly.

Control Arm Upgrades: Higher-quality lift kits can include replacement control arms that are significantly stronger, that contain freer moving joints, and that are adjustable. Some kits offer new lower arms or both lower and upper arms. TeraFlex FlexArms are an excellent example of high-strength, high-flexibility

Four control arms per axle locate the axle and allow movement within the arc of the arms, which are attached to the axle and frame. The stamped-steel arms from the factory are known for bending under hard off-road use and their fixed length doesn't allow for adjustments to alignment or caster. Aftermarket arms can be much sturdier and often offer adjustable ends to allow precise alignments.

adjustable control arms. These heavy-duty arms use the greasable and serviceable FlexArm joint to allow extra articulation while maintaining control. Most of the adjustable control arms allow fine-tuning of the Jeep's alignment by using threaded joint ends. Loosen the jam nut, unbolt the arm, and rotate the end to extend or retract to make adjustments.

Control Arm Limitations: As the height of the lift increases, the angle of the control arm increases, causing a few detrimental effects. Ride quality for street driving is reduced because of the increased angle of the arm; the arm is effectively shorter, forcing the front axle to move forward as the suspension compresses. (This is similar to what happens in a lifted leaf-spring Jeep; the opposing movement causes a harsher ride.) The increased control arm angle also results in the axle's forward and backward movement during articulation. It is not always a problem off-road but can cause the tires to come in contact with the body and other components. Typically, the maximum lift with stock-length control arms is 4.5 inches.

Long-Arm Modification

A long-arm kit is an answer to the limitations and effects of stock-length control arms. These kits can require some extra garage skills. Generally speaking, a long-arm kit abandons the stock control arm mounting location in favor of a new location farther toward the center of the Jeep. The new location increases the distance from the frame mount to the axle mount by using a longer arm. The increased arm length lowers the arm's angle; this improves ride and, in some cases, allows more

Some long-arm kits replace just the lower control arms while others replace both arms with longer arms. This requires removal of the old mounts and installation of new mounts. Some kits use mounts that are integrated with a center skid plate while others require welding of new mount brackets. Longer arms allow for more suspension movement, better suspension geometry, and smoother off-road operation.

wheel travel.

Several long-arm kits use special bracketry that mounts to the center skid plate mounts and some use special bracketry with a new skid plate. The variations in kits are endless; kits from TeraFlex and Rubicon Express are some of the most tested and best-developed kits available. Long-arm kits can put the driveshafts to task because of increased wheel travel; they most often require replacement shafts with longer slip joints and the replacement of the NP231 transfer case slip yoke.

Some long-arm kits go even further to alter the geometry of the control arms. Common designs are those that combine the upper and lower front control arm into a single Y-style arm, effectively creating a two-link system. This design allows the axle to move without the alteration of the axle's orientation, as happens with the four-link design. A common custom-geometry system found in the rear is a triangulated four-link system that eliminates the need for a rear track bar. These systems use a differential-mounted truss for attaching the upper arms. The triangulated system allows incredible amounts of suspension travel, which is often limited by the shocks and even lim-

iting straps. These custom-geometry systems are for hard-core off-roaders and require excellent garage skills because the complex installation often requires cutting and welding.

Track Bar

The track bar keeps the axle centered and prevents lateral movement. It is mounted to the axle on one side near one spring mount and to the frame on the opposite side. The track bar causes the axle to move (slightly) laterally within the bar's arc during the suspension's up-and-down travel. Therefore, the track bar operates best when it is parallel to the axle. When adding a lift, the angle on the bar increases; this causes excess lateral movement that presents itself as something like bump steer. When hitting a bump, it is noticeable in the rear as a shoving feeling to the right.

Another side effect of a lift is that the increased angle causes the track bar to become effectively shorter, which alters the lateral centering of the axle. An axle that is off lateral center can cause the tires to rub the body, frame, or other parts because there is not enough clearance. Many Jeep owners install aftermarket adjustable track bars. Choose a bar from a quality manufacturer because

A track bar in a coil suspension keeps the axle located side to side and is mounted to the axle on one side and to the frame on the opposite side. Because the track bar travels in an arc during suspension travel, keeping the track bar as parallel to the axle as possible will give the best handling. An easy way to accommodate an added suspension lift is to relocate the bar's mounting location to return it to a more level position.

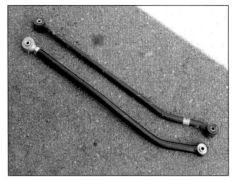

The factory track bar is not adjustable and installing it after a lift can be a challenge because of slight pitch changes in the axle. Installing an adjustable track bar will allow better side-to-side adjustment to center the wheels and allow easier installation. Most aftermarket track bars, such as this one from TeraFlex, are much stronger; they increase rigidity for better handling and use a threaded end with a flexible joint.

4 inches or lower use a heavier adjustable front track bar that will perform well. Some 4-inch or higher kits offer a drop-steering pitman arm that should be used with a drop–track bar bracket.

In the rear, most kits compensate for the added lift by installing a track bar relocation bracket. This bracket often mounts to the axle-side track bar mount; it reduces the track bar angle by raising the bar's mounting location. This increases the stress on the mount but, fortunately, most brackets can be bolted on and used without incident. A few tack-welds on a bolt-on bracket will keep it extra secure.

A rear adjustable track bar isn't absolutely necessary, but it will make fine-tuning the lateral alignment possible and aid in installation. When a Jeep is lifted, the track bar installation can be extremely difficult and the bar will not be able to rotate even slightly. Installing the bar by force can lead to mount holes that become oval, stressed mounts, and worn bushings. Bars from Tera-Flex use a Flex Joint at one end that allows rotation and adjustment.

some inexpensive bars can bend easily and cause poor drivability. Tera-Flex, Rubicon Express, and JKS offer high-strength adjustable bars.

Solutions to this problem are handled differently in the front than in the rear because of the steering system. For the best street performance, the track bar and the steering drag link should run parallel to each other; otherwise you may experience severe handling and steering issues. Most lift kits

Installing and Adjusting a Front and Rear Track Bar

Start with the front and remove the old track bar, which on the TJ uses a ball joint at one end and a bolt at the other. These can typically be removed with the Jeep on jack stands and the tires removed.

With the bar in place, tighten both the upper nut and lower bolt to the proper torque specs. Install the cotter pin in the upper ball joint. Assuming that both front and rear bars are being changed, leave the front adjuster loose and support the rear of the Jeep for a similar procedure. Often, it's necessary to remove only the passenger-side tire to replace

1 *When changing only the track bar, it is important to support the front of the Jeep properly and remove the front tires. While end removal doesn't particularly matter, loosening the upper mount keeps the bar in place when removing the lower bolt. Remove the cotter pin and loosen the nut. Use a pickle fork to drive the ball joint apart; leave the nut loose to keep it from coming out completely.*

2 *Remove the lower axle side bolt. A factory bolt will have a nut attached to a metal arm to act as a stop for loosening and tightening. Pull the bolt out and pry the bar from the mount. Remove the top nut and remove the entire bar.*

5 *Installing the new rear bar is rather easy. With the old bar removed, you can maneuver the new bar into place and install the upper bolt. Tighten it loosely. It helps to install some anti-seize compound on the bolts to allow easier removal in the future.*

the bar. Unbolt the lower bar bolt and then the upper bar bolt. Remove the old bar. As with the front track bar, thread the new bar out to match the length of the factory bar so you can establish a start point.

When both bars are installed and aligned, drive the Jeep and listen

3 *To establish a starting point for side-to-side alignment, line up both track bars and set the new track bar to the same length as the old one. Add a few extra turns to account for the lift. You will have to do an exact alignment with the tires on and weight on the Jeep. Move the new bar into position and insert the new ball joint end into the socket. Be sure to position the ball joint's cotter pin hole in a convenient location so the pin installs easily. Install the castle nut and tighten it lightly.*

6 *With the top bolt installed, install the lower bolt and tighten it loosely. At this point, tighten the upper bolt to the specified torque and remount the tire. Leave the lower bolt loose because this track bar requires removing the bolt from the lower end to adjust it.*

for unusual noises and odd driving behavior. Most manufacturers recommend checking the bolts after 50

4 *To finish the lower end, it's often easier with the tires on the Jeep with weight on them. Install the axle end of the bar. It may be necessary to tap the bar up into the slot with a mallet. After the bar is inserted, align the bolt hole by having a helper steer the Jeep gently in either direction. Insert the stock bolt or supplied bolt when the holes align.*

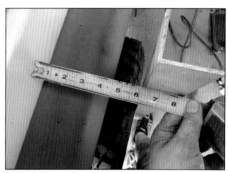

7 *The front and rear bars are installed, everything is properly tightened, and all four wheels are on the ground. To do an alignment at home, simply find a fixed point on each side of the Jeep and measure with a straight edge on the edge of the tire. Adjusting the bar to find a similar measurement will center the axle under the Jeep. Adjust the front and then the rear. A complete alignment will locate the axles more exactly, but this technique will suffice in most cases.*

miles. In addition, it's often recommended to recheck the bolts after trail runs.

Springs

The coil springs are really the stars in the suspension system. Springs play a few roles, which are supporting the weight of the Jeep, establishing the height of the lift, and allowing movement of the axle independent of the chassis. Lift springs raise the Jeep's ride height and increase wheel travel; this allows more articulation, which helps to keep the tires in contact with the surface and not lose traction.

Typical spring kits provide lifts from 2.5 inches and higher; the most common sizes are 2.5 to 4.5 inches. Springs used in higher than 4.5-inch lifts usually require more extensive modification. Most spring lifts will require replacing the shocks with shocks that match the lift; they will have increased travel to allow the suspension to travel farther without topping or bottoming out and stopping wheel travel.

Coil springs for lifts are available in many varieties and colors. Some springs use tighter coils while others use coils that are spaced more. Most springs operate in a variable rate, which means that they get stiffer or lighter when cycled. Many characteristics define a spring's lift and rate differences. Some manufacturers publish their spring rates in the specs for a lift kit.

Some spring lifts use springs that have varying rates to allow tuned movement that changes based upon the spring's extension or compression. These kinds of springs can provide improved handling on-road and improved performance off-road.

The lift you choose for your Jeep will often be in a kit form and the springs will likely be the item that determines the size of the lift. Actual lift sizes can vary from Jeep to Jeep depending on extra weight added from accessories. Quality manufacturers match the springs to the particular Jeep and often set them up for heavier loads than stock because most Jeep owners add components such as a winch and bumpers that increase vehicle weight.

Shock Absorbers

Shock absorbers do not typically play a role in the ride height of the Jeep except in custom applications. Shocks dampen the upward and downward suspension move-

Using shocks designed for the specific kit and for the Jeep will provide the best ride and performance. The TeraFlex 9550 shocks that are part of the kit are well matched for the TJ. The nitrogen charge within the shock increases performance. Using incorrect shocks can cause a poor ride and topping or bottoming out of the shock can potentially cause damage.

ment to help maintain control of the Jeep when encountering changes in terrain. When choosing shocks, it's often best to use those that are designed to work with an entire kit to achieve optimum performance. However, many manufacturers produce vehicle-specific shocks that will work with any lift system. It is important to measure the Jeep to obtain proper shock length. This is best done using an articulation ramp to allow the suspension to compress and extend fully.

The shock is often the limiting factor in regard to suspension travel in a TJ. The coil springs and control arms can allow a considerable amount of movement in both extension and compression. A shock that is too short will limit valuable downward travel and one that is too long can bottom out; both conditions have the potential for causing damage. Damage is more likely from bottoming out, which is easily prevented by using proper bump stops.

Shock technology and offerings have improved dramatically in recent years. From shocks that use external reservoirs to those that offer adjustability, it seems that the number of choices continues to increase. In most cases, the twin-tube nitrogen-filled shock will work exceptionally well and is most common. External reservoirs are designed for applications where shock heat causes a loss in effectiveness; such applications include off-road race Jeeps that experience continuous suspension cycling. Choosing adjustable shocks will allow the Jeep owner to alter the shock's performance to improve both on- and off-road performance. Higher technology and increased features drive the price tag up; deciding on the benefit of the feature compared to the cost is something to consider.

External reservoir shocks have become more popular in recent years. These shocks hold more fluid and allow more travel and cooler operation. Off-road use can produce excessive heat in a shock from the continuous up-and-down movement over obstacles. This heat can cause shock fade, a condition that reduces the effectiveness of the shock that then reduces ride quality.

Bump Stops

Perhaps the simplest and most-often ignored component in the Jeep's suspension is the bump stop. These small bumpers reside within the coil spring to stop the suspension compression softly and prevent the suspension or tires from coming into contact with items such as the frame, engine, or fenders.

Many Jeep owners overlook bump stops unless they actually come with a kit. Even then, many Jeeps are seen with a lift and stock bump stops. Jeep owners often say that they don't want to hinder travel with a larger bump stop. In truth, they will limit travel, which will save damage to fenders and/or the tires. Unless high-clearance fenders are used, using the specified bump stops is recommended.

Most lift systems include bump stop extensions that move the stop downward a shorter distance than the lift. This may seem to have the effect of reducing upward suspension travel, but a higher lift often includes the addition of larger tires that may come in contact with the fenders. For example, a 3-inch lift may use 2-inch bump stop spacers that result in an extra inch of upward travel.

Bump stop extensions are available in a variety of forms and can be attached in several ways. Some use a spacer to move the bump stop mount and some use a separate block that is opposite the bump stop; either way is effective.

For extra bump stop performance, replacement stops that act like a small shock absorber allow increased compression at a faster rate without the harsh bump when the suspension hits the stop. These bump stops will come in contact earlier and begin slowing compression before the end is reached. Some of these speed bump stop systems require welding and fabrication for proper installation.

Sway Bar

The sway bar is used to control body roll when cornering on the street. However, it is a suspension articulation hindrance off-road. The TJ uses both front and rear sway bars; both will interfere with articulation, but the front is often the only one modified because it's much heavier and has a stronger effect.

Installing sway bar disconnects is the easiest way to detach the sway bar from the front axle to allow full movement while off-road. Driving on the road at street speeds with the sway bar disconnected is never recommended.

Several varieties of sway bar disconnects are available; most differ in the way they attach and disconnect. The best ones either have links that remove completely or have a disconnect mount that keeps everything up and out of the way. The Rock Lock system from Skyjacker uses a clever lockout hub that allows the sway bar to be disconnected by just turning the hub dial.

The sway bar controls body roll; it improves handling on the street but limits axle articulation off-road. Several companies, including TeraFlex, make sway bar kits that use a disconnect system that effectively removes the bar from the suspension system.

Installing Sway Bar Disconnects

This will vary from kit to kit but the essence remains the same. The factory sway bar links are replaced with detachable or removable links to allow the front axle to move freely. In this install, a TeraFlex Sway Bar Disconnect system is used. The TeraFlex system uses links that disconnect from the axle mounts and attach to installed frame mounts to keep the bar and links secured.

1 *You can remove the sway bar links with the wheels on the Jeep, but it may be a bit easier with them off. Simply take out the lower bolt and upper nut and then use a mallet to drive the upper bolt from the sway bar.*

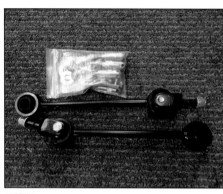

2 *Sway bar disconnect kits are available in many varieties with numerous methods for detaching. The TeraFlex system use links that remove easily from fixed bars installed on the axle end. This particular kit mounts the disconnected bar to a newly installed fixed mount on the frame.*

3 *Check the movement of the sway bar in the frame mounts. It should move with some force but not have excess slop. If it's very difficult to move, the bushings may need replacement or some lubrication. If the bar is in good shape, install the upper bolt into the sway bar and tighten to spec.*

4 *The lower part of the kit requires installation of a stud that mounts to the inside of the axle mount. Tighten the stud using a pin to hold the stud secure. It should be in a good position for installing the snap pin when the bar is connected.*

5 *The TeraFlex disconnect kit uses a secondary frame mount to secure the bar and links when it is disconnected. This requires drilling and tapping a hole into the frame for the studs. The sway bar will connect to these studs and be secured with the snap pins from the lower mount. It's best to install one side and align the other side while it is disconnected.*

6 *When the disconnect rods are connected, sway bar operation is the same as stock. The TeraFlex kit includes grease fittings to keep the extended links lubricated and operating smoothly. Checking and maintaining the lubrication after off-road trips (especially following excess water or mud) will keep contaminants out and prevent wear.*

The Currie Antirock is a replacement sway bar that finds a balance between off-road performance and street performance. This system is not disconnected off-road. Instead, it offers a lighter amount of anti-roll that actually improves off-road traction by allowing weight transfer in off-camber situations to help vehicle stability and traction. Some aftermarket bumpers are not compatible with the Currie system.

A body lift uses discs or spacers to raise the body but does not increase ground clearance for the chassis. These spacers can increase clearance for larger tires. Several items on the Jeep will be impacted by a body lift, including the fan shroud, shifters, brake lines, and more. Body lifts of more than 1 inch will cause more clearance issues.

Sway Bar Disconnect Alternatives: A few alternate sway bar systems are available for the TJ; some are quite clever and they add performance off-road. With the sway bar disconnected for off-roading, the Jeep will have a tendency to be top heavy and experience body roll in off-camber situations that can lead to a rollover. The sway bars for on the trail use a lighter-tension torsion bar to control some body roll while still allowing flexible suspension movement.

The TeraFlex Dual Rate sway bar uses a unique bar within a bar system; the larger, stronger bar is used for the street but is then disengaged to allow use of the lighter bar off-road. To engage or disengage, turn a knob on the driver's side. Currie also makes a trail sway bar that remains engaged all the time. It allows adjustment to the firmness of the torsion bar by moving the links to different holes in the arms.

Body Lift

Interestingly, a body lift doesn't technically fit into the suspension category because it merely increases the body height above the frame to allow installation of larger tires without changing any suspension components. A body lift alone will not increase the Jeep's performance significantly because the increased ground clearance is only from the tires and not from the suspension. The stock suspension is only so capable off-road and the limited articulation will provide no off-road performance improvement compared to a true suspension lift. Many Jeep owners use a body lift combined with a suspension lift to further increase tire size without increasing suspension lift over usable height.

Installation of a body lift is relatively straightforward, but it can be a time-consuming and frustrating job with an older Jeep that has seen a lot of winter weather resulting in seized body bolts. A seized bolt or a broken, loose, or embedded nut can be a huge headache and you can waste a fair amount of time dealing with them. It's best to try to remove the bolts with an impact wrench before deciding on a body lift. Using an impact wrench may loosen a stubborn bolt without snapping it off. If the bolts won't budge with the impact, more work is needed and the odds of snapping the bolt increase. A gas torch can come in handy with stubborn bolts.

In general, installation of a body lift requires removal of the TJ's body bolts and new, longer bolts installed with the body lift spacer pucks. In addition to the pucks, most body lifts require installation of new radiator support brackets and relocation and trimming of the fan shroud. You may also need a new transfer case shift bracket and transfer case shifter linkage adjustment. Kits and requirements will vary with different manufacturers.

Jeep owners often combine a body lift with a suspension lift to allow installation of even larger tires without adding excess spring lift. A common body lift size is 1 inch to 1.25 inches with extra sizes up to 3 inches. More than 1 inch of body lift can give the appearance of the body being on stilts; it's especially obvious with a 3-inch lift. The extra space causes unsightly gaps between the body and frame. TeraFlex, Rough Country, and Rugged Ridge are well-known makers of body lift kits.

Installing a Lift Kit

This TJ Unlimited is completely stock with factory-size 30-inch tires. It will receive a new 3-inch TeraFlex kit that includes TeraFlex 9550 shocks, all-new front and rear adjustable control arms, sway bar disconnects, and front and rear adjustable track bars. The TJ and TJ Unlimited share all suspension components, so they are 100-percent compatible across all of the models.

The lift being installed in this TJ is one step below a long-arm kit. This is a complete system from TeraFlex that includes upper and lower adjustable control arms. These control arms are not only adjustable but also include the TeraFlex Flex Arm joint that allows increased suspension movement with less resistance.

Also included in the kit is matching shocks, sway bar disconnects, and a front adjustable track bar. Installation of this kit can be completed with normal garage tools but will require a four-wheel alignment when finished. Proper support for the Jeep is essential for safety because the Jeep will not sit on the suspension during installation. In this particular install, the axles were removed from the Jeep for installation of ARB Air Lockers, which was covered in chap-

ter 5. When installing the lift alone, removing the axles is not necessary.

Jeep owners can choose to do the lift in two different ways: take everything out then install new or just do the front first then the rear. It depends on your comfort level and ability to support the entire Jeep without a suspension. In this case, the axles were getting Air Lockers and lower gears so they needed to be removed. In addition, the frame and underside were getting a good cleanup and some paint. Access is much easier without all that stuff in the way.

It's best to place fasteners in zip-type bags and label them to make installation simpler and less confusing. Moreover, using some never-seize coating on fasteners will make future removal, if needed, much simpler. Rusted, seized bolts are some of the most annoying things that you will encounter when working on a Jeep.

1 With the Jeep supported, the starting point is removing the shocks. Next remove the sway bar links, lower track bar mount, and the axle breather tube. The axle can lower sufficiently to allow spring removal and installation without a spring compressor.

2 Removing the stock or old shocks can be a challenge when the upper nut is seized to the shock's shaft. It's difficult to get a grip on the shaft's hardened steel. Locking pliers (such as Vise-Grip) locked tightly in the area at the top of the shaft are usually enough to get the nut moving. Thread lubricant such as PB Blaster will help. It is possible to get a socket on the nut from above.

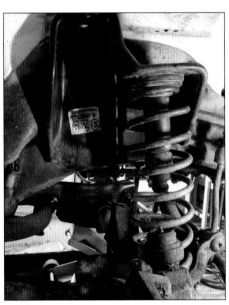

3 Remove the top nut and then the lower two shock bolts. Now you can remove the shocks from the Jeep.

4 Remove the lower sway bar link bolt, followed by the upper nut. In most lifts the link will be replaced with longer links that may or may not be part of a sway bar disconnect kit.

5 At a minimum, unbolt the lower part of the track bar to allow the axle to move more freely. This Jeep will be fitted with a TeraFlex adjustable track bar, so it was fully removed.

6 With the shocks, sway bar links, and axle-side track bar end removed, lower the axle carefully to allow the springs to extend fully and become loose. Use a pry bar to work the spring off the pad and remove it. If only the lift springs are being installed, you can put the new springs right back into place. It is best to leave pressure off the spring at this point.

7 If you are replacing the control arms, remove them one at a time to prevent the axle from falling out or rolling out of the way.

8 As with many things on a Jeep, rust will make a job take 10 times longer. Removal of the control arms was almost impossible because the bolts were seized to the inner sleeve. Attempting to remove the bolts with heat didn't work, so the decision was made to cut them off. A blade capable of cutting the hardened steel bolt will save time and blades.

9 TeraFlex provides starting measurements for the control arms. Begin installation of the arms by tightening the frame-side mount only enough to keep the arms in place. If you are installing the arms with the axle still in the Jeep, it's best to do one arm at a time to keep the axle stable.

10 Most kits include bump stop extensions or blocks to account for the lift and prevent excess upward travel. The TeraFlex kit uses blocks installed within the spring. A hole in the top of the lower spring mount must be drilled and tapped for the bolt. Leave the bump stop out for now.

11 *Place the new spring in the upper mount; hold the bump stop inside the spring and place the lower part of the spring into the lower mount. At this point, install the bump stop and the bolt to secure it.*

12 *With the springs installed, raise the axle up slowly to allow the weight of the Jeep to compress the springs to ride height.*

13 *Installing the nitrogen shocks can be a challenge because they want to remain extended. Use a ratcheting strap to pull the shock together to make the job easier. Install the new lower bolts and upper nut.*

14 *The front installation is nearing completion; the springs are installed and are supporting the weight of the Jeep. At this point, it's a matter of reinstalling the sway bar links, track bar, and any other temporarily removed components.*

15 *Install the lower track bar bolt. It can require some muscle to align the holes. Having a helper turn the steering wheel gently will usually allow the holes to line up more easily.*

16 *This kit included front sway bar disconnect links. They were installed in place of the factory sway bar links.*

17 All of the components are now installed. Everything that was touched should be tightened to the lift manufacturer's specifications and checked.

18 With the added lift, the brake lines can pull tightly and potentially damage the lines. This kit included extension brackets to allow use of the factory brake lines. These brackets lower the hard-line section of the brake line slightly to prevent overextension.

19 Rear installation is not quite as complicated because the front has more components. The disassembly process begins with removing the shocks, sway bar links, and springs.

The rear shock bolts are notorious for seizing and breaking off the welded nut on top of the frame. Getting to the location is impossible without raising the body and/or removing the fuel tank. Another more aggressive (but time- and work-saving method) is to cut a hole approximately 2 x 3 inches above the shocks to allow access from above. In the future, you'll have easy access if you fabricate small covers after completion.

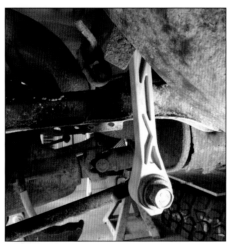

20 Remove the lower shock bolt to allow full removal of the shocks. To prevent stretching and potential damage at this step, pull the axle breather tube.

21 Remove the sway bar links. The factory links are a plastic material that will be replaced with longer steel links that are part of the kit. Lower the axle gently and remove the springs.

22 Similar to the front installation, new control arms are being installed. Remove each control arm and replace with the new arm.

23 In this particular install, the axles were removed completely for the installation of ARB Air Lockers. Seeing the Jeep from below with no suspension components is a rare site. This is the perfect opportunity to clean up the frame and add some paint to pretty up and preserve the underside.

24 Both the front and rear will have bump stop extensions installed, each in slightly different ways. The front bump stop is installed on the axle-side by drilling a hole and installing the extension with a self-threading bolt. It's best to drill the hole and run in the bolt first. The bump stop shouldn't be fully installed until the spring is in place. The rear bump stop extension installs on top of the factory stop.

25 The TeraFlex control arms are installed and ready for spring installation. In addition, the new sway bar links are installed. Leave them hanging until the axle is raised up to ride height.

26 The track bar extension bracket allows the track bar to remain at an angle that is very close to parallel to the axle. You'll have to drill a single hole to allow the supplied bracket to bolt in place.

27 Use the supplied bolts and sleeve to install the bracket. The axle is now ready for the new springs.

28 With the track bar bracket and new control arms installed, place the rear springs inside the spring buckets. Begin with the upper side and work the lower part onto the mount. With both sides installed, raise the axle gently to allow the springs to support the weight of the Jeep. The new sway bar links and new shocks can now be installed.

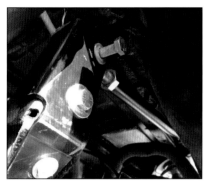

29 *Reinstall the lower part of the track bar to the new bracket. In this install, an adjustable TeraFlex track bar replaced the factory track bar.*

30 *Tighten all of the fasteners according to the lift manufacturer's specifications and inspect everything. After some brief driving, double-check everything again. You'll likely need an alignment of the track bars and the new control arms.*

Steering Systems

The TJ factory setup will work fine for a street-driven Jeep, but one that is exposed to off-road conditions will benefit from an upgrade, modification, or both. The factory design uses a Y-type tie rod/drag link configuration where the drag link connects to the passenger-side steering knuckle and the tie rod connects to the drag link and to the passenger-side steering knuckle. This configuration is supposed to improve bump steer but it actually creates a weak point where the tie rod connects to the drag link.

The TJ's steering gear is extremely exposed and has no protection from leaf springs. The gear is often rammed up on trail obstacles, causing it to bend or break. The steering gear is often ignored until it becomes damaged. Severe damage can cause the tires to experience excessive toe-in, making the Jeep undriveable.

On-trail repairs often involve attempting to bend the gear back and/or repair it. Jeepers get very clever with this repair, welding or clamping anything they can find to rods to get them as straight as possible. It's also common for a Jeep owner to carry a spare set.

In addition to the linkage, the steering box is exposed, sticking out from below the front of the frame. Similar to the linkage, the steering

box on a TJ doesn't have the added protection of leaf springs.

Steering System Upgrades and Modifications

The steering gear is vulnerable and exposed to obstacles on the trail. Upgrades and modifications to the Jeep's steering components can beef up strength to handle abuse and larger tires.

Heavy-Duty Gear

A few companies make high-strength steering gear that will take the off-road punishment much better than the stock gear. Companies such as Currie, Rugged Ridge, and Synergy manufacture replacement gear that is more substantial than stock. Currie's Currectlync Heavy-Duty Tie Rod System uses a 1.25-inch-diameter

The stock steering linkage on this muddy TJ uses a Y-style design where the tie rod connects directly to the drag link. This setup can cause toe-in changes when the suspension is cycling and/ or when a lift is installed. The stock setup is prone to bending because of the light materials and the fact that the steering gear is very low and has little protection.

Currie's Currectlync Heavy-Duty Tie Rod System may be regarded as one of the strongest steering upgrades for a TJ that still uses the factory configuration. The larger-diameter hardware and chrome-moly tie rod reduce the likelihood of damage or bending from impact with trail obstacles or larger tires that increase leverage on the system

forged chrome-moly drag link and a 1.25-inch chrome-moly bar stock tie rod; they provide an extra-strong replacement system for stock.

Installing a Currie Currectlync Heavy-Duty Tie Rod System

This is not a complex procedure, but is easier with a few specific tools, particularly a tie rod puller. With the Jeep supported and the front wheels removed, begin by removing or disconnecting the steering stabilizer and removing the cotter pins from the rod ends.

1 *Remove the cotter pins to free the rod ends. Use a tie rod puller to make getting the rod end out of the socket much easier. The trick is to apply enough pressure to the threaded end and give the puller a smack on the top. This will break the tapered end loose without beating on the threads. Remove the axle ends and the end of the pitman arm.*

2 *It's usually best to install the drag link first. Attach the new rod end to the steering knuckle and then attach the other side to the pitman arm. Align the cotter pin holes for easy pin installation and tighten the nuts loosely.*

3 *Note that in this system, the tie rod has a left and right side. The grease fitting is the key to identifying which end is which. The end that attaches to the steering knuckle has a grease fitting on the bottom of the rod end; the drag link side has a fitting on the side to allow access.*

4 *Installing the TeraFlex 9550 steering stabilizer requires the stabilizer mount kit provided with the Currie system. It is important to line up the mount to allow full steering movement on the stabilizer; tighten all of the bolts.*

5 *When these upgrades are complete, the Jeep will have a substantially stronger system that is ready for abuse on the trail. Be sure to lubricate and check the joints regularly to prevent failure. A good off-road driver is aware of the Jeep's low-hanging components. Remembering that the steering is extremely vulnerable can help to prevent damage.*

6 *You can perform a crude home toe-in alignment with a tape measure and a straight edge across the tires. The front of the tires should measure about 1/8 to 1/4 inch less than the rear of the tire. Toe-in is adjusted by rotating the tie rod in or out. This system allows the Jeep to drive correctly until a professional alignment can be performed. Tighten the tie rod clamps when alignment is completed.*

Stabilizer

A steering stabilizer operates similarly to a shock absorber and helps control abrupt steering movement both on- and off-road. Factory stabilizers are designed primarily for street driving and can be less effective when larger, heavier tires are installed. Replacing the stock stabilizer with an aftermarket model, especially one matched to the lift, will improve street driving as well as off-road performance. These stabilizers often mount directly in place of the factory stabilizer for an easy installation. The TJ stabilizer is mounted above the steering linkage, which keeps it reasonably protected from trail obstacles.

High-Steer Systems

For the more adventurous, a few varieties of high-steer systems are available for the TJ, or you can home-build one. Similar to the tie rod flip solution in the CJ, the tie rod/drag link ends can be fitted to mount to the top of the steering knuckle instead of the below the knuckle location, which is stock. This can result in raising the linkage about 3 inches higher. It requires reaming

A steering stabilizer designed for off-road, such as the TeraFlex 9550, will provide excellent street handling as well as off-road performance. When installed on a Jeep, they can handle the added stress of larger tires.

or altering the rod end taper on the knuckles to allow proper installation.

Some caveats with these systems on a TJ exist and must be dealt with. The flip typically requires at least 2.5 inches or more of lift. The gear will often have clearance issues with other components such as the track bar mount, steering stabilizer, and sway bar mounts. Another potentially more severe issue is bump steer. This is a condition that causes the Jeep to unintentionally steer in one direction or another when hitting a bump. Unlike the CJ, for which this flip is a piece of cake, raising the drag link on a TJ will change the plane alignment from the track bar. This will result in different directional movements when hitting bumps, causing bump steer.

TeraFlex makes a high-steer system that replaces the stock steering knuckles with custom knuckles that allow use of a separately mounted drag link and tie rod. This system was originally intended for Jeeps with 4 inches of lift and will require extra modification.

These systems are often saved for Jeeps used more off-road than on-road. A smart Jeep owner is always aware of the underside of his or her Jeep and positions it accordingly on the trail to avoid or minimize damage situations.

Steering Box and Pump Upgrades

The factory steering box is more than capable of handling 35-inch tires but, on occasion, an upgrade to the system will benefit the Jeep to ease steering in rocky conditions. Performance steering boxes are available that alter steering ratio and increase piston size to reduce steering effort. AGR manufactures a few versions of performance boxes for the TJ. A

noticeable improvement results from a combination with an AGR performance power steering pump.

Cooling

Off-road driving requires constant steering and frequently steering against objects, which causes the pump to work harder. The extra work will cause the power steering fluid and pump to heat up, potentially leading to reduced capacity and possible failure. Installing a steering cooler in the system will help keep the temperature of the fluid down. Derale makes a compact cooler that can be installed inline and mounted in the grille area or tucked into the bumper area.

Ram

When running extra-large tires, a steering-assist ram can be added to the steering linkage to help the steering box. Extra-large tires can be extremely heavy and, combined with the situations they are often used in, can cause difficult steering for the driver. The ram provides extra muscle for the system to help overcome the difficulty. These systems are typically used only on dedicated trail vehicles with heavier aftermarket axles and steering gear and can cause damage to stock steering gear because of the increased power. Special steering pumps with extra lines need to be installed with ram-style systems. PSC Motorsports makes an almost-complete system for the TJ.

Steering Shaft

This is another often-overlooked item on a Jeep. The factory shaft is often sufficient and can generally serve the Jeep for a lifetime. Heavy-duty shafts with improved joints are available from Borgeson and Flaming River.

Alignment

For the best handling and tire wear, a Jeep owner should pay attention to the suspension and steering alignment. Aligning the TJ suspension is much easier than in older Jeeps equipped with leaf springs.

Caster

Put simply, caster is an angle set within a vehicle steering system that is offset from the centerline of the wheel that causes the wheels to force a self-centering action. When installing a lift, the added height can reduce or eliminate the caster angle and cause the Jeep to wander when driving down the road. A TJ equipped with factory control arms allows for caster adjustment by rotating the cam bolt at the axle-side mount of the front lower control arm. Aftermarket control arms typically allow adjustment at one end to enable even more precise alignment of caster.

Camber

Solid-axle Jeeps have no factory camber adjustment provision and, in most cases, little or no camber is set. Camber is the angle of the wheel when looking from front to rear. Negative camber places the lower part of the wheel outward of center; positive camber places the top of the wheel out. Camber will affect steering performance and tire life. Because a Jeep typically has zero camber, the tire will sit flat on the ground. This provides the best performance for the type of driving a Jeep sees most. If an alignment shows excess camber, it's likely the axle tubes are bent, which indicates a larger problem.

With all of the suspension work and the upgrades to the steering system now complete, the Jeep's capability has been increased dramatically. After all the work, the Jeep now has ARB Lockers front and rear with 4.56:1 gears, a 3-inch lift, steering gear upgrade, adjustable track bars, 33-inch tires, and proper-fitting 16-inch wheels. Compare this photo to the photo on page 74, and the differences are obvious.

Toe

Toe is the alignment of the driver- and passenger-side front tires. Proper toe alignment will keep the steering straight and minimize front tire wear. The Y-style steering linkage causes toe to change, even with just a lift. This is because the increased angle on the drag link causes the tie rod angle to increase, which reduces toe. When installing new steering linkage or a lift on a TJ, the toe must be re-aligned.

Track Bar

As discussed earlier, the factory track bars offer no adjustment; this will cause an axle offset to occur after a lift. Installation of stronger aftermarket track bars that allow adjustment will enable the Jeep owner to center the axles properly under the Jeep.

Putting It All Together

A lift is almost mandatory on a TJ, since we are building a TJ to max-imize performance on- and off-road. A 3-inch short-arm lift will often perform best and allow for 33-inch tires and plenty of ground clearance with little risk for tire contact with the body or other components.

The 3-inch lift will minimize handling compromises and bump steer.

Adjustable track bars allow for fine-tuning of axle alignment to maintain tire clearance and help with handling.

Almost all 3-inch kits use a drop-rear track bar bracket to improve handling.

Using matched replacement shocks will allow for increased wheel travel and good ride.

Proper bump stops are essential.

Replacement control arms will allow better alignment and increased suspension flex.

A complete alignment is essential after installation.

Installation of a heavy-duty steering tie rod/drag link system with an off-road–style stabilizer will reduce linkage damage potential.

CHASSIS AND BODY PROTECTION

It doesn't take much off-roading experience to recognize the sound of rock and steel meeting underneath the Jeep. In reality, there are many things lurking on the trail that are just waiting to do some damage. Those of us who use our Jeeps as they were intended must accept the eventual damage that will come from off-roading. A skilled driver can avoid severe damage (for the most part) but limits will be reached and

having the proper equipment to protect the Jeep's vital parts and body will keep it moving on the trail and the parts budget in check.

Jeep did a basic job of protecting the underside with skid plates and some light side protection was included on the Rubicon. Unfortunately, you can quickly exceed the capabilities of these lighter parts. Fortunately, the aftermarket is full of options to add armor to the TJ. It's stuff that works well and looks great.

Protecting the Underside

Many components lie below the iconic Jeep body. Some owners are

unaware of where everything is and what everything does. Doing the work on your Jeep will help you to become familiar with what is underneath and perhaps keep all that in mind when navigating a rock garden at your favorite trail spot. Some upgrades to underside protection are more important than others. Differentials, the center skid plate, the steering components, and the fuel tank are most vulnerable.

Center Skid Plate

This component serves two purposes; it is a crossmember that provides the mounting point for the transmission/transfer case, as well as

If you find yourself facing a sign like this on your favorite trail, remember that off-road driving exposes a Jeep to damage like no other driving conditions. Obstacles on the trail can come in many forms and sizes. Protecting the underside of the Jeep, especially in the vital areas, along with some exterior protection, will keep the damage away and allow you to proceed with confidence.

A Jeep owner should take the time to study the underside of his or her Jeep before setting out on the trails. Knowing where low-hanging components are is essential to avoiding damage when traversing obstacles. Being able to steer clear of an obstacle, rather than plowing through or over it, is always a better option.

The factory center crossmember, more commonly called a skid plate, is quite capable of providing protection to the transmission and transfer case area. Its biggest flaws are that it is hanging lower than it should be and its irregular shape can cause the Jeep to hang up on obstacles.

Replacing the factory skid plate with a high-clearance plate can increase ground clearance without additional lift. Some of these replacement skids are almost flat and will allow the Jeep to slide over an obstacle without becoming snagged. Many of these require installation of a body lift and engine lift.

The automatic transmissions found in the TJ leave a vulnerable, thin-walled fluid pan hanging low. The factory included a light-duty skid plate to protect the transmission pan that will work rather well, but this formidable aftermarket plate from Under Cover Fabworks (with added support) will provide superior protection for both the transmission pan and engine oil pan.

being a skid plate to protect them. The factory TJ skid plate is quite strong and capable of supporting the weight of the TJ. A drawback of its design is that it is not flat, which causes an increased likelihood of becoming stuck on an obstacle. In addition to the plate's contours, the bolts for the transmission/transfer case mount are exposed and subject to damage.

Belly Up, Tummy Tucker, or High-Clearance Replacements: It's a common practice on a TJ to replace the factory center skid plate with a style that increases ground clearance. These are commonly referred to as belly up skid plates. These plates are manufactured from thicker steel than the factory plate or aluminum. These skids increase rigidity with the strength ribs mounted above the plate rather than below and that allows the skid to be almost flat on the bottom. The Jeep can then slide over obstacles easily in high-center situations.

The transmission mount is often raised to protect the bolts from dam-age. These skid plates may require installing an engine lift and/or body lift. This lift raises the engine and transmission, which then allows installation of the belly up. The result is increased ground clearance for the engine, transmission, and skid plate. Some extreme versions can raise the skid plate more than 2 inches.

The Nth Degree Tummy Tucker uses a replacement transmission mount along with a modified exhaust mount to allow a 2.75-inch gain in clearance without an installation of a body lift or engine lift. This kit does require a slip yoke eliminator, a CV-style driveshaft, and the ability to adjust the rear pinion angle for proper driveshaft alignment, which is usually done with adjustable lower control arms.

Skid Plate Armor: For Jeep owners with some fabrication skills, adding a flat section of steel to the factory plate is a less expensive but very effective option. It will add strength to the bottom of the plate and pro-tect the bolts by allowing them to be slightly recessed. The smooth bottom

allows the Jeep to slide over obstacles instead of catching on them.

Automatic Transmission: A Jeep equipped with an automatic will have a thin, metal, low-hanging fluid pan. The pan is extremely vulnerable because of its location. The factory skid plate is a simple flat piece of steel that bolts to the center skid plate and a small crossmember. This protection isn't capable of support-ing the full weight of the Jeep and will crush when pushed over its limit. Replacing the factory protec-tion with something stronger such as the transmission skid made by Nth Degree or TeraFlex will protect this delicate area.

Differential Protection

A Jeep's axles, and especially the differential housing, are usually the lowest part of the Jeep and the most likely to come in contact with an obstacle on the trail. The factory differential covers are constructed of relatively light-gauge steel that can

A comparison of an aftermarket differential cover (left) compared to the factory cover (right). The ARB cover is fabricated from high-tensile solid nodular iron that is tougher and harder than solid carbon steel. This cover and others like it will protect the vulnerable ring and pinion and look good doing it.

The front (pictured) and rear factory differential covers on a TJ are constructed of relatively thin steel that will bend and/or crack when smashed against a trail obstacle. The differential housing is one of the lowest points on the Jeep; the front is especially subject to punishment on the trail. A Jeep owner who knows that the front differential is on the driver's side can maneuver it around obstacles.

An alternative to a replacement cover is a skid such as this one from Four X Doctor. These bolt to the differential housing using the lower bolts. Skids have a dual purpose: They act like a bumper during an impact with a trail obstacle and also provide a skid to allow the differential to slide up and over the object. You can see this one is well used.

bend easily when impacting a large obstacle. This damage can result in lost gear oil and/or cause the cover to come in contact with the gears, which is potentially expensive damage. Several varieties of differential protection are available; some are better than others but anything is better than stock.

In addition to the low-hanging housing, the factory axles used a low-pinion design that placed the pinion yoke and its snout on the low side of the differential housing. The yoke area is extremely susceptible to damage when sliding over an obstacle or coming off an obstacle with a tire.

Differential Guards: Guards usually bolt to the factory differential cover and provide a thicker steel plate that protects the cover. These covers are easy to install and provide excellent protection.

Heavy-Duty Covers: Replacement covers are a popular means of adding protection. They are often manufactured from considerably thicker material with extra-strength ribs to prevent damage. Installation is as simple as draining the oil, removing the old cover, and installing the new one. In addition to the protection, these covers are often more attractive and available in a variety of colors.

Differential Skids: Differential skid systems take protection a step further by protecting the differential cover as well as providing a skid to help the axle move up and over an obstacle. A simple skid acts as a cover guard; it bolts to the cover and uses tubular steel to create the skid. The protection and ability to allow the Jeep to move over the object is very effective. Four X Doctor offers well-made differential skid guards.

For broader protection, complete skids are available, such as the one from Nth Degree that bolts to the axle tubes and yoke snout to provide protection to the entire differential housing and yoke area. A small amount of ground clearance is lost with these kinds of skids but the added protection can make up for it.

Lower Control Arms and Mounts

The lower control arms will take abuse, especially on a Jeep equipped with a long-arm kit. Lower control arms often unintentionally act as ramps for obstacles. These can cause the factory arms to bend easily because they're made from simple stamped steel. Using strong replacement lower arms such as the TeraFlex FlexArms will protect from damage and allow axle adjustment.

Like the differential housing, the lower control arm mounts sit very low on the axle tubes and the frame side mounts, which makes both areas very

The Wrangler TJ's lower control arms can receive a fair amount of abuse because they sit close to the tires. Very often, when running a tire over an obstacle, the control arm can act like a skid, which increases the potential for damage. Stronger arms and smart driving will help reduce damage.

Like the models before, the TJ uses a steering box mounted to the forward-most part of the frame. Unlike previous models, the TJ doesn't have leaf springs to help protect the box. It's easy to ram the steering box into obstacles on the trail and cause damage. Good driving and adding a guard will help keep the box safe.

The fuel tank hangs low between the rear sections of the frame rails. The tank on a TJ Unlimited sits in the same location as a regular TJ with some additional frame section to the rear. Keeping the tank more forward on the Unlimited helps reduce potential damage because of the lower departure angle.

susceptible to damage. Skid plates for the axle-side control arm are available from Rancho and Skid Row. Frame-side mount plates will need to be fabricated.

Steering Box and Linkage

The TJ is similar to its predecessors in that the steering box sits exposed at the front of the frame. Unlike previous generations of the CJ and YJ, the TJ does not have added protection for the steering box courtesy of the leaf springs. Nose-diving the TJ will cause the steering box to come in contact with an obstacle and potentially cause major damage.

A simple solution is to install a steering box skid plate from Skid Row, TeraFlex, or Rugged Ridge. The skid plate mounts to the frame and bumper area to protect the box. Installation is rather simple; some kits require minor drilling.

As was discussed in chapter 6, upgrading the TJ steering gear to something more rigid is the best way of protecting it. The Currie replace-

ment linkage is much more formidable than the factory steering gear.

In addition to the gear, converting to a high-steer system will move the linkage farther away from the ground. These systems are much more complex and often require replacement of the steering knuckles. High-steer kits usually require 4 inches of lift as well as other modifications.

Fuel Tank

The departure angle is a measurement from the bottom of the rear tires to the lowest point on the rear of the Jeep, usually the bumper or something on the bumper. A TJ has a high departure angle even when stock. Add a lift and larger tires and that angle gets even better.

A TJ Unlimited has a lower departure angle than a standard TJ because of the additional 5 inches of body behind the rear wheels. The fuel tank is mounted in the same location on the Unlimited as on a standard-length TJ, which helps reduce the potential

for fuel tank damage.

The fuel tank is located between the frame rails at the rearmost section of the Jeep; it is subjected to abuse because of the decreased departure angle, especially when dropping off of an obstacle. An experienced driver knows the importance of control when navigating an obstacle that provides a sudden drop. Failure to maintain control can cause the weight of the rear of the Jeep to land suddenly on the fuel tank, possibly causing damage or a failure. The factory skid plate is pretty robust, but it will not support all of the weight.

Several companies, including TeraFlex, Warn, and GenRight Off Road, make replacement fuel tank skid plates that use heavier-gauge steel and a fully boxed design that increases strength and, for some models, increases ground clearance. Those that increase ground clearance typically require a 1-inch body lift. Most of these systems require removal of the fuel tank and dis-

Many aftermarket fuel tank skids are available; some add protection to the existing skid and some replace the entire unit. These skids are made of heavier-gauge steel with added supports for rigidity to stand up to trail abuse. This skid from Poison Spyder is a good example of one that slips over the factory skid.

connecting the fuel lines and other related connections. It's a potentially messy job but likely worth it to prevent a loss of fuel on the trail.

Engine Oil Pan

The engine oil pan isn't particularly low but it's fairly thin-gauge steel that is just waiting for a puncture. A higher lift on the Jeep helps to get the engine even farther away from harm, but flying debris and obstacles can still be a threat. Several companies make bolt-on skid plates to protect the oil pan's most vulnerable area, lower sump, or even the entire bottom of the engine. TeraFlex, Nth Degree, and Skid Row make skid components to protect the engine oil pan.

Bump Stops

Bump stops were discussed in chapter 6 but are worth mentioning again. These often-overlooked components prevent damage to the suspension as well as the tires and body. Bump stops come in many forms; some attach to the axle while some attach to the frame. Properly sized bump stops slow and limit wheel travel during suspension compression, typically preventing them from coming in contact with the body and/or other vehicle components.

Most lift kits include properly sized bump stops, but some Jeep owners may use special compressed air stops like ones from Fox that add dampening as well as a stop. Most of these require modification for mounting.

Protecting the Ends

Bumpers serve many functions on a Jeep beyond simply protection. They establish a stylish look, hold the winch, lights, spare tires, pull points, and so on. In addition to lift kits and tires, bumpers are often among the first things that a Jeep owner replaces. Tubular bumpers were the style many years ago. More recently, rock-style bumpers are protecting the Jeep's front and rear.

Front Bumper

The front bumper defines a Jeep so much that it's no wonder they are among the first modifications a Jeep owner makes. The factory bumper isn't very strong and the plastic ends will deform or rip out, even with slight contact. Fortunately, the aftermarket is full of bumper choices with many options to suit everyone's needs. Bumpers can range from full width to stubby and from simple to complex. Some bumpers double as air tanks; they provide air storage for running tools, lockers, and airing-up tires.

Bumpers that increase approach angle, especially right in front of the tire, will prevent damage to the bumper and allow the tire to climb a larger obstacle. Bumpers that fit this style are narrower than full width to right down to stubby models. In addition, some wider bumpers can improve approach angle by angling the ends of the bumper or raising the bumper ends in a step fashion.

When choosing a bumper for your Jeep, you should choose one that fits the application. Bulky bumpers are very heavy; adding a winch and some extras can add an excessive amount of weight to the front of the Jeep and (potentially) cause a loss of ground clearance and poor suspension performance.

A front bumper is often a key visual element on a Jeep in addition to protecting it. This bumper from Bulletproof Manufacturing provides many useful features, such as a winch mount with grille and winch protection hoops, tow points, 2-inch receiver, and light mounts. A formidable bumper is a must on an off-road-used Jeep. Overly intricate and bulky bumpers can add a substantial amount of weight to the front of the Jeep.

Tow tabs are the safest style of a pull point on a Jeep. These tabs should be mounted through the bumper and welded on both sides. Tabs provide a secure mounting point for a D-ring shackle that will prevent the line from falling off during use.

Many aftermarket bumpers integrate the winch mount directly into the bumper, which reduces costs and allows for an easier install. The unique location of the TJ's sway bar means that the winch will be farther forward than you might like. This Barricade bumper includes both a winch and fairlead mount.

Bumpers with provisions for tow points are typically a better choice for a Jeep that is used off-road. Tab-style tow points are preferred for safety and efficient attachment methods. The D-ring shackle used with the pull points will keep the pull line attached even if the line goes slack. A bumper equipped with tabs should be rated for using the tabs as pull points. The strongest tab mounts typically pass through the bumper and are welded on both sides.

What used to be known as a brush guard is now more commonly referred to as a stinger or a hoop. These arch-shaped guards serve multiple purposes, including protecting the winch and providing additional mounting points for accessories such as lights. In more extreme cases, they can prevent end-over rollovers.

Additional mounting points for accessories such as lights and a winch are a plus when selecting a bumper. Some bumpers use integrated winch mounts and a fairlead attachment while others require a separate mount; the combination can save

money. The TJ is unique compared to other Jeep models in the way that the front sway bar crosses over the frame behind the bumper. It is an obstacle that interferes with a tighter bumper design and winch mounting. Most bumpers and winch mounts will take this into consideration.

Notable manufacturers for front bumpers are JCR, Barricade, Rock-Hard, Smittybilt, ARB, and Warn. Keep in mind that there are many more. Selecting a bumper is a task. Go to a Jeep event and look around; you can often find something that fits your Jeep's needs.

Installing a Front Bumper

The Barricade bumper's styling matches the TJ well. Its integrated tow points, winch mount, fairlead mount, and hoop put everything in one package. The heavier steel is very strong but not super heavy. The integrated LED lights and the excellent price tag are a bonus. All mounting hardware as well as a wiring harness for the lights are included. Installation takes an hour or so; removing the factory bumper can actually be the biggest time consumer. The exact procedure will vary with different bumpers but the procedure is pretty much the same.

1 *Removing the factory front bumper can be a challenge on an older Jeep that has seen a lot of weather. Removing the six Torx bolts takes some patience and time to avoid breaking. Sometimes a little heat and an impact gun are needed to remove stubborn bolts.*

2 *With the bumper removed, begin fitting the new bumper and installing the new bolts loosely.*

3 *Occasionally, certain things require some custom fitting because they just won't line up. The lower mount tab was slightly off from the frame bolt hole, which required some elongation of the hole with a die grinder. A larger washer was used to prevent the regular washer from deforming.*

4 *With everything fitted, tighten the bolts to the bumper according to the manufacturer's recommended torque specifications.*

5 *With the bumper installed, the sway bar cover required some trimming to fit. The winch was ready for mounting and the auxiliary lights just needed wiring up. Because this TJ had factory driving lights, the existing wiring was used for a clean and easy job.*

Rear Bumper

As for the front bumper, many aftermarket options are available for the rear with many different features and options. In addition, the rear bumper is also subject to abuse on the trail, probably even more so than the front. Dropping off obstacles is common and the fact that it's almost impossible to see the rear bumper area means that it gets a real workout.

Aftermarket rear bumpers are as popular as the front ones. With so many varieties and options, choosing a bumper can be difficult. Bumpers that integrate a tire carrier, tow tabs, and a hitch are the most popular. Some have optional components that allow attachment of accessories such as jacks and fuel tanks. This bumper includes provisions to mount a Hi-Lift Jack behind the spare tire.

Spare Tire

A replacement hinge system for the spare can save damage to the tailgate and body. Even though this system isn't part of the bumper, it relates to bumper choice. All TJs used a tailgate-mounted spare tire that swings open with the tailgate; it's easy and rather convenient. For a little bit of trivia, the latch on the tailgate is a longtime holdover from the AMC years. This paddle-style latch has been found on many AMC vehicles since the late 1960s. When adding larger tires, increased stress on the tailgate can cause wear on the hinges, the latch, and the tailgate itself. Over time, the area around the hinge and the tire mount can start to crack from fatigue. Vibration from the tire is the biggest enemy. The solution to a larger tire can be handled in two ways: a stronger reinforcement hinge system or let the bumper handle it.

Bumper-mounted spare tire systems often use a sophisticated hinge system that allows the tire to swing away and grant access to the tailgate. The Smittybilt XRC Bumper uses a strong hinge and latch system to prevent rattling. This bumper also integrates tow tabs and a receiver hitch.

The stock tire carrier is integrated into the tailgate. A larger spare increases the stress on the tailgate and its hinges. Replacement hinges such as these from Rugged Ridge can help with worn-out hinges but a tire larger than 33 inches can put too much stress on the whole assembly. High-strength hinge systems are a good alternative to a bumper-mounted spare tire.

Tactik and Rugged Ridge each manufacture a hinge system that decreases stress to the tailgate mounting points dramatically by using a large single-piece hinge system that mounts to the hinge points and tire mount with one solid, rigid piece. The new hinge supports most of the weight, which relieves the stress on the tailgate. It's important to use the rubber bumpers with the tire to prevent it from wobbling and rattling. Most of these replacement hinge systems can handle a 33- to 35-inch tire. Along with the bumper, its tow points, and ability to carry the spare, many include extras such as a standard 2-inch receiver to allow towing or anything else that can fit in. Mount points for cargo racks, high-lift jacks, rearward lights, and fuel/water containers are a plus and add the ability to carry more gear. Owners need to remember the extra weight. It's easy to overpack and start to make the Jeep's rear droop and lose valuable departure angle and ground clearance. To combat added weight, a Jeep owner can add a small spacer above the rear spring or install a heavier spring. Some lift makers offer special springs for heavier Jeeps.

Many Jeep owners choose swing-away bumper-mounted tire carriers to deal with the larger tire.

This method often requires the tire carrier to be opened first and then the tailgate. It's extra work and bulk added. If you decide to relieve the tailgate of tire duty, a bumper that integrates a swing-away spare tire carrier is the best choice. Some of the best bumpers use a bearing-style hinge in the swing-away system. These allow for a tight, rattle-free fit that moves easily. Latch mechanisms vary greatly too; finding one that holds tight and prevents rattles will be best. Some people find this tedious but it works well for many. Warn, ARB, and Rock-Hard 4x4 are some of the companies that make quality rear bumpers with swing-away tire carriers.

Protecting the Body

The sheet metal of a Jeep isn't particularly heavy or tough. An obstacle such as a rock or tree will bend the

sheet metal and ruin paint very easily. Some Jeep owners have little regard for their Jeep's body; however, most want to keep appearances intact. Protecting certain areas will give you peace of mind on the trail and you'll know that the body will come out looking as good as when it went in.

Fenders

Often, the fenders' worst enemy is the tires. Without proper bump stops, larger tires will hit the fenders, flares, or both with the likelihood of causing damage.

The rocker area is extremely vulnerable to trail obstacles. High rocks can easily damage the thin steel of the Jeep's body, which makes for an expensive repair. Protecting this area can reduce damage and improve the Jeep's appearance at the same time.

Jeep owners often replace the factory fenders with flat-style fenders to increase wheel travel and reduce the chance of fender and/or tire damage when the suspension cycles. These fenders from Fishbone use tubular steel as the edge of the fender, which adds strength and rigidity while reducing damage from obstacles and tire contact.

Several varieties of high-clearance fenders are available in the aftermarket. This one from MetalCloak uses a unique high-clearance bump where the tire will come up during compression; it allows more tire travel before contact. Other high-clearance fenders use replacement fenders and a different hood.

The Rubicon flares are 1 inch wider than the stock TJ flares. This allows using a wider tire that won't stick out too far, which could cause issues with local vehicle laws. The Sahara and other special model TJs used the same wider-width flare.

Flat Fenders: An option to allow some extra clearance without damage to the tires or fenders is replacement flat tube fenders. These fenders use strong tubular steel to make up the outer section of the fender with a small section of flat steel to complete the top. The smooth bottom of the tube steel will not hurt a tire with gentle contact and its rigid structure will not bend from the pressure of the tire. Tube fenders alter the look of the Jeep to a point that some do not like; it's a matter of preference. In addition, because the front signal light and side marker light are part of the fender, provisions need to be made to move the lights if the fender kit does not include them. Most flat-fender kits require reusing the factory inner section of the fender, which requires cutting and welding. JCR, Poison Spyder, and GenRight Offroad make flat tube fender kits.

High-Clearance Fenders and Hood: Although the availability of high-clearance kits is disappearing, a few high-clearance kits are available. Adding a special high-clearance hood and raising the fender line with special fenders allows more upward tire travel before contact. TNT and JCR Offroad make high-clearance kits. MetalCloak's unique approach is high-arch fenders that retain the stock hood but create a larger arch in the area that the tire will move into.

Fender Flares: The factory fender flares are well known for their ability to fade and become chalky after years of sun exposure. Factory flares are 3.25 inches wide except for Rubicon and Sahara flares, which measure in at 4.25 inches. Replacing the flares on a Jeep with the wider flares is often sufficient to cover larger, wider tires with properly spaced wheels.

Flares protect the Jeep from thrown objects as well as serve as a bit of a barrier to the steel of the body. A flare will flex with light contact and suffer no damage. The Sahara and a few other models used painted flares that will scratch during contact.

Many companies, including Bushwacker, Rugged Ridge, and Xenon, make replacement flares that create a flat-style look or a pocket-style flare. Many of these flares are more durable and wider for better tire coverage.

Side Rockers

The side rockers are an extremely vulnerable part of the Jeep body. This is the area between the front and rear wheels under the door opening. Centering the Jeep high on an obstacle in this area will cause serious, difficult-to-repair damage. Unlike the front fenders, rockers are an integral part of the body tub and replacement can be expensive. Two general methods exist for protecting the side of the Jeep; each has advantages and disadvantages.

Frame-Mounted: Frame-mounted guards are more similar to a step, and they often double as a step

The Rubicon featured factory rocker protection that was made of relatively thin diamond-plated steel. This did provide better protection compared to no protection (as on any other TJ) but stronger replacements will provide the best protection.

Rocker protection is available for the TJ and typically two main types exist: frame mounted or body mounted. Body-mounted skids, such as these from Treks, require drilling into the body; this allows more clearance and often a stronger mount. Rocker guards that protect the underside of the body

and include a side skid will provide maximum protection.

Tub-Mounted: Tub- or body-mounted rocker guards mount to the Jeep body directly, usually with a combination of drilled body bolts and the Jeep body mounts on the frame. Installation differs with manufacturers and styles. Tub-mounted guards are available in a variety of styles, ranging from simple straight protection to integrated steps. Heavier steel guards will offer the best protection. Poison Spyder, JCR Offroad, and RockHard 4x4 are a few makers of tub-mounted rocker guards.

The extra 10 inches of a TJ Unlimited creates a larger in-between body space, which reduces the breakover angle and increases the potential for contact. Rocker guards are even more crucial on an Unlimited.

while providing protection. These guards mount to the Jeep frame, usually in two or three places; drilling is often required. An advantage to these is that they do not require drilling holes into the Jeep body, which is a potential invitation for rust. The mount point also puts these lower and that allows better use as an actual step.

The main disadvantage is that there is a loss of ground clearance, usually by several inches. This will cause an obstacle to come in contact with the guard when it would possibly miss a body-mounted guard. Heavy impact to a frame step can drive the step up into the bottom of the body, possibly causing damage to the body or (even worse) bending the Jeep frame.

The advantage of these guards is that little or no ground clearance is sacrificed and that allows the Jeep to avoid a much taller obstacle than the frame-mounted guards. Drilling into the Jeep body and attaching a steel object to it can invite rust from both the drilled holes and the metal-on-metal contact. Some Jeep owners install a thin rubber gasket between the guard and the body to help preserve the paint and keep water out.

Installing Tub-Mounted Rocker Guards

Installation will vary from type to type, but most use a similar mounting method. The Poison Spyder Ricochet Rockers offer excellent protection as well as an integrated step and overall good looks. These rockers come unpainted so the purchaser can color-match them to the Jeep, if desired. These were painted satin black after fitting to match the monochrome theme of the Jeep.

1 *The Poison Spyder Ricochet Rockers mount to the side of the tub and extend underneath to use the 3 side-body mounts. Removing all 11 body mounts is necessary to raise the tub for installation. Patience and some heat may be needed to avoid broken body bolts. An impact gun can usually remove stubborn bolts without breaking them.*

2 After raising the body and sliding the guards into place, gently lower the body and begin fitting the guard. These particular guards almost self-align because of the body mounts. Use clamps to pull the guard into the body so you can mark holes.

3 With the guard lined up, begin drilling holes. Drilling one hole at a time and installing the nut and bolt will keep everything lined up as you go.

4 Go easy when installing the bolts; use the clamp to hold the guard to the body. It's likely that the guard will need some force to pull in properly. Using the bolt to pull it in may cause the tub sheet metal to stretch outward because it's thinner than the guard.

5 The Poison Spyder Ricochet Rockers are unpainted and require fitting before painting. After they are completely fitted, remove them and apply paint to protect the steel. In addition to painting the parts, apply some paint to the drilled holes to prevent rust. When they are completely dry, complete the installation and admire your new protection.

Rear Corners

Like the rockers, the rear corners are a section of the Jeep tub that is easily damaged but not easily fixed. Dropping off an obstacle or backing onto one is a good way to incur some damage. As with many other Jeep accessories, numerous versions of rear corner guards are available that bolt directly to the body and provide protection to this sensitive area. These corners usually wrap around the body from the tailgate to the fender area and are manufactured from a variety of materials and different textures.

Much like the rocker guards, installation requires drilling into the body and creating a metal-to-metal condition that invites rust. Use a thin rubber gasket during installation to help save the paint and keep out water.

Companies generally offer several versions of corner guards to allow custom installation. Most are pre-cut to allow the tailgate hinges, taillights, and fuel filler to fit in the factory locations. However, some are available that have no cutouts to allow a completely custom install. In addition, most will line up with the factory flare edge for a clean install.

Similar to the rockers, the rear corners on the TJ are vulnerable and damage easily. A variety of corner protection is available. All require drilling into the body but will provide considerable protection to the area. These rare Mopar guards for the TJ are difficult to find. The small side bar provides some extra protection.

Installing Poison Spyder Corner Guards

Installing these guards requires some careful drilling and mounting to line up everything. The Poison Spyder corners are pre-painted but a fresh coat of satin black was added after fitting to match the rest of the Jeep. While not totally necessary, using a nutsert tool will allow much easier installation of the threaded nut inserts in the body.

1 Fitting the Poison Spyder rear corners with clamps will get them in the proper spot. Take into account the location of the taillight fitment, fuel filler, and tailgate hinges. Loosening the flare may be necessary for installation of some corner guards.

2 With the clamps holding the guards in place, start drilling holes and installing the bolts just tight enough to prevent movement as you go. Observe the alignment to make sure the guard has not moved.

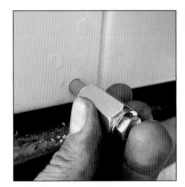

3 The Poison Spyder corner guards include nutserts that make bolt installation easier in a few areas where rear access is not possible. You can use a nutsert installation tool or install them carefully using the manual method of a long bolt and oversized nut.

4 With the guards fitted, they were removed for a better coat of paint that matches the other components on the Jeep. When the paint was fully dry, they were installed permanently along with the taillights, fuel filler, and license plate holder. Small sections of the body were painted the matching black to make the installation more uniform.

5 The guards are a functional and attractive addition to the Jeep that will provide excellent protection to the corners. The TJ Unlimited has 5 inches extra body in the rear that can make this area more vulnerable than a regular TJ.

Protecting the Occupants

The irreplaceable parts of the Jeep are the driver, passengers, and other occupants, such as a dog. Many Jeep owners put so much into protecting the Jeep and forget about protecting the occupants. Wearing a seat belt when driving is always recommended, but taking some extra steps to protect the Jeep's occupants in the event of a rollover is a small price to pay. Several items can make the Jeep safer for the occupants on the trail. Many of these products are not billed as actual safety devices but a little extra is always better.

Sport Bar

The Wrangler TJ came equipped with a sport bar (also known as a roll bar) that is only marginal at supporting the Jeep in a rollover. "Roll bar" is rarely used officially because it implies an actual function in a rollover situation. From this point forward, I will refer to the sport bar/ roll bar generically as the "roll bar." When Jeep altered the design of the YJ Wrangler's bars to accommodate rear passenger shoulder belts, the triangulation point was lost. Triangulation in a roll bar adds strength and rigidity. Compare a CJ roll bar to a TJ; the side view on a CJ is more of

The factory sport bar is attractive but isn't as strong as a Jeep owner might like. The rear bars offer minimal support in a side rollover because they will move inward easily. Several aftermarket systems are available to reinforce the sport bar. Bolt-in systems are functional, good value, attractive, and easy to install.

a triangle shape while the TJ is more square.

During a low-speed rollover in a TJ, the factory bar does seem to do its job of supporting the weight of the Jeep and keeping the occupants from being crushed. However, the forward section at the windshield does little. The forward bars in the factory design are simply bolted to the top of the windshield, which offers little resistance to being crushed in a rollover. In the past, having access to a tubing bender and a welder or investing in a professionally built cage were the only ways of enhancing the system.

Remember that an off-road Jeep would benefit from the kind of protection that can protect its occupants in a slow rollover situation. This is most likely what can happen when

on the trail. Roll cage systems that can protect the occupants at high speeds are expensive and intrusive within the Jeep; the factory spends considerable money on crash design that actually does work on the street.

Companies such as Smittybilt and RockHard 4x4 make bolt-in roll bar systems that, again, are not billed as actual roll bar systems but that do dramatically enhance the ability of the system to protect the occupants. These systems make use of very strong clamping components to add bars to the factory bar. Along with the standard kit, optional components can be added to further enhance the system. Finally, these systems look great but are as unobtrusive as possible; there is little interference to the occupants from installing these systems.

Installing a Smittybilt Bolt-In Sport Bar System

The Smittybilt and RockHard 4x4 system are similar, so installation will not vary too much between the two. The main part of the system consists of several components: the front center bar section, forward drop bars with grab handles, and rear strengthening bars. This installation is rather involved and can take 6 to 10 hours. The fine details take extra time; these include padding trimming, fitting the covers, and door surrounds.

1 *The first step is removing all of the factory foam from the sport bar. The amount used is rather impressive. Gentle removal will prevent the press-in nylon rivets from pulling out of the foam.*

2 *Installing the front-bar section requires a bit of force with a rubber mallet. It will be necessary to support the rear section until the overhead couplers are installed.*

3 *Installing the side grab-bar sections requires some muscle and partial disassembly of the outer dash area. Install the bolts loosely to allow movement as the installation continues. Installing the dash crossbar required pulling back one side of the grab bar section to allow clearance.*

4 *An overhead view shows the upper section, rear spread bars, and dash bar. Keep all of the bolts loose as you go because fine adjustments will be needed.*

5 *Carve the foam carefully to allow fitment of the foam around the couplers. You may think about removing all the foam but the foam is part of the safety device that can protect occupants in a crash. Don't do it. Hitting your head on a bare roll bar is never a pleasant experience.*

6 *Fitting the foam into the bars is a time-consuming job but will produce excellent results with a factory look. Install the covers gently as you go. It will be necessary to cut the cover at the areas where the bars pass through. The rear spread bars should pass through the cover on the small end of the bar.*

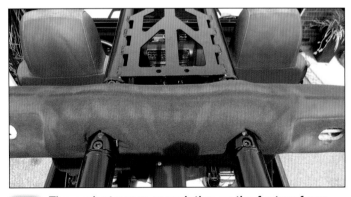

7 *The project nears completion as the factory foam and cover is fitted and installed. Reinstallation of the seat belts and sound pods is next. Continue to tighten all the bolts as you go.*

8 *The installation is complete with all of the new foam covers and the fitted factory door surrounds. As the material relaxes, you'll have to fine-fit the foam covers.*

Seat Belts

The factory seat belts are sufficient for an off-road Jeep like our build. Some owners replace the factory belts with competition-style systems that are actually extremely restrictive; they work to keep the driver firmly in the seat. In slow-driving off-road situations, the ability to move in the seat is a benefit. For street driving, these systems are even more inconvenient.

For Jeep owners who like to take a pet along, a pet restraint that uses the seatbelt latch will ensure that the animal stays in the Jeep.

Cargo Nets

Cargo nets can serve as occupant protection, especially in their ability to keep stuff, even animals, in the Jeep during a rollover. These will be discussed further in chapter 11. However, securing items inside the Jeep is always a must, particularly while navigating rough terrain or in the event of a rollover. Being hit in the head by a toolbox during a rollover can make a bad day worse.

Putting It All Together

Protecting the Jeep underneath and above is an extremely important part of building and modifying a Jeep. In our TJ, one that is built for maximum performance on- and off-road we can put together some best practices of protection.

Adding protection for the following areas should be considered first on the list:

Differentials: front and rear
Steering box

With all of the protection on the TJ Unlimited project inside, outside, and underneath, this Jeep is much better equipped for the abuse it will see on the trail. The bumpers, guards, and sport bar enhancements are just a few of the installed components.

Rockers: body-mounted will offer most clearance
Corners
Bump stops

Secondary steps are:
Center skid plate
Roll Bar
Fuel Tank
Engine

A lighter-weight front bumper will provide protection and proper pull points. A bumper that can provide mounts for a winch, lights, and other accessories will save money. Finally, a bumper that increases approach angle, especially in front of the tires, will help off-road.

Deciding on a rear bumper that provides a spare tire mount (or doesn't) is a big decision. Dealing with the tire mounted on the bumper can be a consideration. Similar to the front, a rear bumper should include pull points and provisions for accessories. Look for bumper-mounted tire carriers that provide a rigid wobble- and rattle-free mounting system.

If you want to keep the tire on the tailgate, a larger tire (even a 33-inch) will likely require an enhancement to the hinge system.

Enhancing the factory roll bar will help protect the Jeep's occupants and also look great.

TIRES, WHEELS, AND BRAKES

After all the discussion, I have reached the point where the power of the Jeep finally gets to the ground. In addition to getting moving, stopping the Jeep is an especially useful feature that is often taken for granted until there is an issue. Like bumpers and lifts, tires and wheels are often some of the earliest items replaced on a Jeep. These components are so visual that they can and often do define a Jeep at first glance.

Tires are the final point on the Jeep before the terrain, and their ability to get the power to the ground is all a matter of traction. If you have sufficient traction, the Jeep will move; if not, the tires will spin and possibly result in a stuck Jeep. Tires, especially the tread, make such a difference that you should exercise careful consideration when making a choice. The contact patch of a tire is such a small area; making it count

is often the difference between stuck and not stuck.

On a paved road, almost any tire will provide sufficient traction in many conditions, even rain and snow. This is far from the truth in many off-road conditions when mud and rocks are involved. Add a little slick mud to a street-style tire and the traction nearly disappears due to the mud filling the tread and creating a slick-style tire. Since the off-road terrain is so varying, a tire that can properly deal with the changes will keep you moving and keep getting stuck for situations way more challenging.

Purpose-built tires allow for a Jeep to tackle off-road obstacles such as rocks, mud, and hills more easily so you can take on more difficult trails. Thanks to modern engineering and designs, off-road, purpose-built tires have excellent on-road manners in both noise and handling. Tread life is also better thanks to improved construction compounds and clever tread design.

Tire Types

Tire types can be broken down into three categories: street, all-terrain, and mud-terrain. Spend a

The mud bog is a favorite for many Jeep owners. It's a true test of traction that is pretty much in the hands of the tires alone. This may be the ultimate test of a mud tire for those who love to spend hours cleaning five minutes' worth of fun.

spring weekend at a Jeep trail run in the Northeast navigating soft muddy terrain sprinkled with tree roots and you'll quickly understand the difference between tire types. Those with mud-terrain tires will keep moving while almost anything else will become a mud-filled slick. By contrast, spend some time navigating a rock garden and it will be evident how well a mud-terrain tire will work here too. In some ways, the mud-terrain should be considered the all-terrain.

Street Tires

Street tires are really a type of tire that doesn't have a place on the Jeep we are building. Their road manners might be nice, but take them off-road and they will leave you stuck even in the most mild of challenges. If your Jeep has factory tires, they will fit into this category unless the Jeep is a Rubicon. The Rubicon was the only model to come with proper off-road–style tires. At a minimum, all-terrain–style tires belong on a Jeep that is used off-road.

The all-terrain tire, such as this BFGoodrich All-Terrain, has a less aggressive tread than a mud-terrain tire, which reduces its effectiveness off-road but increases street performance. These tires perform very well on mild trails in mostly dry conditions.

All-Terrain Tires

All-terrain tires fill the area between street tires and mud-terrain tires. This style uses a more aggressive tread design without too much compromise to street driving. The tread often uses smaller and shallower grooves between the treads. This keeps the tire from making more noise on the street like mud tires.

All-Terrain Tire Performance	
Rain	Better than street tires
Snow	Better than street tires
Ice	Good
Mud	Marginal
Rock	Good
Sand	Good

The smaller treads and voids collect mud within the voids; this makes less tread available for digging in. These tires are often equipped with sipes, which are small cuts in the tread that improve the tire performance in slippery road conditions such as rain, snow, or ice.

Off-road performance can be good with all-terrain tires in certain conditions. Dry conditions and rocks are handled well by the all-terrain tire. Some all-terrain tires move closer to the mud-terrain–style and will naturally perform better off-road. These use extra features such as wider voids and side tread. The BFGoodrich All-Terrain has evolved over the years and definitely gets closer to a mud-terrain without too much street sacrifice.

In the Middle

Perhaps the most interesting tire in recent years is the Goodyear Dura-Trac and the Toyo Open Country R/T tire. These tires resemble a mud tire but maintain a slightly tighter tread to reduce road noise. They also add siping for better snow and rain performance compared to true mud tires. Mud and general off-road performance is not quite as strong as a true mud tire, but these two are very capable. The aggressive looks and excellent overall performance make these tires great for a daily driver as well as all-around trail tire: all in one package. ∎

A few tires are available that exist between mud- and all-terrain styles. These tires are excellent daily-driver tires that are still aggressive enough to keep up off-road. The Wrangler DuraTrac is a prime example of this in-the-middle–style tire. Aggressive but tighter tread reduces noise and siping improves rain and snow driving.

Goodyear DuraTrac and Toyo Open Country R/T Performance	
Rain	Good
Snow	Good
Ice	Good
Mud	Better
Rock	Better
Sand	Better

Mud-terrain–style tires, such as the Toyo Open Country M/T, dominate on Jeeps that are used off-road. Many brands are available; each provides its own twist on the style but almost all feature large tread blocks with wide gaps that allow mud to be thrown away from the tire to maintain traction. Mud tires perform best on rocks as well; the tread blocks can grab the rock surface to keep traction.

Mud-Terrain Tires

The mud tire is likely the most common tire found on a Jeep, especially one that is used regularly on the trail. Interestingly, the mud-style tire is generally the favored variety off-road, regardless of the type of terrain the Jeep experiences. From thick mud to snow to sand to rocks, this style of tires excels in a variety of poor-traction conditions.

The thick tread blocks and large voids allow the tire to grab onto the surface and search for traction while allowing mud and dirt to be thrown away with minimal wheel speed. The ability of the tire to clean itself when it's in sticky, muddy conditions will mean the difference between being stuck and not stuck. Jeepers learn that in heavy mud conditions some extra wheel speed causes the mud to fly from the tire tread, which allows the tread to continue finding traction.

Mud-Terrain Tire Performance	
Rain	Poor
Snow	Good
Ice	Poor
Mud	Best
Rock	Best
Sand	Better

The large tread blocks are the reason that this style of tire is so notoriously loud on the street. Better brands of mud terrain tires, such as those from BFGoodrich, Toyo, and Mickey Thompson, use special designs that cut down on the noise without compromise to traction. Altering the size and spacing of the tread blocks prevents the tire from keeping a constant hum on the highway. As mud-terrain–style tires wear, they tend to get louder. Rotating them regularly helps control uneven wear and reduces noise. The reality is that many Jeep owners come to appreciate the tire noise and often it is not considered a problem.

Mud-terrain–style tires are constructed from stiffer compounds to deal with the punishment of off-road use and the tread blocks usually lack sipes, which helps to lessen chunking (chunks of tire tread torn off by rocks, etc.). This style usually performs poorly on-road in slippery conditions such as rain and snow. Jeeps equipped with mud-terrain tires must be driven with caution in these conditions because the tires will slide very easily. Deep snow may be an exception with mud-terrain tires; in these conditions, the treads will dig quite well through the snow.

Tire Size

Tires are available in many sizes but often the most popular size on a TJ that is used on the street and trail is in the 33- to 35-inch range. There

A larger-size tire than stock will improve off-road performance and increase ground clearance. Even a few inches larger will combine well with a suspension lift and alter off-road capability dramatically. In addition, a larger tire improve off-road ride quality because it can traverse obstacles more easily and the additional sidewall allows the tire to absorb bumps.

are many considerations to keep in mind when choosing a tire size that the decision can be extremely difficult. It's easy to succumb to tire size envy when you're at a Jeep event. The JK Wrangler has caused a surge in tire sizes because fitting 37-inch tires is easy, even with a mild lift. Prior to the JK, 37-inch and taller tires were considered something only found on extreme off-road vehicles.

Size Lies

Nearly all tires are smaller than their advertised size; some are much more than others. Careful comparison on tire spec sheets will allow you to better understand the actual size of the tire. A tire that is off by 1 inch can mean loss of valuable ground clearance, which can be even worse when the tire is aired-down.

The actual measurement of a tire will almost always measure less than the advertised size. Vehicle weight, rim width, tire pressure, and construction variations all play a part in the actual size. Researching actual tire size can show the wide variations between manufacturers.

On a TJ, a 35-inch tire is about the maximum tire size without more serious modifications. This size pushes the limits of the factory axles. Running 35-inch tires typically requires regearing and a 4-inch minimum lift. Most commonly, a 4.5-inch lift and 1-inch body lift will allow 35-inch tires to run comfortably.

For example, a 33-inch BFGoodrich Mud Terrain KM2 tire for a TJ is advertised as 33 x 12.50R15. Decoding those numbers indicates that the tire is 33 inches tall, 12.5 inches wide, and fits a 15-inch wheel. It seems simple enough, but in reality the specifications of the tire show the tire as actually 32.8 inches tall when mounted. That particular tire is pretty close to advertised size; research will show sizes that are all over the place. Understanding and choosing tire sizes that use metric measurements can be more difficult and deceiving.

Mounting the same tire to different width wheels will impact the height of the tire. Generally, wider wheels will reduce overall height because of the wider spread of the sidewall. In practice, using a narrower wheel will benefit tire height and protect the wheel because the wheel bead will be farther inward from the sidewall. Running low tire

pressures off-road with wide wheels can increase the likelihood of popping the tire off the bead.

So, How Big?

In general a 33-inch tire is the optimum size for a TJ that is used both on- and off-road. This size will allow the tires to clear the fenders when used with a 3- to 4-inch lift. The factory axles are strong enough to deal with the 33-inch size as well.

For those looking for a little more, 35-inch tires reach the limit of even the Rubicon Dana 44. To run 35-inch tires, a 4- to 4.5-inch lift is recommended along with a 1-inch body lift. Careful attention should be paid to the bump-stop lengths to prevent the 35-inch tires from causing tire and/or fender damage. Using tubular-style front fenders will help with clearance of 35s.

Some other things to remember when increasing tire size (from factory size) are cruise RPM and backspacing. Larger tires will have a negative effect on cruise RPM and crawl ratio; this often requires changing gear ratios to make street and off-road driving better. In addition,

larger tires often come in wider sizes that cause clearance issues in several places, the most common being the rear upper coil spring mount.

Spending some time looking at tire sizes at a Jeep event or an online forum is a good way to determine the proper size for your Jeep. Make sure to note the size of the tire, the rim size and width, and the amount of lift. A popular size on a TJ is 33 x 12.50R15 or 285/75R16; both measure about 33 inches. The popular sizes for a 35-inch are usually 35 x 12.50R15 or 315/75R16.

Metric Versus Actual

The TJ used the 15-inch wheel in almost all models except the Rubicon, which used 16-inch wheels. In years past, most 15-inch wheel and tire sizes were measured in actual sizes that were quite easy to interpret. A 33 x 12.50R15 was easily decoded to be 33 inches tall, with a 12.5-inch sidewall width, and fitting a 15-inch wheel. Many sizes still follow this measurement, especially larger sizes, but metric sizes are more common and decoding these tires often requires a calculator.

Metric-size tires use designations that require some calculation to decode actual size. The first number is the section width followed by the aspect ratio. This will vary with different size rims so a 315 tire on a 16-inch wheel may not be the same as a 315 tire on a 17-inch wheel.

A 33-inch tire on a 16-inch wheel may come in a size 285/75R16; it is much more difficult to decode over the actual measurement. Metric tires are sized by a measurement of width and an aspect ratio. The first number is the width and the second number is the aspect ratio. Converting the metric size to an actual size isn't difficult. The formula is (width x aspect / 2,540 x 2) + wheel size. In an example using the size 285/75R16 (285 x 75 / 2,540 x 2) + 16 = 32.8 inches tall. Charts can be found online, and to make it even easier some calculators will do it for you.

Sprung Versus Unsprung Weight

These terms are used most often when talking wheels and tires, but other components can be impacted by these differences in weight. The coil springs on a TJ do the job of isolating the chassis from the axles, which takes the abuse of the terrain directly. The springs allow the axles to move independent of the chassis; that makes the ride comfortable and allows more control of the vehicle. Imagine a Jeep with no provision for suspension movement and axles attached to the frame; the ride would be rough!

Nearly all of the Jeep's weight is supported by the springs (known as sprung weight) with the exception of the components attached below the bottom spring mount, including the wheels, tires, and axle assembly. These components are part of the Jeep's unsprung weight, meaning they take the full pounding of whatever terrain the Jeep is traversing. Installing larger, heavier tires, different wheels, and heavier-duty axles increases the Jeep's unsprung weight. Some folks wonder why this matters.

The heavier unsprung weight requires the application of more force to move the suspension, which results in a decrease of road handling. Thankfully, that unsprung weight is more of an issue in higher-speed sports cars than in a Jeep. These vehicles were never designed for high-speed driving and handling so decreased performance may not be noticeable with a Jeep. In fact, slightly higher unsprung weight can help lower the overall center of gravity, which helps with stability off-road.

Type, Weight, and Weight Rating

In addition to the size of a tire, the tire type and its weight rating are also indicated. To use as an example, a BFGoodrich Mud Terrain has markings LT285/75R16 Load Range E. I already discussed the 285/75 and the 16, so what does the rest mean? The first letters indicate the vehicle type for which the tire was designed: P for Passenger and LT for light truck. In most cases, tires for a Jeep will be the LT. In this example, the R is often misunderstood to stand for rim size, but it actually stands for the tire construction type: R for radial and B for bias ply. Bias-ply tires are still common in some off-road–style tires. These tires tend to take more off-road abuse; their on-road handling and manners are less than desirable.

Finally, the last rating is the load range, which is an indicator of the designed weight rating for the tire. The higher the rating will mean that the tire can support more weight. A drawback of using a tire with high weight ratings on a Jeep is that the Jeep is rather light compared to a pickup truck for which the tire may be intended. This can cause the tire to weigh more and have stiffer sidewalls, which reduce ride quality. Most Jeep tires are C rated but many larger off-road sizes are D or E rated, especially those in the 16- and 17-inch wheel size. Examining all of the specs of a tire including its weight rating can help with a decision.

Larger tires weigh more and higher weight ratings will increase the weight of a similarly sized tire by 10 to 15 percent more. This will add to the Jeep's unsprung weight, impacting driving characteristics and potentially wear.

Air Pressure

It's often best to run recommended air pressure on the street with factory-sized tires but it's difficult to know a recommended pressure when larger tires with different weight ratings are used. Usually, tires on a Jeep with higher weight rating can run at lower street pressures to help with ride and wear. To properly determine the best street pressure, a simple contact patch test will give excellent results.

Reading the Tire Contact Patch

There are many ways of doing this but the basic idea is to mark the tire with something that will leave an impression on the surface to show the contact patch. Using a piece of white paper and a little latex paint gives the best impressions.

Examine the patch created by the paint. The pattern will indicate the size of the contact patch and whether pressure is too high or too low. Look for a patch that allows nearly the whole tire to contact the surface for best street traction and tire wear without excessive low pressure, such as less than 25 psi. In addition to pressure, this test can indicate poor camber. Note that the factory Dana 30 and Dana 44 typically have no camber and no factory provision for adjustment. Indication of positive or negative camber can indicate a bent axle tube or worn ball joints. Further investigation is warranted if excess camber is detected.

Make any pressure adjustments and run the test again, using new paper. Compare results to find the happy spot in the contact patches for your Jeep.

1 *Using some latex paint or art paint, coat a small section of the tire to cover a region of tread. Tape some paper to the floor to prevent it from sticking to the tire. This works best on a smooth surface such as a concrete garage floor.*

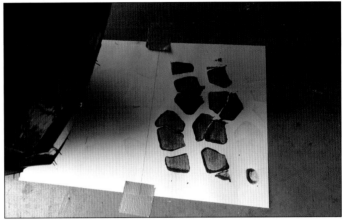

2 *Roll the Jeep over the paper, allowing the paint to mark the paper. Mark the tire pressure on the paper for reference. Wipe the paint off the tire with a wet rag and repeat the test at different pressures. Note the contact patch differences.*

3 *At 35 psi, the contact patch shows that the outer tread is barely touching the surface. This may cause the tires to wear in the center more and make the ride rougher. The decreased patch size, along with the stiffer tire (from the pressure), can negatively impact handling when driving in rain and snow.*

4 *At 24 psi, the tread coverage is almost complete, which indicates that this pressure is creating the best patch without being too low for proper on-road handling. In this particular Jeep, 28 psi offered a similar patch with better street manners.*

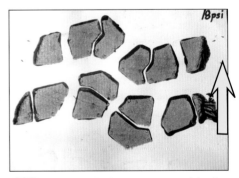

5 *At 18 psi, the outermost blocks are making good contact with the surface. This pressure is likely too low for good street driving manners, but it would allow the tire to use all available means of traction on the trail.*

Running an aired-down tire while off-road is regular practice for a Jeep owner. The lower tire pressure allows the tire to conform to the irregular terrain, which helps to maintain traction. In addition, the softer tire helps absorb bumps, allowing for a more comfortable ride and increased control.

Off-Road Air Pressure

When driving off-road at slow speeds, it's common to air-down the tires. This means that the air pressure is lowered to a level that allows the tire to conform to the surface but keeps the tire from coming off the bead. An aired-down tire will become much softer and, as it conforms to the terrain, the tread blocks will actually grip the surface like fingers, which results in increased traction.

A secondary result of airing-down tires is that because the tires are softer, they will help absorb bumps from the terrain and help the handling of the Jeep. This will then reduce the possibility of damage to components, especially those that are unsprung. Control arms and axle tubes are essentially unsprung, and striking obstacles off-road will transfer a fair amount of energy to them. The softer tire will help absorb some of that energy.

How Low?

Knowing the kind of terrain where the Jeep will be used will help

At 35 psi, the high pressure keeps the sidewall of the tire firm and prevents the tread from conforming to the obstacle. Off-road driving with this kind of pressure will impact traction and cause a rough ride because the tire cannot help absorb the bumps.

with deciding how far to air-down the pressure. In addition, standard wheels can't be aired-down as much as bead lock–style wheels. Lower pressures are better for rocks, hills, and sand; medium pressures will handle mud and dirt roads. Most non-beadlock wheels and tires can handle approximately 15 psi; going lower can cause the tire to separate from the bead, causing a flat and possibly damage. If you are using beadlock wheels, it can be possible to push pressures into the single digits.

Lower pressures cause the tire to bulge under the weight of the Jeep, which effectively reduces ground clearance. This is a compromise that a Jeep owner must deal with when airing-down: low-enough pressure for traction and ride but not too low to cause excess reduction of ground clearance. This alone can be the rationale for a larger tire instead of a smaller tire.

An additional consideration relating to running low air pressure is the need to air-up after the trail to drive home. Unless you have a method to air-up before leaving the trail, it may be necessary to drive some distance

At 18 psi, the tire still maintains its form and is likely safe from being pushed off the wheel. However, the pressure is low enough to allow the tread to conform to the obstacle and grip it with the blocks. Moreover, the lower pressure will allow the sidewall to flex to absorb bumps and help maintain vehicle control.

on the street with low tire pressure. Tires with less than 15 psi will feel extremely spongy on the street; you will have to drive very carefully. In this case, running 15 to 20 psi will keep the tires street-drivable without being dangerous.

Rotation

Rotating tires at regular intervals will keep tire wear even and allow for their max life. In general, rotating tires every 5,000 miles is sufficient. Following a four- or five-tire rotation scheme will achieve the best results.

Rotating four tires is slightly different than five. Jeepers often only rotate the four with the thought that the fifth will not wear and will save them from having to purchase five in the future. This thinking often leads to a dry, rotted spare that is likely to not match and will become dangerous. Unless you have access to a vehicle lift, using an impact wrench, floor jack, and several jack stands can make rotation easy.

If the Jeep only runs four tires or if the spare is of a different size/type, implementing a four-tire rotation scheme will help maintain even wear while allowing the tires to serve in a location for a set amount of time. Follow the arrows.

Running a matching spare will prevent possible damage to the drivetrain if the spare is needed. Including the spare in the regular rotation will extend tire life and allow all tires to wear evenly. Checking the pressure in the spare regularly will prevent the unfortunate event of having two flat tires on the trail.

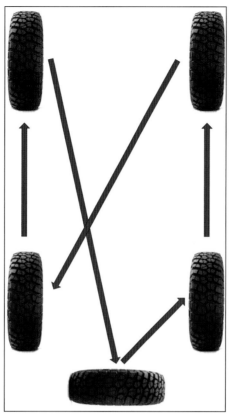

When all five tires are matching, rotating the spare with the others will keep all the tires wearing evenly. As with the four-tire rotation, each tire will spend a set amount of time at each location, including the spare, which accrues no miles.

Four-Tire Rotation

Rotating four tires is a simple process. The rear tires move forward on the same side and the front tires move to the rear, opposite side. Using this method, each tire will eventually be used in every location; they will return to the original position on the fourth rotation.

Five-Tire Rotation

Rotating five tires is a little more complex, and it is best to keep a reference. Similar to the four-tire rotation sequence, the rear tires are moved forward on the same side. The spare goes to the rear passenger's side and the passenger-side front goes to the rear driver's side. The driver-side front becomes the new spare. In this method, every tire is eventually used at each position and the "spare" tire receives no wear during its time as the spare. This rotation can allow tires to wear longer because one sits out for 5,000 miles at a time.

Spare Tire

For some folks, a spare tire is seen as an extra expense; this type of person may use something cheap, likely the wrong size, or even a different type of tire. This might be fine on the street, but not having the proper spare if you need it when you're out on the trail (and away from civilization) can make for a long day. Running a spare that is the same size and type is always recommended, along with rotating the spare within the set. Maintaining tire pressure in the spare is also important. Having to air-up a flat spare on the trail wastes time and could indicate that the tire is damaged.

Running a smaller-sized spare can cause problems with certain kinds of lockers and limited slip differentials because of the variation in tire diameter. If you are running a different-sized spare, it's best to stop using the locker or switch the smaller tire to the axle that has a manual locker or no locker.

Wheels

The terms wheels and rims are interchangeable, and both are commonly used. On the surface, it may seem that the only purpose the wheel serves is as a mounting place for the tire, but this is not true. Wheels are important for locating the tire within the wheelwell; this measurement is the backspacing. In addition to function, wheels are an important and significant part of the Jeep's overall appearance. For some folks, choosing a set of aftermarket wheels can be a long process because so many options are available.

The TJ was fitted with 15-inch-diameter wheels from the factory; the exception was the Rubicon, which was equipped with 16-inch wheels. Many aftermarket wheels in 16- and 17-inch sizes will offer the greatest variety. Today, 15-inch wheel choices are diminishing because they are less popular.

Construction

The TJ used both steel and aluminum wheels during the span of the model. Typically, the steel wheels were used on the less expensive models, such as the X, while aluminum were upgrades or standard on higher models, including the Sport and Sahara. Factory aluminum wheels usually have a name designation such as Canyon, Ravine, and Moab.

Most aftermarket wheels are typically constructed of aluminum but all-steel choices are available. Aluminum wheels are attractive, lightweight, and strong; these factors combine well with larger, heavier tires and off-road use. Aluminum wheels are almost always more expensive than steel wheels.

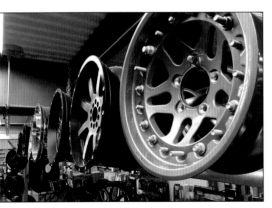

These Quadratec Rubicon Xtreme 16-inch wheels are inexpensive and have the proper backspacing for a TJ with larger and wider tires. The simple design is stylish and looks great on the Jeep. The wide spoke openings allow mud and debris to fall from the wheel easily.

A popular steel wheel is the black D-window–style made by Tactik and Pro Comp. These inexpensive wheels are durable and look good on a TJ. Steel wheels will not shatter or crack as aluminum wheels can and will often take more abuse on the trail before failure.

Choosing the construction type often comes down to looks and budget. Aluminum wheels are available in more styles and are generally considered better looking on the Jeep, which makes them the more popular choice.

Searching for wheels for your Jeep can be a daunting task. So many options are available that it can be difficult to make a decision. The reality of wheel damage on an off-road–used Jeep can help in the decision to purchase less-expensive wheels. Simple wheels that allow dirt and mud to escape often work best.

Backspacing and Offset

Backspacing is the distance between the mounting point and the inner edge of the wheel. This measurement indicates how far in or out the wheel will be located. Knowing the optimum measurement will help you choose the proper wheel for your Jeep. Jeep spaced the TJ wheels to bring the tire to the edge of the flare. This can cause issues when changing wheels because most wheels, when combined with larger tires, will exceed the flares. This is a potential issue with vehicle inspection requirements in some areas.

Factory backspacing is most commonly 5.5 inches; it is difficult to find aftermarket wheels in this size. Tires wider than 11.5 inches will often create rubbing issues with the rear spring buckets and front sway bar when used with the factory wheels. An optimum backspace for the TJ using larger tires (up to 12.5 inches wide) is 4.5 inches. This spacing will allow clearance of the rear spring bucket and keep the tires close to the flare edge, exceeding it only minimally. Installation of Rubicon or Sahara flares, which are 1 inch wider, often brings the tire back within the flare. The Quadratec Rubicon Xtreme

Factory backspacing on most TJ wheels is 5.5 inches. This will keep the tires within the flares, but tire widths wider than 11 inches run the risk of coming in contact with the frame-side rear spring bucket.

wheel is an example of a wheel designed specifically to fit the TJ; the 4.5-inch backspacing falls within the optimum size.

Many aftermarket 15-inch wheels use a 3.5-inch backspacing. This can cause the tires to exceed the flares by several inches. This issue can be troubling enough, but 2 inches less can cause excess wear on the wheel bearings and the steering knuckles because of the changes in leverage. Larger, heavier tires can magnify the problems. Finally, less backspacing can interfere with steering geometry and handling because the factory steering system is designed to work with the factory backspacing. Reducing the backspace moves the wheels farther from the steering centerline, increases tire scrub, and reduces steering performance.

Offset is an additional measurement found on some wheels; it measures distance from the mounting hub to the centerline of the wheel. Positive offset is when the centerline of the wheel is located farther inside from the mounting point. It is most common on modern vehicles including the TJ.

Wheels such as the Quadratec Rubicon Xtreme 16-inch wheel that use a 4.5-inch backspacing will allow up to 12.5-inch-wide tires without rubbing. This size will keep the tires as close to the flare edge as possible with minimal excess.

Width

Factory Jeep aluminum wheels on the TJ were generally an 8-inch width, while the steel wheels were 6- and 7- inch widths. Most of the larger tires will need at least an 8-inch wheel to be mounted properly. It's always best to follow the tire manufacturer's recommendation regarding wheel width. Mounting a tire on a wheel that is too wide or too narrow can cause the tire to wear incorrectly and possibly cause a failure.

Beadlocks

Beadlock wheels are designed in multiple pieces. The tire bead is placed into a channel; the outer section bolts to the channel and clamps the bead to the wheel. This prevents it from popping out because of an impact or extremely low tire pressure. Beadlocks do allow the ability to run extremely low pressures in extreme off-road conditions. These wheels are often expensive and most brands are not legal for street use. Most beadlock wheels only clamp the outer bead but dual locks are available. Hutchinson is one of the few companies that manufacture street-legal beadlock wheels.

Staun and Desert Enterprises make an internal, street-legal beadlock system that doesn't require special wheels. These beadlocks work by using an inflatable inner tube that inflates to apply pressure to the inner and outer bead of the tire, thereby preventing it from separating from the bead. These are installed at the same time as the tire and require wheel modification for the addition of a separate valve stem.

Wheel Spacers (Adapters)

For those looking to retain the factory wheels when using larger and wider tires, wheel spacers, also known as adapters, can be very effective. Spac-

Beadlocks are the ultimate in off-road wheels. These wheels use an outer locking ring to clamp the tire to the wheel, which prevents air loss at extreme low pressures. Most true beadlock-style wheels are expensive and are not legal for street use.

ers are usually 1.25 to 1.5 inches wide and are constructed from an aluminum alloy. Spacers that are most commonly used are technically more of an adapter because they bolt to the factory hub and provide different lugs for the wheel to mount to. A true spacer sits between the hub and the wheel and acts like a large washer. Spacers require care during installation; using thread locker combined with proper torque will keep them tight and safe. Spidertrax and TeraFlex make spacers for the TJ; these versions allow installation of newer 5-bolt on 5-inch wheels to be adapted to the TJ's 5-on-4.5 hub.

Brakes

With all the stuff we add to our Jeeps to make them go, it's nice to have something capable of stopping the Jeeps when we need them to stop. Fortunately, the TJ came equipped with capable power brakes and some TJ models were equipped with factory rear disc brakes. All TJs used disc brakes up front. Some TJs were factory equipped with an anti-lock brake system (ABS) to help the driver

Wheel adapters (wheel spacers) can be used to move the wheels outward to increase clearance for wider tires. These can also be used to adapt the TJ 5-bolt on 4.5-inch lug pattern to other lug patterns. Using 17-inch Wrangler JK 5-bolt on 5-inch wheels is popular on the TJ. These adapters bolt to the existing lugs and provide new lugs for mounting the wheels.

in extra-slippery conditions. Jeeps with the Dana 44 rear and Trac-Lok were equipped with disc brakes; this includes all TJ Unlimited models. The factory system is able to handle 33- to 35-inch tires comfortably.

Parking Brake

The TJ parking brake uses a center console–mounted handle connected to a cable system to actuate the parking brake. Disc brake–equipped Jeeps employ a small drum brake located within the rotor. Maintaining a strong parking brake is essential for safety and use on the trail. The parking brake can often be used when navigating obstacles and slowing the Jeep when both feet are needed on the other pedals.

Brake Upgrades

While most TJ owners leave their factory brake systems alone, there are a few upgrades and modifications possible that can improve performance on the street and trail.

Factory rear disc brakes are a hidden gem found on some TJ models. This rear brake offers better stopping force and better off-road self-cleaning ability. TJ Rubicons, Unlimiteds, and Dana 44–equipped TJs often used factory rear disc brakes.

Disc Brakes

If you aren't lucky enough to have a TJ equipped with rear disc brakes, some conversion options are available. Stainless Steel Brakes Corporation (SSBC) makes a bolt-on kit for the TJ Dana 35 and Dana 44. The kit includes calipers with a built-in parking brake, mounting hardware, dust shields, and lines. Other companies, such as Currie, offer kits that use new hardware combined with other manufacturers' hardware, such as from the Ford Explorer.

Swapping Dana 44 with a disc brake from another TJ is an option that can be easy; this conversion replaces the weaker Dana 35 with the stronger Dana 44 and adds the better brakes. When swapping a Dana 44 from another TJ, often the only changes needed are a new rear driveshaft and installation of new parking brake cables. Keep in mind that front and rear gear ratios need to match. Similar, almost-bolt-on conversions can be made using axles and parts from a 1993–2004 Grand Cherokee.

Hydroboost

If you are looking for the strongest brake performance in a TJ, a

The parking brake is another tool at the disposal of a Jeep owner. In many situations, the driver can use the parking brake to assist when navigating an obstacle. Maintaining proper parking brake operation is essential in both manual- and automatic-equipped Jeeps.

Hydroboost system is the ticket. Vanco makes a Hydroboost system that is a direct fit for the TJ. The kit replaces the stock vacuum booster with a unit that is driven by the power steering pump. In addition, the stock master cylinder is replaced with a high-capacity, high-flow unit. This system produces more pressure to the brakes with less pedal effort.

The system is designed to not feel over-sensitive and can be driven normally. When higher pressure is applied to the pedal, the system pressure is increased. In addition to the Vanco equipment, a high-flow power steering pump is required for proper operation.

Brake Lines

Aftermarket brake lines are a nice addition to a Jeep. Most lines are made of braided stainless steel that offers more protection from trail obstacles. Most aftermarket brake lines are available in longer lengths to accommodate lift kits of all sizes. The front lines are especially susceptible to line stretching when the axle is moving away from the frame during suspension cycling. Goodridge is a popular brake line manufacturer that offers lines in many lengths.

Brake Line Brackets

Many lift kits include brake line extension brackets for the front brake lines. These brackets shift the frame mounting location for the end of the hard brake line mount down by about 1 inch to allow the flexible brake line to gain back additional length lost with a lift kit. Testing brake line stretch with a new lift is extremely important because a damaged line on the trail will make for a bad day. These brackets are available from most lift manufacturers if the kit installed didn't include them.

Putting It All Together

Wheels, tires, and brakes mark the completion of the drivetrain discussion. Power has made it from the engine to the tires; finding traction is less of a problem with the right combination of components.

Tires are a big and expensive decision, choosing a set can be extremely

Brake lines that are longer and wrapped in braided steel, such as these from Rubicon Express, will prevent stretched lines after installing a lift kit. The braided covering will further protect the lines from trail debris and damage.

Some lift kits include brake line brackets that relocate the hard brake line downward approximately 1 inch to prevent the factory lines from pulling tight when the suspension is extending from the Jeep. Checking for tight lines during articulation and replacing with longer lines if necessary will prevent a ripped line off-road.

challenging for a Jeep owner. Many find a favorite brand and stick with it for many years. Consider the type of trails the Jeep will see as well as the amount of on-road time. This can help with the decision. If the Jeep will not see wet weather and winter driving, the absence of sipes on the tires is less important.

Radial mud-type tires will provide the best performance off-road and on-road.

Aluminum wheels provide good looks, light weight, and many styles. Wheels that are 8 to 9.5 inches wide with 4.5-inch backspace work best with most tires up to 12.5 inches wide.

Proper maintenance on the Jeep's braking system will keep it stopping. Disc swaps on the rear can add stopping power without being a major project.

A Hydroboost system can provide brake pressures much greater than the factory vacuum-assist systems. The popular system by Vanco uses the power steering pump to increase the pressure applied to the master cylinder, which results in easier driver effort and greater stopping power.

Good choices of tires and wheels will help control expenses and equip a Jeep for excellent off-road performance. The 33- to 35-inch tires on wheels with 4.5 inches of backspace are a good choice for a TJ. This size will reduce the potential for drivetrain failure and will fit with most 3- to 4.5-inch lift systems.

ELECTRICAL AND LIGHTING

The heavy stuff on Jeeps, such as the tires, lifts, and armor, has now been covered. The Jeep's electrical system may be physically lighter but is a heavyweight system that can mystify a Jeep owner. As Jeep models have evolved, their electrical systems have become more complex; understanding and dealing with these systems has become increasingly difficult. If you ever had (or have) the pleasure of owning a CJ, you'll know that its electrical systems is very basic and almost minimalist compared to the TJ's electrical system, which is quite different and much more complex.

Like almost every other vehicle, the TJ uses a 12-volt electrical system in which the chassis of the Jeep serves as a common ground. The system consists of mostly blade-style fuses and a few circuit breakers to protect from overloads that could lead to an electrical fire.

All of the TJ series Wranglers use a Powertrain Control Module (PCM) to operate most of the engine functions through constant monitoring of sensors and switches located throughout. The PCM manages the engine timing, dwell, air/fuel ratio, idle speed, and electrical charging system. The PCM is located under the hood on the passenger-side cowl just behind the battery.

The TJ charging system uses a 117- to 136-amp alternator, depending on particular model years, engines, and options.

Manual-transmission Wranglers are equipped with a clutch safety switch that prevents the starter from engaging without the clutch pedal depressed. Automatic-transmission Wranglers are equipped with a starter lockout if the transmission is not in park or neutral.

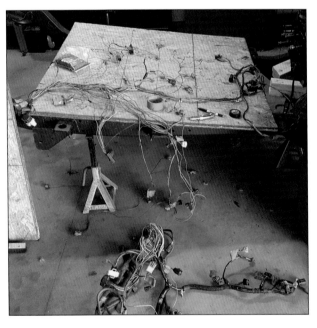

The wiring harness on a TJ is rather complex when compared to the past Wrangler and CJ models. Taking the time to label everything when you are going to do extensive wiring work is extra important to prevent a potentially expensive mess and a great deal of frustration. (Photo Courtesy Ben Mann)

The PCM is located in the engine compartment behind the battery. This sealed module controls many vehicle functions. These modules are typically very reliable and can serve the Jeep for a lifetime.

Wiring Basics

Entire books are written just on vehicle electrical wiring, so it's almost impossible to cover the whole topic here. Some common-sense items and good wiring habits will minimize electrical failures and reduce the chance of electrical fires dramatically. If you look under the hood or dash of many Jeeps, you may see wiring hack jobs. These poor wiring techniques create nightmares when it's time for troubleshooting, as well as the potential for disaster. Here is a generalized list of some essentials for proper wiring.

- Neat and organized wiring is much easier to troubleshoot and trace.
- Always use automotive stranded-core wiring instead of the solid-core wire that is usually used in home wiring. Solid-core wire can fail over time because of vibration.
- Maintain matching-gauge wire to circuit capacity to prevent the wiring from overheating and to prevent failure and possible fire.
- Use proper gauge automotive-style connectors and avoid home-style connectors to keep connections from working loose from vibration.
- Solder connections and used shrink-wrap; this is always the best way to ensure a solid electrical connection that is reliable over time.
- Use dielectric grease to lubricate and protect the connection; it allows a better electrical connection and prevents corrosion from moisture.
- Secure wires and use a plastic automotive loom to prevent rubbing and wear. Keep wires protected from heat sources and always use grommets when passing the wires through metal.

Take a peek under the dash of the TJ and you will find tightly wrapped bundles of wiring. This is a good example of the efficient assembly-line design. These bundles keep the wires together and reliable but can be very difficult to troubleshoot and modify. Tapping into these parts of wiring is not recommended.

Plastic wire loom will keep wiring neat and organized while protecting the wires from wear from rubbing. Loom is inexpensive and available in many sizes, lengths, and colors. Loom can be a bit maddening to work with but the end result is worth the effort.

- Good grounds are often overlooked. It may be the first thought to ground to the chassis; however, in some cases, especially with high-draw devices, a direct ground to the battery or a ground bar will provide better and safer performance. ∎

In general, the TJ electrical system is rather robust and reliable. Minimal maintenance is required, even after years of use. Like almost everything else on the Jeep, upgrades and modifications to the Jeep's electrical system are available and can offer some advantages. Jeep owners often add a variety of electrical accessories that draw power from the Jeep, such as lights, winches, compressors, and a whole array of small electronics.

One of the biggest challenges with the TJ electrical system is finding a suitable and safe location to tap power for additional accessories. Fortunately, some clever ways and aftermarket electrical system add-ons are available that make adding components easier and safer. It's common to find poorly installed electrical hack jobs on aging Jeeps. Some owners don't take the time to properly install additional components, which leads to unprotected circuits and fire hazards. It's bad enough to lay your Jeep on its side on the trail; it's much worse watching it burn up on the side of the road from a preventable electrical fire.

Electrical System Upgrades and Modifications

Electrical system modifications and upgrades are somewhat unnoticed because the modifications don't have an outward appearance like a lift kit or larger tires. Nevertheless, despite the hidden nature, these upgrades improve reliability, safety, and performance.

Battery

A Jeep owner may start his or her Jeep on the trail more times in one day than in a month of street driving. This alone puts a load on the battery and starter that is not normally experienced by a street-driven car.

Battery technology has improved over the years and many upgrade options exist for a Jeep owner. When adding high-draw accessories such as a winch or a compressor, extra load will be put on the battery that can lead to quick charge drain, premature failure, and reduced life. Several brands of heavy-duty aftermarket batteries are available that can handle the additional load introduced. Optima and Odyssey manufacture batteries that are well suited for the demands of an off-road–used Jeep. Both offer unique features that will serve the Jeep exceptionally well for many years. A common feature of both is the sealed design that allows the battery to be installed in any orientation; in addition, their design makes them unaffected by vibration, heat, and bouncing so commonly experienced on the trail. Either battery is an excellent choice for an upgrade in a TJ.

Both the Optima Red Top and Yellow Top batteries are good choices for a TJ. The dual–terminal post–design allows simplified attachment of a winch and extra accessories. It is important to use the main terminals, which are usually the top terminals, to attach a winch because they are attached directly to the cells. The secondary terminals are connected with a small length of wire. The Red Top will perform well for normal trail use, while the Yellow Top will tolerate heavy winch use better thanks to its deep-cycle design.

The Odyssey battery claims three times the service life of conventional batteries and exceptional cranking power, even at very low temperatures. The pure lead composition of the battery's plates allows for thinner plates and a denser interior, which creates more power in a similarly sized package. Unlike the Optima Red and Yellow model batteries, the Odyssey is both in a single package.

An often-overlooked item related to the battery is the need to secure the battery within the battery tray. Many trail facilities will inspect the Jeep for a proper battery hold down. Using a bungee to secure the battery is an invitation for an electrical fire. Bouncing on the trail and the possibility of a rollover can cause the battery to fall out of the tray, opening the potential for a massive short. Retaining the factory hold down or a quality aftermarket retainer is cheap insurance.

Dual Batteries

The addition of an extra battery is for the serious trail-Jeep owner. This setup allows the batteries to keep up with high-drain/draw accessories such as a winch or onboard welder. For extended trail time, the extra battery will help provide reserve power when the Jeep may not be running; a good example is an overnight trail campout. With a battery isolation system there is little risk of draining both batteries, which will prevent not starting.

It may be a simple thought to install the two batteries in a parallel circuit, but this will lead to problems and the potential early failure of both batteries. High-tech dual-battery systems, such as the Genesis Offroad dual-battery kit, feature a secure battery tray and sophisticated isolator system that controls charging and discharging automatically. These kits allow both batteries to function until one drops below a certain voltage, at which time one battery will be cut off to save power for starting. In addition, the isolator system controls battery charging to prevent excess load on the charging system when both batteries are low.

The Optima Red Top battery has been a favorite with Jeepers for years. Its power, reliability, and long life make it an excellent addition under the Jeep's hood. The dual terminals are especially useful when adding high-draw accessories such as a winch or onboard welder.

Odyssey Extreme's batteries (right) are relative newcomers to the off-road realm. Their unique design allows them to deliver extra power with long life. The Odyssey Extreme series are available with dual terminals, such as the Optima, that allow easier attachment of high-draw extras.

Wrangler Power Products offers a clever dual-battery setup for the TJ that creates a better fit in the tight battery space under the hood. This setup uses two small-footprint Odyssey batteries that pack a lot of power in a small footprint. This setup includes an isolator and cables. (Photo Courtesy Wrangler Power Products)

The TJ electrical system is demanding, even from the factory. Adding high-draw accessories along with extra lights and electronics can exceed the capacity of the factory alternator that can lead to a potential dead battery. Mean Green and Powermaster alternators offer extra charging power to keep up with the added demands.

When running dual batteries, it's important to use a battery isolation system. This will prevent both batteries from draining while reducing the load on the charging system. The Genesis Off-Road system is fully automated and designed for the demands of off-road use. (Photo Courtesy Genesis Off-Road)

Companies such as Smittybilt and Rugged Ridge make dual-battery trays that are designed for direct fit into the TJ. Most stack the batteries in the fender area and require the batteries to be mounted on their sides because of the tight space. Wrangler Power Products makes a direct-fit mounting kit that uses two Odyssey batteries mounted side by side. This kit also includes an isolation system for a complete installation.

Alternator

The factory alternator is actually capable of running the Jeep, even with added accessories, up to a point. In the past, some of the highest continuous-draw add-ons were lighting. Thanks to LED lighting technology, replacing the older high-draw–style lights and adding auxiliary lighting to the Jeep barely impacts power requirements. Winches, compressors, and onboard welders are a few remaining high-draw but limited-use items. Under normal trail conditions, a good battery and a healthy alternator will power these accessories without problem. A Jeep that sees heavy winch use will benefit from a higher-output alternator. Mean Green and Powermaster make higher-output, heavy-duty alternators that can put out 170 to 200 amps. These alternators, combined with a dual-battery system and auxiliary circuits, can provide the extra power needed for added accessories and high-draw extras such as a winch or a welder.

Starter

It's inevitable that a Jeep used off-road will encounter water and mud. This stuff gets into a starter because it's low on the Jeep's engine where contaminants eat away at the starter over time, usually resulting in a failure in the worst of places. It's common for many Jeep owners who expose their Jeeps to mud and water to remove the starter on a regular basis to clean and inspect it, which helps to extend its life.

In general, the factory starter (and even good replacement starters) will have little issue starting any of the factory engines. Upgrades to the factory starter are available from Mean Green and Powermaster. These starters provide more cranking power with less draw. Both manufacturers boast increased water and corrosion resistance. A higher-performance starter will perform well with a manual-transmission to start the engine on an incline and prevent the Jeep from rolling backward.

Wiring Harness

The TJ wiring harness is rather complex; hacking into it can cause problems that can lead to expensive repairs. As vehicles have become more complex, it's become increasingly difficult to add accessories safely and properly. Resisting the urge to splice into a switched or unswitched positive wire will reduce the likelihood of electrical problems.

The TJ electrical system uses two main fuse boxes, one located on the passenger-side fender under the hood and the other behind the glove box. Tapping into the underhood fuse box is tricky and isn't really the best idea. The main power pole is a good place to wire to, if necessary.

Circuit taps, extra circuit blocks, and ground bars are a few of the common electrical modifications that will make adding extras easier and safer.

Grounds

If you add additional components inside the Jeep or under the hood, having a good ground source will improve performance and reliability of the components. Almost all of the metal parts of the Jeep can provide a ground, but the quality and distance from the ground point may increase resistance and decrease component performance. Installation of a ground bar or grounding block will provide a tidy location for component grounds. Ground bars are usually connected directly back to the negative side of the battery with a heavier-gauge wire.

Extra Circuits

The most complete method of adding extra circuits to power all of the added components is with the use of an extra circuit system. Painless Wiring makes a variety of extra circuit systems. The installations are very neat and clean and there is a variety of circuits in both switched and unswitched types. These systems, as opposed to individual wires, use in-line fuses that make attaching extras simple and troubleshooting a snap.

Circuit Tap

A circuit tap is a simple, inexpensive, and safe way to tap into an existing circuit for use with extra accessories. It's important to tap a circuit that is not used or has low draw/occasional use. A common circuit to tap on a TJ is the rear defroster circuit, which is usually found in the fuse block located behind the glove box.

A circuit tap essentially uses a replacement blade to access the hot side of the fuse, adding a fused output wire that is then usable for an extra circuit. When doing this, a

In this case, the circuit tap is installed to the circuit that feeds the rear defroster. This particular Jeep is not equipped with a hard top so this circuit isn't used and is an excellent choice to power an accessory. This tap is used to power the low-voltage side of the ARB Air Locker system.

A fuse tap is a clever and inexpensive component that allows tapping power from an existing circuit while maintaining the integrity of both the original and new circuit. The tap still provides fuse protection to the original circuit and adds a second fuse for the tapped lead.

second fuse slot for the original fuse is provided to protect the original circuit. The tap fuse should never exceed the amp rating of the tap.

Whether the tap requires switched power or unswitched power will determine the best location to install the tap. The rear defroster circuit is switched but the door switch circuit is unswitched. ∎

These circuit systems typically attach directly to the battery and use a small relay to engage the switched circuit. The direct battery connection provides full power to the system and doesn't rely on any taps into the Jeep factory wiring harness. Each additional circuit is protected by its own fuse.

Painless offers simple circuit blocks that are available with three

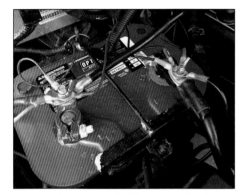

Excess taps on a battery can be trouble in many ways. These wires seem to go in all directions and are not secured well. In addition, these taps make tracing and troubleshooting difficult. Using an add-on circuit block would clean up this installation and lessen the likelihood of a failure.

and seven circuits. These systems use a relay for switched circuits.

For a more complete system, Painless makes an eight-circuit system called Trail Rocker. It provides a switching system that can be installed inside the Jeep while the power distribution module can be located elsewhere, such as under dash or under hood. This sophisticated system minimizes wiring headaches and provides a clean and safe distribution system.

Dome Light and Door Alarm

Every Jeep owner likes running with no doors from time to time, if not all the time. Jeep's official position lately is that driving with no doors should be limited to off-road use, but during the summer months it's hard to resist the enjoyment of an open-air Jeep.

The TJ has an annoying feature when the doors are off. The interior lights stay on and the open-door alarm sounds when the key is inserted because the door switches are in the door-open position. A few

options are available to deal with this when you take the doors off.

Door-switch clips are spring-loaded clips that install on the plastic door switch plunger to hold the switch in the door-closed position. These clips are unreliable and can fall off.

A fuse can be removed on most-year TJs that will defeat the light and alarm so that the doors can remain off with no dead batteries or annoying alarm. Pulling the fuse will prevent the dome light from lighting when the door is open. The light will then have to be turned on and off manually.

A more-sophisticated method is to install a fuse tap in the door circuit that integrates a switch. When completed, a simple flip of the switch turns the door system on or off.

Headlight Relays

This wiring modification can increase the brightness of your headlights dramatically. The factory headlight wiring uses a long route of wiring to power the headlights. This increases resistance, draining power

Painless Wiring circuit blocks are available in several sizes. This seven-circuit block is protected with a main circuit breaker and provides several switched and constant-hot circuits. This installation is clean and provides wiring to add ons that is easy to troubleshoot and trace.

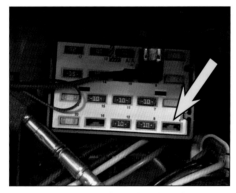

By removing the fuse for the door switches, the Jeep can run doorless without the worry of the interior lights draining the battery and the door chime constantly being a bother. For extra convenience, some Jeep owners wire a switch into the fuse to allow easy on or off of the circuit.

A completed headlight relay installation is extremely tidy. These relays are securely installed on the back side of the grille on the driver's side. Labeling and clean installation makes for a reliable and easy-to-troubleshoot setup. Each relay is dedicated to the high or low beam headlight mode.

Installing Headlight Relays

Installing headlight relays is not very difficult, but it requires some planning and neat electrical work for best results. Routing wiring in safe locations to avoid heat and wear will ensure proper operation and understanding the wiring modification will help with troubleshooting in the future.

Parts and Supplies

The procedure requires two automotive-style weatherproof relays. Choose quality relays from Bosch or Hella to avoid driving in the dark. One relay will be used for low beam and one for high beam. A 20-amp fusible link for the high-power side of the lights connects directly to the battery.

Over time, the headlight plugs and wires degrade from weather and age. When installing headlight relays, it's recommended to replace the headlight plugs with new, readily available plugs from automotive stores. You can purchase relays for the setup with plugs that make installation easier.

Use 10- to 12-gauge wire for both the positive and ground wire. Stay consistent with gauge; choose one and stick with it for the complete circuit. Replacing the headlight connectors during the project will replace the old connectors that are likely brittle. If you are looking to change to a different style of headlight, such as H4 or LED, check the plug type; it may be necessary to use a different light plug.

Wiring Diagram

Relay Pin Layouts	
86	The relay switching (control) circuit input
85	The relay switching (control) circuit output (ground)
30	The power circuit input
87	The power circuit output

Headlight Socket Pin Layout	
56a	The high beam feed
56b	The low beam feed
31	Ground

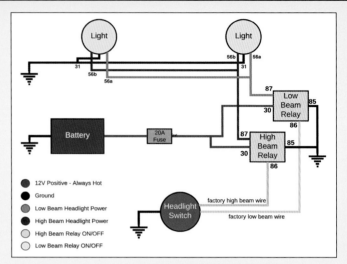

The diagram shows a typical headlight relay installation. There are variations in installation design, but the basics remain the same. It is common to use the driver-side headlight plug that is cut off and used as the switched feed for the low/high beam circuit to the relays.

Routing

On a TJ, the headlight wiring runs on the driver's side of the Jeep from the firewall connection. Mounting the relays on the driver's side of the grille will allow the use of the factory headlight switch feeds to switch the relays. Running a fused positive and ground to the new relays in an organized way is often best by running down the passenger-side grille supports and across the inside of the grille. Place both wires an within automotive-style wire loom for protection.

Using the driver-side headlight plug as the source trigger for the relays is often best. There is typically room on the backside of the driver-side grille to mount the relays. The passenger-side headlight plug will be unused and can be secured out of the way. Both headlights will receive power from the new harness fed from the relays, directly from the battery.

Relay Wiring

Attach the high beam circuit feed (typically orange/red) from the headlight plug to the 86 terminal on the high beam relay.

Attach the low beam circuit feed (typically violet/white) from the headlight plug to the 86 terminal on the low beam relay.

Attach the new high-power feed wire to the 30 terminal on both relays.

Attach the 85 terminals to the new ground source.

NOTE: It may be easier to remove the headlights and their bezels to work on the inside grille wires.

Assuming a standard automotive headlight plug, attach the 56a wires to the high beam relay.

Attach the 56b wires to the low beam relay.

Attach the 31 wires to the new ground source.

Final installation steps include making sure that the wiring is protected and secured. Test the light operation on both the low and high beam settings. ■

and that causes dimmer headlights. A trick for getting the most out of your lights is to make sure that all of the power possible is available to the lights and not to heat the wires. A simple modification to the lighting system will reduce the distance of wire carrying the high power. It involves the installation of a set of relays to engage the high-power side.

In this setup, the headlight switch is simply powering the relays while high power is delivered right from the battery using higher-gauge shorter wiring. It's an inexpensive modification that only requires some relays, wire, and replacement light sockets. This can work with standard lights, H4 lights, and LED.

Headlight Upgrades

Jeep owners often upgrade the TJ headlights to something with more light output than the factory lights. The Halogen-style lights were very popular for a number of years, but as LED technology has become less expensive, this new light technology is taking over.

Factory Lights

The factory headlights, even with a relay upgrade installed, have minimal light output compared to newer, more modern vehicles. The sealed-beam incandescent lights have a typical rating of only 35 watts (low) and 65 watts (high). Higher-wattage

The factory headlights used sealed-bulb lights that were 45–55 watts. The light output was marginal. Installing headlight relays improved output, but replacing these with newer LED lighting results in a significant improvement.

versions of sealed-beam lights are available, but the improvement will only go so far.

H4 Halogen Lights

H4 headlights are a more-modern high-light-output bulb design that uses about the same power as sealed-beam bulbs. Most H4 systems use a separate bulb and reflector system. The multi-surface reflector systems allow better light distribution along with the higher-output bulbs. The systems from KC HiLites, Rampage, and Delta are available in direct-fit models. H4 systems are more expensive than standard sealed-beam incandescent lights, but their increased light output is dramatic.

As LED headlight prices have dropped, they have become more popular. New Jeeps use these as standard equipment direct from the factory. Many styles of LED headlights are available. These Quadratec LED headlights are a direct installation on a TJ.

LED Lights

A relative newcomer in automotive use, the LED light has reached a level of sophistication and affordability to justify installation in an older Jeep. LED technology provides a much higher light output while only using a fraction of the power. LED lights often use only 15 watts for low beam and 25 watts for high beam, perhaps avoiding the need for the headlight relay modification. LED lights are much more expensive than traditional systems but can last considerably longer. Typical sealed-beam lights last for 300 hours, while LED lights can last 30,000 hours. Many LED kits are available for the TJ that are direct fit. Notable LED systems are from Quadratec and JW Speaker.

Extra Lighting

Adding extra lighting on a Jeep is as common as lift kits and bigger tires. Increasing the ability to see when out at night is useful from a navigation and safety perspective. Jeep owners add extra lighting almost everywhere on their Jeeps, even underneath and rearward. On a night trail run is at hand, the only light source is often the vehicle itself.

Thanks to the advancement and popularity of LED light technology, adding extra lighting that puts out incredible amounts of light with low power draw is affordable, reliable, and long lasting. LED technology often uses varying numbers of small LED bulbs to make up everything from light bars to miniature under-body lights.

Forward

Forward-facing lights are usually the most common type of light that Jeep owners will add and, most often, they come first. Many Jeeps came with factory bumper-mounted driving lights that were operated from inside the cabin. Most of these will only operate when the headlights are on with the low beam setting. Replacing these lights and using the

Auxiliary Light Types

There are many types of lights a Jeep owner could add; knowing the type of light and what they are used for will help you decide what to buy. While more types are available than I can discuss here, many of the extras are slight variations of the main types.

Spot: These lights use reflectors to focus the light into a very narrow beam that can travel longer distances. There are two common applications for this type. One is when used as a mounted light on a moveable arm allowing the light to be moved in nearly any direction. These are useful when light is needed in an area not directly in front or rear of the Jeep. The second is when mounted to the front of the Jeep for long-range sight, which is especially useful when driving at higher speeds in very dark conditions.

Driving: Driving lights allow a more complete view of the area directly in front of the Jeep. The rectangular pattern often lights the side area, which allows better visibility of the front of the Jeep. They are extremely useful when navigating obstacles at night.

Flood: These lights will light a large area with less focus on forward lighting. Floodlights are commonly mounted rearward to provide visibility for backing and lighting up the area when not driving. Floodlights mounted high and facing forward will often over-light the Jeep's hood, possibly creating a distraction.

Fog: These lights are similar to floodlights but the reflector design prevents the beam from illuminating particles in the air, such as fog or dust, that cause a loss of vision. These lights spread the light at the lower areas directly in front of the Jeep. ∎

The Quadratec TJ winch bumper features mounts for a set of JK factory driving lights. These factory lights put out nice coverage and are an excellent replacement to the TJ factory driving lights. They are available with plugs that match the TJ factory driving light wiring.

Small LED floodlights can provide light coverage that fully illuminates the area directly in front of the Jeep. These are very helpful on a dark trail for getting a good view of the terrain to help navigate obstacles.

The windshield hinges are good locations for mounting small lights; this adds height that allows the light to project farther forward. Spot-style lights work best in this mounting location because fog- or flood-style lights can put too much light on the hood, which can be a distraction.

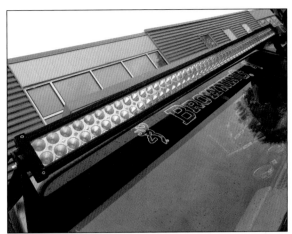

An LED windshield-mounted lightbar can light up the night, perhaps better than any other light on the Jeep. The 50-inch lightbar is commonly mounted to the Jeep. These bars are compact and add minimal height to the Jeep when compared to older incandescent lights. LED lightbars are available in many widths and can include colors.

factory wiring will cause the lights to operate under the same conditions.

Forward lights are commonly mounted to or are part of the front bumper. Almost all light types can be used on the front bumper, and it's popular to outfit the bumper with multiple types of lights for different situations.

Common locations not on the bumper are the windshield hinges and above the windshield. Thought should be used with the type of light mounted to the hinges because the hood is so close. Flood, fog, and driving lights will illuminate the hood, which could possibly become a distraction. Spot-style lights work best in the hinge mount location. KC and Rigid auxiliary lights are popular and are available in many combinations.

LED Lightbars

As stated earlier, LED lighting technology is relatively new to the automotive arena and prices have become very affordable because of its increasing popularity. The aftermarket is now flooded with LED products that can fit nearly any need.

LED lightbars are an extremely effective and flexible product for use all over the Jeep. These bars are available in many sizes and configurations from 3 to 50 inches. KC and Rigid are popular makers of lightbars.

Over-the-windshield LED lightbars have all but replaced the old-school lightbars. A 50-inch LED lightbar can put out incredible amounts of light with minimal power draw. These bars often contain approximately 100 LED bulbs with varied reflectors to spread light in different ways.

Rear, Under, Side, and More

Lighting other areas not in front of the Jeep is useful when off-road at night. This additional light is useful to the driver as well as a spotter who may be assisting in a tougher area of a trail.

This is a wooded area lit by just the Jeep's main headlights. This may be sufficient to light up a street when driving at night, but better visibility is needed on the trail.

This is the same wooded area with 50-inch lightbar added. Much more is visible; it will make navigating the area much easier and safer. LED bars draw much less power than traditional lightbars but last much longer.

Small under-body mounted lights can light up the area directly under the Jeep to aid both the driver and a spotter in challenging off-road areas. These compact LED lights often come in sets that include wiring and switches.

With enough lighting to sufficiently light up the area around the Jeep, some night off-roading is much more enjoyable and safer for both the Jeep and its occupants. Jeep owners are known to go crazy with lights and cover all directions, in some cases more lights than needed. If it's your thing, why not?

Rear lights are useful to light up the rear area of the Jeep when backing and also when the Jeep may not be moving. Flood-style lights are most often used for rearward lighting. Common mounting locations are the spare tire area and the bumper. Roof-mounted racks commonly have rear-light mount provisions included as standard.

Under-lighting is obviously useful to light up the area below the Jeep when navigating obstacles. This allows better vision for the driver and especially a spotter. Small, bright, under-Jeep LED light kits, often called rock lights, are available from Rigid. Lighting the area around the tires will give an excellent view of the obstacles the Jeep may have to navigate.

Side lighting is a good use of flood-style lights mounted high on the Jeep, such as on a roof-mounted rack. Increased side vision is good for a spotter or when the Jeep's occupants are out of the vehicle.

Lights in other areas such as under the hood, inside the cab, and even under the dash can be extremely useful. There really is no end to the amount of places a light can be used.

Wiring Lights

Using LED lighting makes wiring lights easier because the power draw is so much less and the switch is often a digital connection that does not carry the power to the light. Still, using an auxiliary circuit system (such as the previously discussed Painless Wiring options) to power the lights makes for a cleaner and safer installation. Using switch panel kits designed especially for the TJ or universal panels prevents random switches within the TJ cab.

Clutch Starter Switch

A manual transmission in a TJ will be equipped with a clutch switch. This switch will prevent the starter from engaging unless the clutch pedal is depressed. This safety feature is designed to prevent the Jeep from starting in gear and should not be considered useless.

It is a common practice off-road to restart a stalled Jeep using the starter with the clutch engaged when fording water or especially on an incline. This prevents the Jeep from rolling backward when the clutch is disengaged.

The only way to do this with a TJ is to bypass the switch, which is not something that should be done without consideration to the safety reasons. The year of the Jeep and whether or not it's a Rubicon will dictate the process of bypassing the switch. Jeep designed this ability into the TJ and the user manual will indicate the proper way of doing it for the particular year. The Rubicon will automatically bypass the switch when the transfer case is in low range.

Putting It All Together

This chapter covered a great deal of relatively ignored and unglamorous topics. Good electrical practices will reduce the likelihood of an electrical-related fire and ease troubleshooting. Some other things to take away from this chapter include:

Headlight relays will dramatically increase light output of traditional headlights.

Extra lighting, especially underneath, rearward, and to the side, will make running trails at night safer and more enjoyable.

Installing varied forward lights will help with different situations.

Using new LED lighting will reduce power load while increasing light output and light longevity.

Always maintain good grounds.

A good battery is essential when on the trail.

Use caution when bypassing the clutch safety switch.

RECOVERY AND AIR SYSTEMS

Some accessories are just for looks but a few serve such an important and useful purpose that it's difficult to call them accessories rather than essentials. Recovery and air systems prove to be invaluable when part of your Jeep; not just for your use but also for helping others.

Recovery

"It's not a matter of if but rather when" is a saying that fits many things in life, but it is especially true when using your Jeep off-road.

Eventually, you will get stuck. Building and modifying a TJ is more than just lift kits and big tires. Those things that help your Jeep do more are often the things that allow you to get deeper into challenging areas and eventually get you stuck. Many Jeep owners tell tales about how their Jeeps never get stuck; the truth to this is those owners never truly challenge their Jeeps.

It's also a fact that building a Jeep to be more capable will result in more opportunities to get stuck. Lockers, lift kits, and big tires will get you into more trouble than a stock Jeep. Having the right equipment will get you moving again quickly and safely. Recovery equipment can vary from high-powered winches to manual pullers. A combination of both will fit the needs of varied situations and assist in the recovery effort.

Winch

The look created by a winch on the front of the Jeep seems to complete the front of the Jeep so much that you might wonder why one

Tackling tougher challenges off-road will increase the likelihood of encountering a situation that will render your Jeep stuck. Hill climbs, rocks, and mud are just a few of the obstacles that can get in the way of progress. This driver tests his TJ on a steep hill at Anthracite Outdoor Adventure Area (AOAA).

A winch on the front of a Jeep looks so natural that it's a wonder Jeep didn't just stick it there from the start. The TJ has a front crossmember that forces mounting the winch forward or higher for clearance. A quality winch is worth the investment for reliability and long life.

wasn't there from the beginning. A Jeep owner who has equipped his or her TJ with a winch can tackle a trail with increased confidence, knowing that the Jeep can get out of a situation that may have left others stranded or reliant on others. With the quick attach of a line and some pulling, the Jeep can often pull itself away from the obstacle and be on its way.

Many winches are available in varying configurations and manufacturing quality. Relying on a "cheap" winch can be a risky move because failure in a remote area can create trouble and inconvenience. Quality brand-name winches with years of development, such as Warn, Superwinch, and Ramsey, will serve a trail Jeep reliably and safely.

Many factors come into play when selecting a winch for a TJ, such as line-pull rating, line length, construction, and electric versus hydraulic. Many of these are answered by common practice while some come down to a matter of preference and application.

Line-Pull Rating

Winches vary in the amount of weight they can pull; higher weight ratings will put less load on a winch and allow increased amounts of pull time. Line-pull ratings are based on the first layer of cable on the winch drum. Line-pull ratings decrease with every layer on the drum because of effective gear ratio changes. A TJ can weigh between 3,000 and 4,000 pounds depending on gear, tops, and accessories. In general, an 8,000-pound winch would be a minimum, while a 9,500-pound would be optimum. Overly high weight ratings can be detrimental to the Jeep because some can exceed the mount ratings and expose the Jeep to pos-

sible damage from the winch. When you evaluate weight ratings, look at the ratings of all layers because some winch ratings fall off more quickly with each layer.

Line Length and Construction

A winch line is often referred to as a rope, which can come in different construction types and lengths. The type is usually a matter of preference. The length of rope often is approximately 125 feet. Longer lengths of rope can reduce the pull rating, especially when the pull is a short distance because of the extra layers from the added length.

Choosing the rope construction usually comes down to two choices: wire or synthetic rope, and each has advantages and disadvantages. Wire rope is the traditional style, which up until recently was the more common choice among Jeep owners. This type of rope consists of strands of steel wire bundled into a larger bundle. A good, common example is 7 bundles consisting of 19 strands each. One advantage of wire rope is excellent tolerance to abrasion; disadvantages include higher weight than synthetic

and burrs that can easily tear flesh. Wire rope is subject to kinks and crushing when spooled incorrectly.

Synthetic rope has become more popular and affordable in recent years, almost to the point that the price difference can be trivial. When compared to wire rope, the same length of synthetic rope can weigh up to five times less. This weight savings is beneficial to the front of the Jeep; it reduces squat from the weight, effectively reducing ground clearance. Synthetic rope isn't subject to the burrs that wire rope can have, and that makes it safer to handle during winching. Nevertheless, you should always wear gloves to prevent friction burns.

Synthetic rope can be damaged more easily from being dragged over jagged surfaces; this is a disadvantage compared to wire rope. Heat from the drum (from heavy winch use), chafing, and sun exposure can damage the synthetic line. Many synthetic-line winches include a line-end cover to prevent sun damage. From a safety perspective, a failed synthetic rope will drop quickly and pose little recoil danger, as does wire rope. Nev-

Wire rope–equipped winches have been the standard for many years. This Warn VR10 winch is available in both wire and synthetic configurations. Wire rope weighs more but is less expensive and can tolerate certain abuse better than synthetic.

The Warn VR10-S winch is a great example of an economy winch with the reliability for which Warn winches are known. The synthetic line cuts down on the weight of the winch and offers some safety advantages not found in wire-rope winches.

ertheless, following safe winch procedures is important regardless of the construction. Synthetic rope floats, which is a nice feature when winching a Jeep stuck in the mud or water.

Gearing

Winches typically contain one of three types of gears: spur, worm, or planetary. The legendary Warn 8274 winch is a long-running model that may be the only spur-gear winch widely available today. Worm-gear winches are very common, and planetary-gear winches are most popular. Planetary gears have advantages over the other types because of their relative light weight, low draw, and smaller sizes. The biggest downside of planetary-gear winches is the need for internal braking to control the load during winching; this raises the drum temperature from high use.

Electric Versus Hydraulic

Electric winches are the most popular by far because of their ease of installation and low cost. There are groups of diehard fans of the hydraulic winch that will swear by them every day. Electric winches are easily installed; simply mount the winch and connect the leads to the battery. Electric winches can put a strain on a Jeep's battery and charging system with extended use. In addition, the motor will generate a fair amount of heat from extended use that leads to potential damage if not left to cool.

The solenoid is essentially a relay that engages the winch for operation. Some winches use an integrated solenoid, which usually appears as a bridge over the drum; other models have external solenoids that mount either to the winch or nearby. In effect, there is little difference, other than appearances.

All electric winches use a solenoid to activate the winch remotely without a heavy cable running inside the Jeep. Some winches, such as this Warn VR8000-s, use fixed solenoids that are housed inside the top part of the winch structure while some use solenoids mounted externally. Integrated solenoids are typically more attractive.

Hydraulic winches require plumbing to connect them to the Jeep's power steering pump, or a replacement pump, to provide the hydraulic pressure. An advantage with hydraulic winches is their ability to operate for extended times with little heat generation. A big disadvantage of a hydraulic system is that the Jeep needs to be running for the winch to operate.

Electrical Needs

I touched on this briefly in chapter 9 because electric winches put a high demand on the Jeep's battery and alternator. Extensive use can quickly discharge a battery and cause extra strain on the charging system. Because all TJs require sufficient voltage to operate the computer system and fuel-injection system, there is a risk to the Jeep's ability to stay running with a completely drained battery. Winching in small sessions is the best for maintaining proper charge, even with a high-quality battery. The addition of a second battery with an

A good battery is important when you're going to use an electric winch. The winch will put a significant load on the battery that can cause damage or failure to a weak battery. A winch should always be attached directly to the battery's main terminals.

isolation system will allow extended use without risking a drained battery and an overloaded charging system (and prevent starting).

A winch should always be connected directly to the battery and the positive lead should be carefully protected from rubbing, which could lead to a short. Installation of a cable disconnect is optional but is a convenient way to disconnect the power to the winch when it's not being used.

Mounting

The TJ has a tubular crossmember near the front of the frame that requires a winch to be mounted above it; this design is similar to earlier-model Jeeps such as the CJ. Because the winch has to be mounted higher, it can impact airflow into the radiator depending on the exact location and the size of the winch. Most aftermarket bumpers integrate a winch mount directly; independent winch mounts are available from Warn, Tomken, and Quadratec.

Most winches use a standard mounting bolt pattern. Most bumpers and mounts are designed for

The tubular crossmember on the front of the TJ interferes with the ability to locate the winch in the frame. This requires the mount to locate the winch forward of the crossmember or above it. Forward makes for a nicer look and allows for better airflow into the radiator but the additional length can reduce approach angle.

A snatch block is useful for changing direction of the cable during use or doubling the pull capacity. Some blocks use different methods of inserting the cable but the end result is the same. This ARB snatch block has a 20,000-pound load capacity.

the standard pattern and this makes selecting a winch a simple process. However, certain winches, such as a Warn Zeon, do not use a standard

Using a winch requires the addition of a fairlead to help guide the cable into the winch. Wire rope often uses a roller fairlead (top) while synthetic rope uses a Hawse-style fairlead (bottom). If a roller fairlead is desired when using synthetic rope, it is important that it is approved for that use to prevent the rope from being caught in the edges of the rollers.

footprint. It requires offset mounting or the creation of extra clearance within the bumper.

In addition to mounting the winch, a fairlead or rope guide must be installed to allow the rope to move smoothly in and out of the winch. A roller fairlead is typically used with wire rope and a hawse-style fairlead is used with synthetic. Special roller fairleads are required for synthetic line to prevent the rope from snagging on the edges of the rollers. Most winch mounts include a mount for a fairlead and both styles typically use the same mounting pattern.

Winch Accessories and Extras

Some winches include extra accessories, such as air compressors and wireless controls, while standard winches include a wired controller that extends into the Jeep's cab for

Carrying a winch kit will keep everything where it belongs for when it's needed. A set of winching gloves, strap, and D-ring should be standard equipment. Don't forget the winch controller. Additional items could include a tree saver and snatch block.

the driver to use. A Jeep with a winch should carry a winching kit when off-road. These kits should include proper gloves, the controller, D-rings, a tree saver, and a snatch block.

D-ring–style connectors are a much safer method of connecting a line than a hook that can fall off easily. Replacing a winch hook with a thimble has become a popular choice among Jeep owners. Thimbles provide a positive cable connection using a D-ring that will not fall off.

A tree saver is a strap made from a short length of wide nylon material that is used when a tree is an anchor. These wide straps will not dig into the tree's bark, thereby preventing harm to the tree. Typical lengths are 6 to 8 feet.

The snatch block is an exceptionally useful winch accessory that serves a few purposes. It's often necessary to pull the Jeep from an angle or corner. A snatch block is a pulley that can be attached to a vehicle or tree to create a direction change for the line. In addition, the snatch block can be used to connect the line back to the same Jeep, effectively doubling the pull capacity of the winch.

Installing a Winch

1 Many aftermarket TJ bumpers integrate a winch mount that can accommodate a standard winch and fairlead. This Barricade TJ bumper has a standard mount ready to go. It is easier to install the winch on this particular bumper before installing the bumper.

2 The Barricade 9,500-pound winch waiting to be installed features synthetic rope and comes complete with a fairlead and externally mounted solenoid.

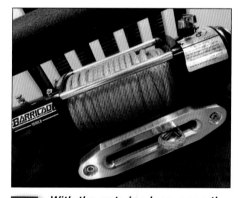

3 Installation of the fairlead to the mounting area on the front of the bumper first will allow easier access to the nuts behind the mount. Tighten it to the manufacturer's specifications.

4 Most winches use captured nuts that are located inside the lower part of the housing. Installing these and keeping them in place during installation can be a challenge. Some Jeep owners glue them in using RTV or a little bit of tape.

5 With the nuts in place, pass the end of the rope through the fairlead and locate the winch over the mount holes. It is often necessary to release the winch spool to pull some rope out. Insert the supplied bolts and tighten it to the manufacturer's specifications.

6 Install the solenoid and wire the terminals to the appropriate posts. Tighten the terminal nuts for a good electrical connection. Keeping the wiring neat will prevent rubbing and make for a nice appearance.

7 Finding a way to get the winch cable into the engine compartment isn't particularly difficult, but there are limited open areas. Squeezing between the transmission cooler lines on an automatic-equipped TJ is a good area. Securing the cables to prevent wear will prevent a potential short.

8 Run the wiring along the fender or use a route that will keep the wires safe from wear. Secure the wires to prevent rubbing. A short on the positive lead can result in a fire because, typically, no fuse is installed on a winch.

9 A dual-post battery, such as this Odyssey battery, allows for easier winch installation. On a dual-terminal battery, always use battery terminals that are capable of handling the load of the winch. It is common for a Jeep owner to disconnect the positive side of the winch when not in use.

10 With the wiring installed and secured, the final installation items are the rope end, which is most often a hook. Check all bolts and admire the improved look of the front of your Jeep. With that, the winch is ready for use.

Manual Recovery

There are occasions when a winch is either not available or usable and the only solution is a manual, muscle-controlled tool commonly called a come-along. This manual winch uses a lever and a ratcheting system to wrap short lengths of cable around a drum. These are available in varied capacities and perhaps the ultimate version is the More Power Puller. The More Power Puller has a 3-ton capacity and is available with synthetic rope. Carrying one of these in your Jeep will enable you to pull the Jeep from almost any direction with only human muscle power. In a pinch, a high-lift jack can be used as a puller. The short length of the jack may require resetting the line if extra distances are needed.

The More Power Puller is the ultimate in manual winches. This tool is extremely handy and a great thing to include in your Jeep. The available synthetic line version saves weight. This puller is useful when pulling or holding from the sides or rear is needed. (Photo Courtesy Ralph Hassel)

Tow Straps

At a minimum, a Jeep owner should carry two tow straps on the trail. A 2- to 3-inch wide strap that is 15–30 feet long can be used for towing and recovery, and a shorter tree saver–style strap can be used for winching from a tree. From a safety perspective, using straps rated for automotive use in the 20,000-pound rating range is sufficient. Cleaning and inspecting straps after use will prevent failures and degradation. Hi-Lift, Smittybilt, Warn, and ARB make quality straps in varying colors and lengths.

Onboard Air

After a long day on the trail that ends with driving your Jeep home, having the ability to air-up the tires quickly will allow you to get along with minimal delay or having to find a gas station. Driving home on under-inflated tires is uncomfortable and potentially dangerous.

Onboard air systems are available in a variety of forms from engine-driven to electric to totally independent. Electric air compressors are often part of a locker system or stand-alone. Engine-driven systems often are

The engine-driven onboard air system from Off Road Only is designed to retain the factory air-conditioning and use the factory serpentine belt system. Its installation is very clean and looks factory. The York-style compressor is seen directly behind the upper radiator hose. (Photo Courtesy Off Road Only)

custom-assembled systems created from readily available parts; the main component in these systems is typically a converted air-conditioner compressor. A common stand-alone system is a high-pressure air tank carried in the Jeep.

Electric Air Compressors

Electric air compressors are often small and easily installed in the Jeep, either under the hood or in the cab. Their compact size limits their ability to air-up tires quickly and operate air tools on their own unless they are attached to an air storage tank. In many cases, the compressor is part of an air locker system that per-

forms double duty as an air source. Electric air compressors can be very noisy and can produce a fair amount of vibration. Choosing a good location under the hood can minimize annoyance to the driver.

Electric compressors are rated by cubic feet per minute (CFM) and pressure. Higher-CFM compressors are able to move more air, allowing for quicker air-up times and storage tank recovery. ARB and Viair produce well-known and reliable electric air compressors.

The ARB onboard air compressor is available in a few varieties and capacities. These compressors are designed primarily to operate ARB Air Lockers but are capable of providing compressed air for other needs. These systems work very well when used with a reserve tank.

An onboard air system makes airing-up after the trail more convenient and serves as power for air lockers and air tools. Choosing between electric and engine-driven is a matter of preference and budget.

The York-style compressor will offer the best performance when used for an onboard air system. The piston pump provides high CFM and its internal oil reservoir can keep the pump lubricated when used as a non-closed system.

Engine-Driven Air Compressors

Engine-driven compressors are most often converted from air-conditioner compressors. These compressors, combined with the power of the engine, can supply a large amount of air that can quickly air-up tires and run tools. Of course, these systems do require the engine to be running to provide continuous airflow. York-style compressors use a piston-style pump that is best suited for onboard air systems. In addition, the York-style pump has an internal oil reservoir that is essential for longer pump life. These are readily available and are still used in a variety of applications. Some other styles of compressors use lubrication held inside the closed system; converting to an air system will not allow for proper lubrication.

Mounting an engine-driven compressor can be a challenge, especially if the Jeep is factory-equipped with an air conditioner. Luckily, a few companies supply mounting brackets and entire engine-driven onboard air systems. Off Road Only offers several versions of systems that use the

This is a close-up view of the Off Road Only York compressor setup for the TJ. The custom bracket and pulley system makes for an extremely efficient and clean installation. (Photo Courtesy Off Road Only)

York-style pump while retaining the factory air-conditioner compressor (if the Jeep was so-equipped).

Running an engine-driven compressor requires many additional components, including an oil catch, a pressure switch, and an air filter.

Air Storage

A good onboard air system will include a storage tank to retain a reserve of air that will allow air tools to run smoothly and speed up air-up times. Depending on the system and size of the tank, a fully depleted air tank can take time to completely

air-up. Allowing the compressor to fill the tank before it's truly empty will make sure the extra air is ready when needed.

The TJ isn't particularly large and finding the space to put all the gear and supplies is always a work in progress. Installing an air storage tank just adds to the clutter. It's tough to find a place to mount an air tank underneath the TJ. In most cases, a 2-gallon tank will fit well on the driver's side underneath the body just behind the skid plate. Some Jeep owners fabricate or use an aftermarket bumper that can double as an air tank. This style conserves space and provides convenient access to air fittings.

Portable Air Tanks

Compressed CO_2 tanks have become more popular because of more affordable prices and ease of use. These tanks require no power and are completely independent of the Jeep. Power Tank, the leader in CO_2 tank systems in the Jeep community, offers tanks in varying sizes to fit many needs. A 10-pound tank is the most common size for its capacities and physical size. Mounting one of these tanks in a TJ is simply a matter of finding a suitable and easily accessible location.

A disadvantage with this style of onboard air is the inability to replen-

Small 2- to 3-gallon air tanks provide a reserve of air that makes running tools and airing-up tires easier. When the tank is depleted, the compressor can run to refill the tank, making it ready for future use. These small tanks can be mounted within the Jeep or underneath.

Designing an Onboard Air System

Designing an onboard air system isn't particularly complex. However, selecting the proper components will help to make the system work reliably. Engine-driven systems are the most complex and will require more design. There is no end to the amount of customizing that you can do with systems of these types.

Engine-Driven Onboard Air

As stated earlier, the big challenge in an engine-driven system is the installation of the compressor. This section lists the most common components that accompany the compressor to make up the system and their functions.

Air filter: This is a necessary component in any install but in a Jeep it is perhaps even more important because dusty conditions are likely. It cleans the air entering the system and reduces wear on the pump.

One-Way Valve: Prevents air from passing back through the pump when the pump is not operating.

Oil Trap: The York compressor will introduce small amounts of oil into the air as it's being compressed; the oil trap will prevent the oil from entering the rest of the system.

Safety Valve: Prevents the air system from exceeding a maximum pressure.

Pressure Switch: Cycles the compressor clutch to maintain a minimum and maximum air pressure.

Connectors: Quick-release connectors for hose connection points.

Air Tank: Storage for reserve air supply.

Optional: Air manifold to divide the air supply, hand throttle to increase CFM.

Electric Onboard Air

When compared to an engine-driven system, these seem simple. Finding a suitable mounting location for the compressor isn't particularly difficult on a TJ. Common locations are under the hood on the driver-side fender and the small platform in the driver-side fenderwell.

Because most electric compressors are self-contained (including a pressure switch and its wiring), it's a matter of installing the extras. Adding an air tank will make the system perform better because you'll have a reserve of air.

Common Options

Some electric compressors will be part of an air locker system while some are for exclusive air use. It may be necessary to install a pressure regulator to prevent excess pressure on the locker seals on air locker–equipped Jeeps that use compressor systems that are not designed for air lockers. Install quick connectors located at the front, rear, and under the hood of the Jeep for added convenience. ∎

Engine-driven systems can be more complex, and additional components are often added for system operation and diverse air use. Seen here from left to right is the oil catch, one-way valve, and air manifold (blue). The manifold can serve a variety of connections.

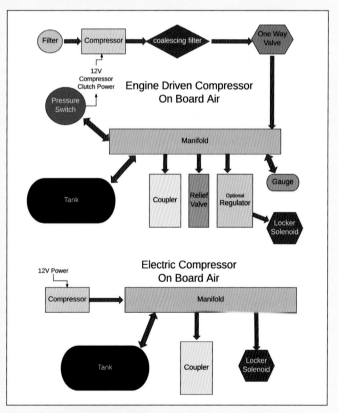

This diagram shows both an engine-driven and an electric onboard air system. The systems can vary from simple to complex installations.

ish the system on the trail when it's empty. According to Power Tank's specifications, a single 10-pound tank can add 10 psi to a 33-inch tire 20 times. In addition to inflating tires, these tanks can run almost any type of air tool. Empty tanks can be refilled at locations such as fire extinguisher service shops and welding suppliers.

Air Tools

A Jeep owner with an onboard air system will likely carry some tools to take advantage of the air system. Because space and weight are always a consideration, careful thought should be put into what tools to take to keep things to a minimum. It's likely that an air chuck, impact wrench, and blowgun are all that would normally be needed on the trail.

Putting It All Together

Investing in quality recovery items for your Jeep will keep the time spent getting unstuck to a minimum and not impede progress on the trail too much. Getting unstuck safely and reliably is much easier with proper equipment.

A winch rated between 8,000 and 10,000 pounds is best for a TJ.

Carry recovery gear that includes winching gloves, tow strap, tree saver, snatch block, and D-rings. Don't forget the winch controller.

Synthetic line keeps the weight down and is safer to hands and during a failure.

Any variety of onboard air system adds convenience for airing-up and operation of tools. Key points of the three systems are: engine-driven systems will provide best performance, electric systems are simplest, and CO2 tanks are the most flexible.

The Powertank offers portability and flexibility over integrated onboard air systems. It can power tools and fill tires quickly, but once emptied it needs to be filled at a specialty station. This system isn't typically used for locker systems.

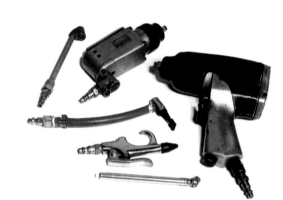

Air tools for the garage will vary greatly from the tools you would take along with you on the trail. Taking only tools that are likely to be used is smart and will save weight and space. Tire chuck, blowgun, air ratchet, and impact gun should be all that's necessary.

The extra equipment on a Jeep are the details that make a difference on the trail, sometimes more than the obvious components such as a lift and tires. The recovery components, especially the winch, will keep trail progress moving for both this Jeep and others. The onboard air system supplies air to the lockers for traction and also doubles as an air supply to air-up tires and power tools.

INTERIOR, TOPS, GEAR, TOOLS, AND OTHER GOOD STUFF

I hope that by now your mind is full of ideas, you have the feeling that all of your money is leaving your wallet, and your garage is warming up for you to get ready with the wrenches. But before you get busy, there are several other items to cover that involve the kinds of items that aren't necessarily part of your Jeep but rather go with it, in it, and on it. These items will help you build your Jeep, keep you connected, protect you, and more. There are so many options when it comes to this stuff that it's difficult to be specific; your situation and needs should help guide you the rest of the way when making choices.

Interior

Before the TJ, Jeeps used rather utilitarian, simple designs when it came to the dashboard and much of the rest of the interior. The TJ maintained much of the traditional exterior Jeep look, but the entirely new interior, especially the dash, brought a modern look to the Jeep. The dash features a centralized instrument cluster and a center bezel that contains the radio, HVAC controls, and more. It was a first in this style vehicle.

The project TJ for this book has come a long way since it was purchased in bone-stock condition. All of the components were chosen to improve on mass-produced performance. Along with the performance items, the Jeep's appearance is much more attractive than in its humble factory form.

The TJ Dash was a dramatic improvement over the previous Wrangler and CJ models. The modern dash located items in an easy-to-view and easy-to-reach manner and added good looks. The new dash allowed better vents that improved HVAC performance.

A slight drawback to this design is that it's not easy to find places to mount extra switches and electronics. The aftermarket offers many options that allow you to add items to your Jeep's dash without needing to hack it up and drill holes. Many accessory options are available for the Jeep interior, including storage bags, consoles, pedal covers, and more. There is no end of options for a Jeep owner to customize a Jeep to his or her liking.

Seats

It's worth mentioning that the factory TJ seats are marginal, and over time they will sink, get lumpy, and just become tired. The seating in a TJ has always been rather low; visibility over the hood is often difficult without leaning up and forward. Luckily, bolt-in aftermarket seats are available from many manufacturers that are more comfortable, increase support options, and look good. Bestop, Corbeau, and Rugged Ridge offer a variety of seats in different styles, fabrics, and colors.

The factory TJ seats came in many styles throughout the years, many were similar and were designed for comfort and durability. Seating position in a TJ is notoriously low compared to older models. Aftermarket seats can offer improvements for comfort and positioning.

Seat Belts and Harnesses

It's common to see Jeep owners who have replaced the factory seat belts with racing-style harnesses. Perhaps this looks attractive, but racing harnesses are extremely cumbersome and limit movement. This may be necessary when racing, but on the trail, the driver needs to be held in the Jeep but at the same time not restricted from movement.

Carpets and Mats

On most TJ models, rubber floor mats sit on top of the factory carpet. Over time, these mats break down and allow water to seep through; it's then absorbed and held in the carpet. Replacing these with the solid mats from WeatherTech, Bestop, or Quadratec will keep the water from getting into the carpet and potentially causing an issue with floor rust. The factory carpet is rather resilient and can withstand abuse. Some Jeep owners remove all or parts of the carpet. Regular removal and cleaning of both the carpet and the Jeep floor will minimize the potential for rust and mold.

Replacement waterproof floor mats will keep mud and water from soaking into the carpet when your shoes are not dry. Soaked-in water can cause mold and worse, rust. These form-fitting mats from Quadratec roll up the side of the carpet to keep water and mud from spilling over the edge of the mat.

Cargo Nets

A good way to keep your gear or a pet inside your Jeep while allowing open-air access is a cargo net. These nets are available in many configurations and colors and are most often constructed of nylon. Most nets are Jeep-model specific and will attach to the roll bar. Dirty Dog and Smittybilt offer several versions and colors for the TJ.

Tops and Doors

Excluding the factory hard top and soft top, a huge array of top and door options is available for the TJ in the aftermarket. Just open a Jeep catalog and you will be so overwhelmed by all of the choices that it will keep you up all night. Choosing from among these options will often depend more on the typical weather than the Jeep experiences.

Bikini Top

A favorite among the Jeep crowd is the bikini top. This top covers the front seats and in some cases also the rear seat area. It allows open air without dealing with the blazing sun. In addition, bikini tops can prevent the interior from getting soaked from rain.

Half Top and Fastback

Tops that reduce the cab area while covering the cargo area tend to reduce the useable interior space but add a unique look to the Jeep and increase heating and cooling efficiency because of the reduced space. These tops are easily removed and stowed away in the cargo area. The fastback top is often called a frameless top because it installs with no real frame, which allows quick removal of the side and rear panels, leaving

A safari-style bikini top will keep the sun from beating down on both the front and rear seat occupants. These tops also can provide reasonable protection from rain and other elements. The Bestop Safari top uses the factory Jeep door surrounds effectively to seal off the front cab when doors are on.

The fastback soft top is typically a convertible top that can serve as a complete top and a bikini top when needed. Most of these do not use a frame for structure but rely on the Jeep's roll bar. The side and rear panels remove easily and store to create an open-air bikini-style top. The entire top can be removed with no need to deal with a frame.

behind a bikini-style top. These tops allow open-air freedom with protection from elements with little to carry. Bestop makes quality half tops, fastbacks, and bikini tops for both the Wrangler and Wrangler Unlimited.

Doors

The factory offered both full steel doors with roll-up windows and half doors with soft uppers. Most Jeep owners have a preference; and both styles have advantages and disadvantages. Hard doors offer better protection from the elements and are more secure while half doors offer increased open-air freedom. Aftermarket, lightweight half doors are available to replace factory doors for easy removal and storage when weather permits. Some Jeepers like the feeling of a door even though they want the open-air feel. This desire is met with a set of tube doors. Rugged Ridge, Bestop, and a few others offer tube doors and lightweight half doors.

Communications

In today's world, almost all of us are connected, and it's difficult for some to think of hitting the trail without a cell phone and the ability to keep it charged. Not long ago, Jeepers tackled trails without any connection to the outside world and the best form of communication was a CB radio.

Even though the ability to communicate and stay connected with a mobile device is common, it isn't the handiest device for communicating while on the trail. CB- and FRS-style radios are still the best way of communicating with friends or groups in close range. These radios allow quick and easy communication to anyone nearby on the same channel. Jeepers often use both on the trail at the same time. It's not unusual for the whole group to use a common CB channel and smaller groups within to use FRS radios. This allows needed trail communication on the CB while chatter talk is kept on the more private FRS. Most off-road parks monitor certain CB and FRS channels in case assistance is needed.

CB Radios

Because interior room in a TJ is minimal, even on the dash, a small, simple CB radio will often work nicely. Investing money in a good antenna will allow better performance than a gimmicky and expensive CB. FCC limits do not allow for CBs that transmit at more than 4 watts; most CB radios use this power. Good examples of compact CB radios are Cobra 19DX, Uniden CMX660, and Midland 1001LWX.

Finding a suitable mounting location takes some investigating and test fitting. When using a small-footprint CB, some of the best locations are on the top left of the driver-side dash, in the area near the transfer case shifter, and overhead.

Small-sized CB radios such as the Cobra 19DX and the Uniden CMX660 make finding a location that is easy to access but out of the way simpler. Mounting a radio to the bottom of the dash is a quick and low-cost way. However, a few CB mounting brackets are available that can help locate the CB in better locations instead of under the dash.

Quadratec makes a mount that places the CB next to the transfer case shifter on the driver's side. This mount makes excellent use of space and is surprisingly out of the way of the driver's leg. This location is convenient for accessing the CB controls and microphone; in addition, the CB speaker orientation makes the CB easy to hear.

The long-running Cobra 75WX CB could be the ultimate in space-saving radios. This CB uses a unit mounted under the dash that connects to power and antenna. The CB's handset contains all the controls and can be almost anywhere inside the Jeep. The CB in the picture has put up with years of trail use (and abuse) and still functions perfectly.

Rugged Ridge makes a bolt-in CB mount for the TJ that locates the CB on the left driver-side dash. This location is well suited for a small CB and is relatively out of the way. A downside to this location is possible weather exposure.

Mounting the CB next to the transfer case shifter is surprisingly out of the way for the driver while providing good access to the mic and audio from the speaker. Quadratec makes a mount for small CB radios to fit right into this spot.

For those with an overhead center roll bar, mounting the CB to the roll bar is an excellent location to keep the dash and floor area clear. Running wires and keeping the CB dry can be a bit of a challenge with this location. A swinging mic cord can be distracting and annoying to some, which may lead the owner to create a way to keep the cord contained.

The Cobra 75 WX ST radio is a unique and popular choice for a TJ. This radio is self-contained and uses an under-dash mount for the antenna and power wires, while the rest of the device is contained entirely in the handset. This design doesn't require any visible installation and the CB can be unplugged easily for removal when not in use. A drawback is that accidental changing of settings is easy because everything is on the handset.

Antennas

The antenna has a larger impact on the performance of the CB radio than the radio itself. A correct antenna with a proper coaxial lead wire in a good location will provide optimum performance for receiving and transmitting. After installation, fine-tuning an antenna with an SWR meter will allow peak performance of the complete system.

It's common for the antenna to be mounted toward the rear of the Jeep and many CB bracket kits for mounting antennas are available. Mounting the antenna higher on the Jeep is always better and using a 3- to 4-foot fiberglass antenna is the best choice; longer antennas will achieve more range. Most fiberglass antennas have a bit of flex, allowing them to tolerate being dragged through tree branches and bushes. Adding a spring to the bottom of the antenna will allow more movement and help to prevent breakage. Antennas from Firestik work extremely well when they are installed on a TJ.

Mounting a CB antenna isn't particularly difficult on a TJ; most Jeep owners locate the antenna on the rear of the Jeep. The antenna should be mounted as high as possible. Several mounting options are available; this mount uses a bracket that mounts behind the taillight. Mounting to the tire carrier is a common and popular location.

Adjusting CB Standing Wave Ratio

Standing Wave Ratio (SWR) is a measured ratio of the output of the CB radio waves that are transmitted to the waves that are reflected back to the transmitter. A lower ratio indicates satisfactory output, which means less reflection. After installing a CB into a Jeep, final adjustment of the system will ensure optimum performance. Tuning SWR is rather easy and only requires an inexpensive SWR meter that is temporarily wired inline with the coaxial line. Adjustment involves slight length alteration of the antenna, usually using a screw at the top of the antenna or by raising and lowering the bottom of the antenna in the base. ∎

To prepare the meter, attach the meter to the CB and place the CB on channel 1. With the meter switch in the FWD position, key the CB and rotate the adjustment knob to move the needle to the SET position. Release the key.

With the CB still on channel 1, move the meter switch to the RF; position and key the CB. Note the position of the needle and release the key.

Change the CB channel to channel 40 and repeat the previous step by noting the position of the needle.

Adjust the antenna length slightly and repeat the procedure to get the two channel readings to be as close together as possible. Some antennas will adjust at the base while others will adjust with a screw at the top.

The coaxial cable that connects the CB to the antenna is as important in the system as the radio and antenna. Using a quality 18-foot coaxial wire run in a secure route to the antenna is best.

FRS and GMRS Radios

Having a set of these small radios for use with groups as a means of more private conversation from the main group channel can make the day on the trail even more enjoyable. Family Radio Service (FRS) radios are relatively new to the market, having been introduced in 1996 as an improvement to the walkie-talkie–type radio market. These radios use higher frequencies that are less prone to interference experienced on CB radios. They have good distances even with their small antennas and offer a wider span of channels to prevent multiple conversations from interfering with each other.

General Mobile Radio Service

FRS and GMRS radios are available in inexpensive forms. These radios are often easier to operate than a traditional CB radio and can offer good range. These radios are especially useful on the trail for more private conversations between vehicles. With many channels and additional privacy channels available, finding an open channel is simple.

(GMRS) radios have become more popular on the trail because of their higher-output power and extended-range capability. GMRS radios feature improvements similar to FRS radios but require an FCC operator license to use the higher-output power and exclusive GMRS channels. Most GMRS radios can use the FRS channels.

Navigation

Thanks to modern technology, you can find your way around without stopping at the local gas station for directions. Carrying a cell phone is often enough to get where you are going, but when the public streets end that cell phone may become less than useful. Having a self-contained GPS system will help you find your way out on the trail. Carrying a good compass (that you actually know how to use) and paper maps can help when the tech fails. If your trail ride is in an off-road park or an organized facility, always take a trail map or two to help you to find your way around. Even taking notes as you proceed can help you backtrack if necessary.

Fuel and Water Storage

When on an extended trail excursion, taking extra supplies is always recommended. Some of the most important things are water and fuel. Storing these items can take a fair amount of room; luckily, the aftermarket offers many ingenious products to make storage much easier. Storing water and fuel outside the Jeep saves interior room. Never mind the fact that storing fuel inside is dangerous. Jerry can–style containers are the most efficient and safe methods of storage. The original jerry cans were metal; that has been replaced

RotopaX containers are available for both fuel and water. These containers use shapes and special mounts that allow them to fit in tight spaces. These containers can fit behind a spare tire on many styles of bumper/tire carrier setups. A few extra gallons of fuel on a remote trail can save the day.

by lighter-weight plastic designed specifically for the liquid they carry.

Mounting these cans requires some planning; mounts are generally available from the manufacturer. Integration into rear-mounted racks and tire carriers is most common. RotopaX offers many options in storage containers and mounts.

Tools

When you test your Jeep's (and your) ability on the trail, you will eventually break something. Having a set of tools on hand can likely help you fix the problem and get yourself underway. Of course, some things are just not fixable on the trail but many are. With some careful thought, selecting and packing the appropriate tools will save space and weight.

Hand Tools

The TJ uses almost 100-percent metric fasteners, so carrying non-metric tools will just add bulk and weight to your tool bag. Carrying a set of metric wrenches and

Soft-sided tool bags are a better way to carry tools on the trail. These bags can conform to the tools and allow for conservation of storage area. In addition, soft sides reduce noise from tools clanking around as well as other items contacting the bag. Strap tool bags down to prevent them from moving around while driving.

A Hi-Lift jack is a ubiquitous tool on a Jeep, much like aftermarket lights or a winch. These jacks can serve a variety of purposes beyond the obvious. Jeep owners often mount the jack to the rear of the Jeep on the bumper or spare tire carrier. Other locations are on the cowl area, front bumper, and next to the door.

ratchets is a good start. A set of deep and shallow sockets with a variety of extensions will allow you to deal with most situations. Adjustable tools, including clamps, locking pliers, and screwdrivers, are standard as are a few pry bars.

Special Tools

A Jeep owner should know his or her Jeep, and knowing the special tools that may be required can possibly save the day. Larger sockets for suspension and axles are among some of the tools that you won't find in a standard toolbox. Puller tools that can be used for replacing U-joints and ball joints are handy because these parts are prone to failure from the stress of off-road.

Jack

The factory jack isn't particularly useful with a lifted Jeep, but it can be useful for doing things on the trail for which it may not have been originally intended, such as being a makeshift press or vise. Keep it in the Jeep because it might

be just the right tool for the job on the trail. Having the ability to raise the Jeep to change a tire or gain access to the underneath is essential for all Jeeps. A Hi-Lift jack is pretty much the standard jack found on off-road–used Jeeps. A Hi-Lift jack is available in lengths from 36 to 60 inches. In addition to lifting, these jacks can be used for pulling and other purposes.

You can mount a Hi-Lift jack on a TJ in one of many ways. The most common locations are on the rear

bumper, over the hood, and on the side in the cowl area. Many mounts are custom, but there are several bolt-on mounts available.

Electrical Tools

Jeep owners should also carry tools to deal with electrical issues that may come up on the trail. A bad crimp, a worn wire, or a needed component can often stop the Jeep. Carrying a set of simple wire tools for diagnosing and repairing electrical problems is insurance for any Jeep owner. Frequently, cutters, crimpers, tape, wire, and connectors along with a set of spare fuses are all that is needed. Knowing your Jeep's wiring, especially for custom-installed equipment, will speed up the time spent diagnosing a problem and get you on your way.

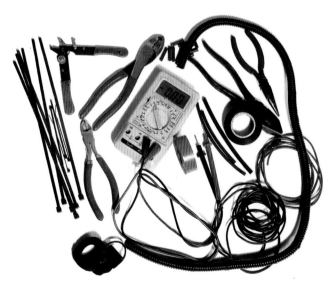

Carrying an assortment of tools and supplies to deal with electrical problems on the trail will help keep you moving and enjoying the day. Lengths of wire, tools, wire ties, tape, connectors, and a meter are just some essentials for the Jeep's toolbox.

Tool List

This list can serve as a starting point for putting together a set of tools to accompany you and your Jeep on the trail.

Hi-Lift Jack	U-Joint Tool	Standard Jack	Breaker Bar
Prybar	Clamps	Engine Belts	Ratchet Straps
Fold-Up Shovel	Knives	Cutters and Pliers	Sand Paper
Socket Sets	Screwdrivers	Penetrating Oil	Adjustable Wrench
Ratchets	Locking Pliers	RTV Silicone	Allen/Torx Wrenches
Socket Extensions	Zip-Ties	Electrical Repair	Metal Saw
Hammers	Tire Repair Kit	Fix-Flat	Wood Saw
Jumper Cables	Multi-Meter	Work Gloves	Vinyl Gloves
Snap Ring Pliers	Multi-Tool	Worklight	Flashlight
Fire Starters	Bungees	Epoxy, Adhesives	Tire Air Gauge
Fire Extinguisher	Lighter/Matches		

Parts and Supply List

You should carry some extra parts and supplies for the Jeep in addition to tools. Depending on your Jeep, you may require other extra things.

Driveshaft U-Joint	Wire	Grease	Engine Oil
Cotter Pins	Paper Maps	Penetrating Oil	Safety Glasses
Axle U-Joint	Zip Bags	Electrical Tape	Gear Oil
Lengths of Hose	Radiator Repair	Duct Tape	Water
Tie Rod Ends	Nut and Bolt Assortment	Electrical Components	Wood Blocks
Chargers/Batteries	Trash Bags	Small Metal Pieces	Hose Clamps
Toilet Paper	Hand Cleaner	Parts Cleaner	

Fire Protection

In the unfortunate event of an unplanned fire on the trail, including non-vehicle fires, having equipment that can stop a fire before it grows is important. A small fire extinguisher or two in a quick and easily accessible location can prevent a bad situation from becoming worse. Common locations are next to the driver's seat on the floor and on the rear roll bar. Periodic inspection for the extinguisher charge will make sure it's always ready for use.

A fire extinguisher is a tool that every Jeep owner never wants to have to use. Having an extinguisher that is quickly accessible can mean the difference between a small problem and a lost Jeep. Maintaining a proper charge in an extinguisher is important; a dead one could mean disaster.

Clothing

Depending on the expected weather, the amount of clothing to pack may vary. Being overprepared with clothing will far outweigh being underprepared. Being cold, wet, or both for an extended time is unpleasant and can be dangerous. A good set of wet weather gear including waterproof boots will keep you dry. Hats, gloves, and some blankets are especially useful on cold-weather trail runs. Carrying packs of hand warmers such as Hot Hands can warm up body areas in extra-cold conditions.

First Aid

Because of the uncivilized conditions on the trail, simple injuries from falls and scrapes can be tended to with a modest first aid kit. In addition to being able to deal with a boo-boo, a first aid kit should carry items for insect bites and known allergies. Additional items include soap, antiseptics, pain medications, eye care, and stomach aids. Bug spray, sunscreen, toilet paper, and personal wipes are not really first aid but can fit into the personal care kit.

Food and Water

It may seem like a common sense item, but it's not uncommon to know a fellow Jeeper who comes unprepared with no food. In most cases, stores and restaurants are not part of an off-road facility, so bringing your own to get you through the day is required. Pack nutritious food that doesn't require refrigeration and provides good energy that will sustain you. A good example is protein/carb bars and granola bars. Avoiding salty snacks and bringing extra water will keep you hydrated. A rule of thumb is to bring food for twice the amount of the trip time.

Storage

Just like older Jeeps, the TJ suffers from a lack of space for storage of the stuff necessary take to the trail.

The Tuffy under-seat storage box is a small but secure box that is an excellent way of keeping small valuables safe in an open-roof Jeep. This box mounts to the seat brackets and is mostly hidden when a door is on the Jeep. Other secure storage options are available for many other areas inside the Jeep.

Some Jeep owners are fortunate enough to have a large garage full of space and the tools to work on their Jeep (or Jeeps) but most owners work on their Jeep in small garages or even outside. The amount of work a determined owner can do with limited resources is impressive.

Careful planning and smart thinking will help you find a good place for all of it. Aftermarket companies make an array of storage items that are a direct fit for the TJ. Some storage systems, such as those from Tuffy, offer extra-secure storage for a Jeep that may not have solid roof. Carrying items in soft-sided bags will conserve space by allowing the bags to conform to each other.

Securing items in the Jeep is necessary because of the likelihood of a rough off-road ride experience. Keeping things secured will prevent injury or loss of items that could fall out. Cargo nets and bungee cords are extremely effective at keeping your stuff in place.

A Jeep Owner's Garage

I discussed tools for the trail but shouldn't overlook the tools that you leave behind, the real tools that you use to build and modify your TJ. Most of us don't have large garages with lifts and expensive specialty tools; we use home garages and a lot of improvisation. While having a few specialty tools in your garage is nice, you can often get by with much less.

Jack and Jack Stands

Safety in the garage is always the number-one concern and using good, properly rated jack stands to support the Jeep when it's off its wheels may be the most important tool to use. Never trust a jack to continuously support the Jeep's weight. Avoid excess pulling, pushing, and rocking when using jack stands, and always place the jack stands in areas that can support the weight of the Jeep, such as the frame or axles. A vehicle-rated floor jack will be a commonly used item in a Jeeper's garage. Using those that provide smooth, reliable operation will make raising and lowering the Jeep much safer.

Hand Tools

Because almost everything on the TJ is metric, it is important to have sets of metric hand tools. Sizes from small to large in multiple sets will cover most needs. Below is a general list of common hand tools.

- Deep and shallow sockets
- Ratchet wrenches in small to long lengths

A good set of heavy-duty jack stands will keep you safe when the Jeep's wheels are off the ground. Never rely on a floor jack to hold the weight of the Jeep on its own. Taller stands are often best for a Jeep because lift kits will raise the stand height necessary to work under the Jeep.

It's not possible to have too many hand tools in your toolbox. Sets of standard hand tools as well as some specialty tools will allow smarter work. Because the TJ uses almost all metric-sized fasteners, investing in sets of metric wrenches and sockets will provide years of use.

- Breaker bars
- Hammers and mallets
- Pry bars
- Clamps
- Screwdrivers, pliers, chisels, drift pins
- Measuring tools
- Torque wrench

Specialty Tools

For the serious Jeep builder, these tools will allow more complex work:

Even a small 220-volt MIG welder such as this Miller Millermatic can fit the needs of most welding that a Jeep owner may do. A good automatically darkening welding helmet and welding gloves will complete the setup.

For the more adventurous Jeep owner, an acetylene torch setup is useful for cutting steel. It may even be more useful for removing stubborn bolts without snapping them off. As the TJ series moves into classic-vehicle status, rust becomes a bigger issue. Careful torch use will prevent fires and damaged parts.

- Brake tools
- Spindle nut socket
- Pullers and ball joint tools
- Shop press

Welder: At a minimum, a 220-volt MIG-style welder should be used. Inexpensive flux core welders are fine for home repairs, but only strong, quality welds on Jeep parts will tolerate the environment experienced in the trail. Welders from Lincoln or Miller are excellent investments that can serve the Jeep owner for years.

Acetylene Torch: Having access to a torch can make cutting steel much simpler but perhaps the best use of a torch is for removal of stubborn fasteners. A snapped bolt can often be removed easily by heating and cooling the fastener, then breaking its bond to the threads. Torches are dangerous and can be intimidating. Always observe the area and avoid flammable objects and fuel lines.

Power Tools

Certain power tools are used constantly in a Jeeper's garage. These

Power tools can save aggravation and time when working on a Jeep. Drills capable of using large-size bits in addition to a smaller compact drill should be in the toolbox. A cutoff wheel and reciprocating saw are invaluable power tools in a Jeeper's garage. Keep a good supply of discs and blades because they can be consumed quickly.

tools can make tough jobs easier and will save time and muscle power:

- Grinder/angle grinder
- Metal chop saw
- Reciprocating saw
- Drill, 3/8- and 1/2-inch size
- 1/2-inch Drill press
- Soldering iron
- Heat gun

Air Compressor

An air compressor is a power tool that has many uses in a garage. Choose one that is capable of maintaining continuous pressure when you use high-demand air tools such as a grinder or a sander. Upright-style air compressors save space and can provide the best performance. Piston-style compressors are the quietest and are typically the best at keeping up with a continuous demand.

Air Tools

An air compressor would be useless without some tools to go with it. A few lengths of hose and a hose reel are a start.

An air compressor is perhaps the most used tool in a Jeeper's garage. Upright-style air compressors save space while still being able to supply the air needed to run tools. Choosing a size will depend on the amount of work and type of tools that you expect to use. Continuous-use tools, such as sanders, will require greater quantities of air than wrenches.

It's often a ritual for a Jeep owner to spend some time under the Jeep with a creeper and an assortment of wrenches before and after a trail run. It's important to inspect the underside of the Jeep and to make sure things are tight. Checking suspension, steering, and drivetrain fasteners are just a few of the items to check before and after.

Air tools can also be used with:

• Impact wrench with impact-rated sockets; flex-head impact sockets are extremely useful
• Air ratchet
• Grinder
• Blowgun
• Tire inflation chuck

Cordless Tools

Battery technology has introduced a variety of tools that were once found only in electric and air versions. The most common are drills, but cordless impact wrenches and grinders are handy and powerful.

Towing

If you choose to tow your Jeep to the trail, you must do it with all four wheels on the ground. Fortunately, the NP231 and NV241 transfer cases are safe for flat-towing. The procedure is outlined in the TJ man-

ual, but all that is required is for the transfer case to be in neutral and the transmission to be in park or first gear. The parking brake must be off and the ignition key should be in the unlocked/off position.

Before and After the Trail

Most Jeep owners have a ritual when they prepare for a trail run, as well for when they get back home. A little bit of organization allows you to be confident when your Jeep is packed and ready to hit the trail.

Prep Before the Trail

Many Jeepers make a checklist and go over it carefully before hitting the trail. Check fluid levels in the engine and drivetrain components as well as lubrication of greasable areas, such as steering linkage, driveshafts, and other suspension parts. Check suspension parts and other items for that may need to be secured.

After the Trail

After returning home from a run, you should inspect the underside of the Jeep and look for damage or components that may have loosened.

It's amazing how a few minutes of playing in the mud can lead to hours of cleaning. Some Jeep owners may not clean their Jeeps, or they leave them dirty to show off like a trophy. Old dried mud is much more difficult to remove and some mud will penetrate paint and/or leave stains. A thorough washing soon after the trip will keep the Jeep looking good and also prevent underneath items from potential wear from contamination. Very often, cleaning a Jeep is performed in a few stages; a bottom to top approach is often best.

Maintenance

After several trail runs (or a season) it's a good idea to perform some deeper maintenance to protect the components from damage or failure. Dust, mud, and water can enter components such as axles, brakes, and almost everything else. Draining and checking differentials that have seen water and muck will prevent contaminates from corroding and wearing gears. If possible, you should lubricate suspension and steering components as well. Always inspect the underside and look for damage or loose parts. This will make your Jeep ready to tackle the trails again without any surprises.

Putting It All Together, What Else?

This chapter and everything leading up to this point should give a Jeep owner ideas and the direction to build and modify his or her TJ for maximum performance on- and off-road. Keeping in mind the balance of what works on the trail as well as the street will allow you to choose the components that best fit your needs as well as your Jeep.

When you hit the trail with a properly equipped Jeep, tackling harder trails such as this "Blue 2" trail at the now-closed Paragon Adventure Park will give you the confidence that the Jeep will get through without damage while you enjoy the challenge of the drive.

Ending Thought

Spending the money first on what matters most is always the best advice for a Jeep that is used off-road. Depending on your budget, forget items such as LED taillights, cargo nets, excess off-road lights, and other items that have little to do with the Jeep's ability. Choose quality suspensions, tires, winches, lockers, armor, etc. These components are the keys to getting your Jeep reliably through the trail and home afterward.

There is no end to what can be done with a TJ. This revolutionary Jeep changed the line and created the best off-road Jeep, which carried over to the replacement models of the TJ. The newer models continue to use a similar suspension design that was mass-produced and proven by the TJ.

The Project Jeep

Writing this book has been an interesting experience, mostly because a Jeep was built. In a matter of months the bone-stock 2004 Wrangler Unlimited with more than 193,000 miles transformed into a trail Jeep that performs wonderfully on the trail and drives better than stock on the street. Careful planning and thought went into the selection of components that allowed the best balance of on- and off-road.

The Components

2004 Wrangler Unlimited, 4.0L, 42RLE Automatic, NP231 transfer case
TeraFlex 3-inch lift with adjustable control arms
TeraFlex 9550 shocks
TeraFlex Monster front and rear adjustable track bars
TeraFlex sway bar disconnects
ARB Air Locker front and rear
ARB on-board air compressor
G2 4.56:1 ratio gears
ARB heavy-duty differential covers
TeraFlex slip yoke eliminator
BFGoodrich 285/75R16 Mud Terrain KM2 tires
Quadratec Rubicon Extreme 16-inch wheels
Bestop Safari Top
Quadratec hood decal
Quadratec winch-ready bull bar front bumper
Poison Spyder Ricochet rockers
Poison Spyder Trail corner guards
Currie Currectlync steering linkage
TeraFlex 9550 steering stabilizer
Cobra 19DX CB, Firestik antenna
Warn VR-8S winch
Smittybilt XRC cage kit
Odyssey Extreme Series battery

The 2004 Wrangler Unlimited project in this book has evolved from bone-stock to a Jeep that is a pleasure to drive on the street and that is very capable. This action shows the suspension flex and how Air Lockers can make three-wheel driving possible.

aFe cold air intake
eFe exhaust system
Quadratec Ultimate all-weather front floor liners

This list may seem like a lot, and it's aggressive to do so much in only a few months. Some great things about the TJ are the low entry price compared to newer Jeep models such as the JK, as well as the modern suspension design that allows this Jeep to perform amazingly on- and off-road. On a personal note, this Jeep has proven to be more fun to drive in all driving conditions than I expected. The combination of components has justified so much of what this book is about. Visit jeepfan.com to follow this Jeep into the future. As with almost every Jeep, more mods are always in the works. ∎

SOURCE GUIDE

Advance Adapters
4320 Aerotech Center Way
Paso Robles, CA 93446
805-238-7000
advanceadapters.com

ARB/Old Man Emu
4810 D Street NW, #103
Auburn, WA 98001
425-264-1391
arbusa.com

Bestop
333 Centennial Parkway,
    Ste. B
Louisville, CO 80027
800-845-3567
bestop.com

BFGoodrich
P.O. Box 19001
Greenville, SC 29602
877-788-8899
bfgoodrichtires.com

Bosch
43811 Plymouth Oaks Blvd.
Plymouth Twp, MI 48170
734-414-0900
hella.com

Cobra
6500 W. Cortland St.
Chicago, IL 60707
773-889-3087
cobra.com

Currie Enterprises
382 N. Smith Ave.
Corona, CA 92880
714-528-6957
currieenterprises.com

Dynatrac Products, Inc.
7392 Count Circle
Huntington Beach, CA
    92647
714-421-4314
dynatrac.com

Enersys
2366 Bernville Rd.
Reading, PA 19605
610-208-1991
odysseybattery.com

Extreme Terrain
1 Lee Blvd., # 2
Malvern, PA 19355
800-988-4605
extremeterrain.com

Firestik
2614 E Adams St.
Phoenix, AZ 85034
602-273-7151
firestik.com

Four X Doctor
1033 N. Victory Pl.
Burbank, CA 91502
818-845-2194
fourxdoctor.com

G2 Axle & Gear
400 W. Artesia Blvd.
Compton, CA 90220
310-900-2687
g2axle.com

Genesis Offroad
P.O. Box 1038
Byhalia, MS 38611
901-214-5337
genesisoffroad.com

Goodridge
174 Gasoline Alley
Mooresville, NC 28117
704-662-9095
goodridge.com

Goodyear
200 Innovation Way
Akron, OH 44316
330-796-2121
goodyear.com

Hi-Lift Jack Company
46 W Spring St.
Bloomfield, IN 47424
812-384-4441
hi-lift.com

JE Reel Driveline
448 S Reservoir St.
Pomona, CA 91766
909-629-9002
reeldriveline.com

Jeff Daniels Jeep Customi-
    zations
495 Indian Creek Rd.
Harleysville, PA 19438
215-256-8090
jeffdanielsjeeps.com

K&N Engineering, Inc.
1455 Citrus St.
Riverside, CA 92507
951-826-4000
knfilters.com

KC HiLiTES
2843 W Avenida De Lucas
Williams, AZ 86046
928-635-2607
kchilites.com

Lokar Performance Products
2545 Quality Ln.
Knoxville, TN 37931
865-824-9767
lokar.com

Lucas Oil Products
302 North Sheridan St.
Corona, CA 92880
800-342-2512
lucasoil.com

Mean Green
3 Imaging Way
Derry, PA 15627
724-694-8290
mean-green.com

Midway Industries, Inc.
2266 Crosswind Dr.
Prescott, AZ 86301
928-771-8422
centerforce.com

Mile Marker Industries
2121 Blount Rd.
Pompano Beach, FL 33069
800-886-8647
milemarker.com

Novak Conversions
648 West 200 North, Ste. 1
Logan, UT 84321
877-602-1500
novak-adapt.com

Off Road Only
1971 Seneca Rd., Unit E
Eagan, MN 55122
651-644-2323
offroadonly.com

OK Auto
2621 NJ-57
Stewartsville, NJ 8886
908-454-6973
ok4wd.com

Optima
5757 N Green Bay Av.
Milwaukee, WI 53209
888-867-8462
optimabatteries.com

Ox Off Road
11405 Challenger Av.
Odessa, FL 33556
727-230-7803
ox-usa.com

Painless Performance
2501 Ludelle St.
Fort Worth, TX 76105
817-244-6212
painlessperformance.com

Poison Spyder
1177 W. Lincoln St., Unit
  100A
Banning, CA 92220
951-849-5911
poisonspyder.com

Power Tank
43 Commerce St., Unit 103
Lodi, CA 95240
209-366-2163
powertank.com

Powermaster
1833 Downs Dr.
West Chicago, IL 60185
630-839-7754
powermastermotorsports.com

Powertrax
1001 W Exchange Av.
Chicago, IL 60609
800-934-2727
powertrax.com

Quadratec
Reseller
1028 Saunders Ln.
West Chester, PA 19380
800-743-4927
quadratec.com

Ramsey
4707 N Minho Rd.
Tulsa, OK 74117
918-438-2760
ramsey.com

Rigid
779 N Colorado St.
Gibert, AZ 85233
855-760-5337
rigidindustries.com

Rock Hard 4x4
Roll Bars
P.O. Box 186
St. Paul, NE 68873
844-762-5427
rockhard4x4.com

Rough Country Suspension
  System
1400 Morgan Rd.
Dyersburg, TN 38024
800-222-7023
roughcountry.com

Rubicon Express
1900 El Camino Av.
Sacramento, CA 95815
877-367-7824
rubiconexpress.com

Rugged Ridge
400 Horizon Dr.
Suwanee, GA 30024
770-614-6101
ruggedridge.com

Smittybilt
400 W Artesia Blvd.
Compton, CA 90220
310-762-9944
smittybilt.com

Spidertrax
174 12th St. SE
Loveland, CO 80537
800-286-0898
spidertrax.com

SSBC
11470 Main Rd.
Clarence, NY 14031
800-448-7722
ssbrakes.com

Steerco LLC
4920 Rondo Dr.
Fort Worth, TX 76106
817-626-9006
steerco.com

Superwinch
359 Lake Rd.
Dayville, CT 6241
860-928-7787
superwinch.com

TeraFlex
5680 West Dannon Way
West Jordan, UT 84081
801-713-3314
teraflex.com

Titan Engines
2120 NW 10th St.
Ocala, FL 34475
877-850-8668
titanengines.com

Tom Woods
2147 N. Rulon White Blvd.,
  Ste. 103
Ogden, UT 84404
801-737-0757
4xshaft.com

Uniden
3001 Gateway Dr., Ste. 130
Irving, TX 75063
817-858-3300
uniden.com

US Mags
19200 S Reyes Av.
Rancho Dominguez, CA
  90221
us-mags.com

Vanco
6342 Jonathan St.
Lancaster, CA 93536
800-256-6295
vancopbs.com

Viair
15 Edelman
Irvine, CA 92618
949-585-0011
viaircorp.com

Warn
12900 SE Capps Rd.
Clackamas, OR 97015
800-543-9276
warn.com

Wrangler Power Products
18930 59th Ave. NE
Arlington, WA 98223
800-962-2616
wranglerpower.com

Wyeth-Scott Company
85 Dayton Rd.
Newark, OH 43055
740-345-4528
wyeth-scott.com